W9-CCI-049

HUMAN NEEDS AND THE MARKET

For my parents, Esther and Con.

Human Needs and the Market

MAUREEN RAMSAY
School of English Studies, Journalism and Philosophy
University of Wales
College of Cardiff

Avebury
Aldershot • Brookfield USA • Hong Kong • Singapore • Sydney

Published by
Avebury
Ashgate Publishing Limited
Gower House
Croft Road
Aldershot
Hants GU11 3HR
England

Ashgate Publishing Company
Old Post Road
Brookfield
Vermont 05036
USA

Typeset by
Neville Young
49 Muswell Avenue
London N10 2EH

A CIP catalogue record for this book is available from the British Library and the US Library of Congress.

ISBN 1 85628 258 9

Printed and Bound in Great Britain by
Athenaeum Press Ltd., Newcastle upon Tyne.

Contents

Figures and tables

Acknowledgements

I would like to thank all those who taught me philosophy. I am grateful for all I learnt from them and the inspiration they gave me. I am particularly indebted to Harry Lesser for his constant encouragement and generous intellectual and emotional support during the writing of this book. I would like to thank him for this, and for his many suggestions and his meticulous and patient criticism. I would also like to thank Norman Geras for suggesting 'needs' as the subject of this book and outlining the problems to tackle; and Roy Bhaskar for the confidence and opportunities he gave me to discuss these problems; my husband, Jules Townshend for his care, time and optimism; and my friends Jeff Girling and Nilou Mobasser for their incessant argument. Special thanks are due to Neville Young who, with rigorous attention to detail, efficiency and creativity prepared the manuscript for publication. Finally I would like to thank my parents, Esther and Con Curtin who will be pleased for me; and my children, Rachel, Matthew and Saoirse, without whom I would have finished this book sooner, but without whom my most important needs would not have been satisfied.

Preface

The weapon of criticism obviously cannot replace the criticism of weapons. Material force must be overthrown by material force. But theory becomes material force once it has gripped the masses. Theory is capable of gripping the masses when it demonstrates *ad hominem*, and it demonstrates *ad hominem* when it becomes radical. To be radical is to grasp things by the root. But for man the root is man himself ... *man* is the *highest being for man*, hence ... the *categorical imperative to overthrow all conditions* in which man is a degraded, enslaved, neglected, contemptible being.

Marx, 1967, pp. 257–258

Introduction

> The only emancipation ... *in practice* is emancipation based on *the* theory proclaiming that man is the highest essence of man ... The *head* of this emancipation is philosophy. (Marx 1967, p. 264)

The presumptions of this book are the beliefs in the centrality of human concerns and purposes, the view that 'man is the highest being for man', and that the task of philosophy is to elucidate these in order to demonstrate what must be done to achieve them so that theory may be actualised and ideas put into practice.

For these reasons I have chosen to examine the concept of needs, for intuitively the satisfaction of human needs seems fundamentally important for the achievement of any and all human purposes.

My aims in this book are to explain and justify the universal and objective character of the concept of needs, identify their empirical content and provide evidence for their existence. A further aim is to show that facts about needs have moral implications. They provide prudential and moral criteria for evaluating social policy and reasons for acting to satisfy them. An underlying aim is to redress the imbalance in current discussions from both the right and the left which reject the very possibility of conscious planning to meet needs and which advocate in a variety of forms allocation of resources a posteriori through market laws.

These aims require analysis of other concepts. The concept of need will be contrasted with the competing concepts of felt needs, wants and preferences. In order to show what needs are required for, the concepts of survival, physical and mental health also require justification and argument.

The structure of the argument is as follows:

Chapter One defines fundamental human needs objectively as means to ends any human being has good reason to pursue, desire or value. These are identified as survival and health; and empirically the concept of fundamental human needs is contrasted with felt needs, wants and preferences.

Chapter Two examines the general connection between facts and values and argues that facts about needs provide prudential and moral reasons for action.

Chapter Three defends the concept of need against the epistemological and empirical criticism of liberal theory and challenges the advantages claimed for liberal theory and the political economy informed by it. It establishes that needs are the proper criteria for deciding and evaluating social policy.

Chapter Four rejects theories of true and false needs as a basis for social criticism. Criticism is based on the limitations on expressions of need and failure to satisfy them. An analytic distinction is made between naturally determined abstract, general needs and socially determined historically specific instances of them.

Chapter Five defines physical and mental health as natural functioning and argues against objections that survival and health are means to ends any human being has good reason to pursue, desire or value.

Chapter Six establishes the empirical content of survival and physical health needs with reference to facts about our biological constitutions and to the nature of these needs as means to ends in given social contexts. It suggests how objective indicators might be developed to identify health needs and what must be done in order to meet them.

Chapter Seven establishes the empirical content of abstract general mental health needs with evidence from common agreement and behavioural and causal evidence.

Chapter Eight suggests how objective indicators of mental health needs could be developed which reflect the causal connections between these indicators and achieving, restoring or maintaining health. It shows that improvements in meeting needs can only come about in a radically transformed socio-economic order.

Chapter Nine summarises the main arguments, points to where further research is needed and concludes the book.

1 Definition of need

Most analytic accounts of need argue that all needs are instrumental. We can need something only for some future end or purpose. Need statements that do not refer to purposes are short-hand for those that do. Statements of need are always of the form, 'A needs x in order to y'. Frankfurt (1984, p. 3) argues that:

> All necessities are ... conditional: nothing is needed except in virtue of being an indispensable condition for the attainment of a certain end (c.f. Barry, 1965, pp. 47–49, White, 1971, pp. 105–6, Flew, 1977, pp. 213–218, Dearden, 1972, p. 50).

If all need statements imply that a need is a means to an end, then what people need is relative to what they want. For this reason instrumental needs, as such, can carry no moral weight. Needs may relate to some undesirable end. They may be the means to evil as well as good (Paul Taylor 1959, Fitzgerald 1977). Richard Hare (1969, p. 256) explains the error of Descriptivists who, overlooking this, suppose than 'good' and 'needs' are intrinsically connected:

> ... We have the pro-attitudes that we have, and therefore call the things good which we do call good, because of their relevance to certain ends which are sometimes called 'fundamental human needs'.
>
> To call them this, however, is already to make a *logical* connection between them and what it is good for a man to have. This, indeed, is why descriptivists have fallen into the trap of supposing that, because the word 'good' is logically tied in certain contexts to the *word* 'needs', it is therefore logically tied to certain concrete *things* that are generally thought to be needs ... The two words 'desires' and 'needs' have both misled descriptivists in the same way – and that because there is an

> intimate logical connection between what is needed and what is desired, so that in many contexts we could say that for a thing to be needed is for it to be a necessary condition for satisfying a desire. It follows that if 'things desired' do not form a closed class, 'things needed' will not either. If, as I said, logic does not prevent us from coming to desire new things, or ceasing to desire old ones, it cannot, either, determine what we do or do not need.

Hare argues that the desires or ends people have are contingent and not logically restricted in the way 'good' is. Therefore 'needs' are also contingent, not necessarily universal, good or worthy of satisfaction.

Springborg (1981) and Fitzgerald (1977) both claim that a theoretical appeal to 'needs' as necessary conditions to achieve an end, while appearing to be empirical, merely pushes back the question of values. They claim that needs defined in this way have so strong an evaluative element that they constitute values in themselves. Any need theory which appeals to empirical data to substantiate its need claims must presume norms. Needs cannot be made empirical because empirical evidence can be brought to bear on the question of needs only after normative assumptions about the nature of human beings, their ends and purposes, have been made. Appeal to instrumental needs is merely an expression of a prior commitment to the values which the ends in question embody. Since there is disagreement about values what counts as a need will differ in accordance with these.

It follows that if classification of need depends on ends, goals and purposes then there cannot be an objective or empirical theory of needs, and reference to need is of no particular importance for supporting claims that they ought to be met and resourced.

In order to avoid the relativity and therefore the redundancy of the concept of need for claims to satisfactions philosophers have argued either (a) that there are some basic needs which are 'absolute' or 'intrinsic', or (b) that objective needs are those which secure ends that are valuable in some objective sense.

'Absolute or intrinsic' need accounts

These accounts attempt to draw a distinction between 'instrumental' needs and 'absolute', 'intrinsic' or 'fundamental' needs which are not necessary merely for a particular end or purpose we happen to want or choose. Non-instrumental needs are said to be those we have by virtue of being human and are necessary irrespective of any particular aim individual human beings may have. For this reason, Braybrooke (1987, p. 31) for example, says:

> ... one cannot sensibly ask, using the language of needs, 'Does N need to live?' or 'Does N need to function normally (robustly)?'. N does not

have to explain or justify aiming to live, or aiming to function normally.

Thomson (1987, pp. 20–21) too, takes up this point:

> If I claim that I *need* to survive, the implication is that my survival is important because it is necessary for the completion of some task or goal ... The normal value of life is not so specific, not dependent on the importance of particular purposes, and is not so easily forgone. This is why the question 'Do you *need* to survive?' and its affirmative and negative answers are normally inappropriate and beside the point ... Thus, in normal circumstances, what we need in order to survive and avoid serious harm are basic or non-derivative fundamental needs.

Earlier writers in this vein have agreed that basic needs relate to survival and the avoidance of harm. Joel Feinberg (1973, p. 111) argues:

> In a general sense, to say that S needs x is to say simply that if he doesn't have x he will be harmed. A 'basic' need would now be for an x in whose absence a person would be harmed in some crucial and fundamental way, such as suffering injury, malnutrition, illness, madness or premature death.

For Miller (1976, p. 30) when we ascribe needs to a person:

> ... we are thinking not of a person's wants, whether actual or hypothetical, but rather of the consequences for the person of *not* having what is needed. We are thinking of the harm which the person will suffer through not being given what we say he needs.

Miller therefore proposes a concept of need which equates 'A needs X' with 'A will suffer harm if he lacks X'. 'Intrinsic' need statements such as 'men need food' translate into 'men will suffer harm if they lack food'. 'He needs someone to understand him' means, 'he will be harmed if does not have someone to understand him'.

Wiggins (1985) and Thomson (1987) rest their accounts of 'absolute' and 'fundamental' needs respectively on these precedents. Wiggins (p. 10) writes:

> I need (absolutely to have x)
> if and only if
> I need (instrumentally) to have x if I am to avoid being harmed
> if and only if
> it is necessary, things being what they actually are,
> that if I avoid being harmed, then I have x.

Thomson (p. 19) similarly claims that:

All fundamental needs pertain to the avoidance of serious harm. The object of such a need must be something the lack of which is harmful to the subject.

Thomson (p. 15) encapsulates the essence of these claims when he argues that:

> 'A needs x' is non-elliptical when the meaning of the term 'need' fixes logically what x is necessary for. This only happens when 'A needs x' entails 'A has a fundamental need for x' for then the antecedents must be the avoidance of serious harm. Since the antecedent is guaranteed by the meaning of the term 'need' under this reading 'A needs x' is non elliptical.

According to these views, human beings need to survive, to function normally and to avoid physical and mental harm, but not for any particular reason; they 'just do.'

We can acknowledge the 'absolutist' point that the value of survival, normal functioning, the avoidance of harm and so on is not dependent on or restricted to any subjective or particular ends. We can argue, though, that need statements both fit the relational formula – 'A needs x in order to Y' and that they can be construed objectively. In this vein, various writers have proposed that needs be defined as the necessary preconditions or instruments for the attainment of any and all particular ends which anyone might want to pursue. Emphasis here is placed not on needs' role as means to ends but on the wide variety of ends they serve. See for example Nielsen (1969, p. 188), Weale (1978, Chps. 4–5), Galtung (1980), Shue (1980, Chps, 1 & 2), Doyal and Gough (1984, p. 14), Daniels (1985, Chps. 2 & 3), Plant et al (1980), Plant (1985) and Sen (1985, a,b). Hart (1955) on 'natural rights', Barry (1965, Ch. 10) on 'interests', Rawls (1971, pp. 90–95) on 'primary goods', Gewirth (1978, 1982, 1984a, pp. 1–24, 1987, pp. 55–70) on 'rights'.

Following these attempts I will argue that needs may be defined empirically and objectively as means to ends any human being has good reason to pursue, desire or value if they are to act successfully to achieve any end or realise any values, whatever they may be. This claim begins from the objective fact of the existence of empirical agents who are in possession of ends (whatever they may be) and who must act to achieve them. In order to act the agent must have the necessary means to and conditions of action. The notion of 'action' employed here is that which is implicit in our everyday understanding of the term and is the object of all moral and other practical injunctions. The type of behaviour we call action is identified by the goal or end result it was the agent's intention or purpose to bring about, so that we could say that the actions occurred because of the agent's intention.

Alan Gewirth (1987) claims that actions in this sense have two generic features and necessary conditions: freedom and well-being.

He proceeds to argue that since freedom and well-being are necessary conditions of action every agent must regard these as necessary goods for himself or herself, since he or she could not act without them. Because of this every actual or prospective agent logically must hold or accept that (1) 'I must have freedom and well-being'. 'Must' here, Gewirth (p. 62) explains, is 'practical-prescriptive in that it signifies the agent's advocacy of his having the necessary goods of action which he needs in order to act successfully in general'.

From this, Gewirth continues that by virtue of accepting (1), every agent must also logically accept that s/he has rights to the conditions of action.

The argument I am advancing at this stage stops short of claiming that from the fact that someone needs something we can establish a right or claim for their having it or for claiming that the need ought to be met. Following Gewirth, though, I would agree that the necessary conditions of action are what constitute the fundamental human needs of every actual, prospective or potential agent. Corresponding to Gewirth's notion of 'well-being', I shall argue that the concepts of survival and health approximate to these conditions. How they may be defined to encompass human needs, why they do and what they consist of will be argued for in a later chapter. For the moment, it is sufficient to say that survival is a fundamental human need because it is the necessary condition of any activity. Physical and mental health are fundamental human needs because they are the conditions of any purposive and successful activity. All persons that are actual, prospective or potential agents in possession of ends have these needs, since the conditions for human activity apply universally to all human agents; for, in order to act successfully such conditions have to be met.

All that can be noted now is that facts about human needs give people reasons from their own point of view for seeking to meet them. That is, in normal circumstances, all things being equal, a person has no rational or practical alternative but to seek what s/he needs. What gives needs this status of practical necessity is their 'natural necessity,' their importance for achieving the ends of survival and health. The question of whether moral as well as prudential obligations follow will be addressed in the next chapter.

Similarly, the question of whether survival and health can be defined empirically rather than evaluatively will be taken up later in the book. I will argue that it is in principle possible to define survival and health needs in a non-evaluative way. Survival and health statements are descriptive rather than evaluative claims which differ between individuals, times, places and cultures. Later chapters will both reveal the empirical content of needs and show how this content has value implications.

Freedom is not here considered as a separate need since the freedom to act to achieve any end involves fulfilling the needs for survival and health which are the means to those ends. Meeting people's needs contributes and is fundamental to their freedom, their ability to achieve their ends and purposes.

This view depends on a particular definition of 'freedom' and will be defended in Chapter 3.

Fundamental human needs are both instrumental and objective. Survival and health are basic needs because they are means to ends any and all human beings have good reason to pursue, desire or value if they are to act successfully to achieve any ends at all.

Strictly speaking survival and health are not always essential means to other ends. There are circumstances in which people will sacrifice their life or health for some other goal. Given this, then can it be maintained that survival and health are essential means to other ends, and therefore universally desired or valued or ends all human beings have good reason to pursue?

I shall take up a selection of counter examples to survival and health being essential means to other ends in Chapter 5 and argue that these do not discredit the claims that survival and health are fundamental human needs, for the following reasons:

1 The fact that people in certain circumstances sacrifice their life or health to attain some other end does not deny but testifies to the fact that what is being sacrificed is something of objective value to the agent, or that in normal circumstances survival and health are needs.

2 People often forgo some aspect of their physical or mental health to secure other aspects of their health or long term survival and health goals. In these cases survival and health remain their objective ends.

3 Sacrifices of life or health sometimes occur when people no longer have ends they want to achieve. This shows only that survival and health are needs when and if people have other ends they want to achieve.

4 Though some goals are not undermined by failing health and failing health can contribute to the achievement of goals it cannot be assumed that people would choose these means if others were available or that generally speaking survival and health aren't objectively important. Failure to meet these needs at least reduces the range of ends open to the agent.

Though there are special occasions when survival and health needs can be overridden, survival and health still remain ends that all human beings have good reason to pursue, desire or value. Human beings can have good reason to pursue, desire or value what they need and not do so. We can therefore accept both the claim that 'people have good reason to pursue, desire or value what they need' and accept that this can be overridden in a particular context without making an exception to that claim. What is needed is practically necessary to pursue other ends. We can choose not to attach any importance to survival and health or to deem other goals more important, but this does not lessen their importance. The fact that needs are universally and objectively important stems from what needs are. The objective instrumental account of needs shows that it is a determinable matter of fact what needs a person has – they are the means necessary to achieve any end at all, and because of this they provide that person with good, though not conclusive, reasons for action.

The claim that there is an 'absolute' or non-instrumental sense of need only succeeds as long as the importance and value of survival and health do not require justification and it is unnecessary to explicate what survival and health are needed for, or where the end for which the needed object is required is incorporated into the meaning of the word 'need'. But, even in these cases the need statements in question can be seen instrumentally. They can be explicated with reference to ends connected with avoiding harm, survival and health. They still fit into the formula, 'A needs x in order to y' where y refers to avoiding harm, surviving or functioning normally.

Both non-instrumental and instrumental analyses of need coincide, in that both hold that the meaning of a need statement is inextricably bound up with notions of survival and health, avoiding harm and functioning normally. The objective instrumental account of need starts from agents with unspecified and differing goals, and explains and justifies the value and importance of survival and health as preconditions for their successful attainment. In contrast, survival and health, are taken by absolutists to be ends which are given, obvious, or embedded in the meaning of what it is to need something. The two positions are not incompatible. Survival and health can be seen both as means to ends any human being has good reason to pursue, desire or value and as ends in themselves, survival and health tend to be valued not just instrumentally but for their own sake. They become goods of intrinsic value that anyone has reason to aim for once their tactical relationship to the differing generalised goals remain in the background. Survival and health are necessary goods to any human agent by virtue of being human. They are characteristic of human existence and as such can be seen both as strategies for the attainment of other goals human beings may have and as ends in themselves; they are integrally related to what it means to be a human agent.

Needs have been defined here in two stages:

1 Fundamental human needs 1: Survival and health are the necessary conditions or means to any and all other ends any human being may have.

2 Fundamental human needs 2: Survival and health become ends any human agent has reason to pursue, desire or value intrinsically as well as instrumentally. What is necessary to fulfil these are FHN2.

If survival and health can be viewed as objective needs because they are means to any and all further ends, and following from this they can be viewed as ends in themselves, goods anyone has reason to pursue, desire or value, then both instrumental and non-instrumental analyses agree that the criterion for being an objective need is the same in both cases: whatever is necessary to achieve survival and health.

Needs/felt needs/desires

Fundamental human needs are the objective requirements for survival and health. As such they are the effects of our biological and psychological constitutions and are therefore relatively unchanging. What changes over time are not fundamental human needs but the specific, socio-historical form those needs take: their actual content and specific ways of satisfying them. The validity of classifying any specific socio-historical need as a fundamental human need will depend on whether the former can be cogently derived from the latter.

Fundamental human needs and their socio-historic forms are to be distinguished from felt needs and wants. Felt needs are what we actually feel our needs to be. They are subjectively experienced and dependent on beliefs about what we need and that we need something which may or may not correspond to what we do fundamentally need. Wants are demonstrable dispositions to desire or prefer something. Wants, though, are not simple psychological facts or private inner feelings. With the exception of those wants that I shall call 'unbidden' desires, that is, instinctive reactions and cravings, desires are the result of deliberation, beliefs, choice or judgement.

Briefly, wants (desires and preferences) are:

1. Instrumental: They require an object wanted and a goal or end for which the object is wanted.
2. Subjectively valuable: Wants and preferences are valuable to the subject of desire.
3. Mind dependent: We are usually aware of them, they are something we feel or experience.
4. Belief dependent: Wants involve beliefs about the desirability and availability of wanted objects.
5. Chosen: With the exception of 'unbidden' desires, desires and preferences can involve an element of choice.
6. Potential reasons for intentional action: A's desire for x is A's reason for action, the fact that x is wanted provides a potential reason for action.

Though wants and needs can coincide in that we can want what we need, and need what we want, fundamental human needs differ from felt needs and wants in the following ways:

1 Instrumental

Both wants and needs are parallel in that they are relational but they differ in the criteria for their justification. They are parallel in that they both fit the formula:

A needs X in order to Y
A wants B in order to C

In both cases of wanting and needing there is a subject of want or need, an object wanted or needed and an end, goal or purpose for which the object is wanted or needed. As others have argued, (Anscombe 1957, Norman 1971, Taylor 1969, and Plant et al 1980) to understand fully what it means to ascribe a want to someone involves being able to specify both an object that is wanted and an end, intention or purpose for which it is wanted.

Though people can claim and often feel that they just want something and that's it, they don't want it for anything, to make that claim fully intelligible requires reference to end for which the object is wanted. G.E. Anscombe's 'Intention' (1957, para. 37) elaborates this point:

> But is not anything wantable, or at least any perhaps attainable thing? It will be instructive to anyone who thinks this to approach someone and say: 'I want a saucer of mud' or 'I want a twig of mountain ash'. He is likely to be asked what for; to which let his reply be that he does not want it for anything, he just wants it ...
>
> It is not at all clear what it meant to say: this man simply wanted a pin. Of course, if he is careful always to carry the pin in his hand thereafter, or at least for a time, we may perhaps say: it seems he really wanted that pin. Then perhaps, the answer to 'what do you want it for?' may be 'to carry it about with me', as a man may want a stick. But here again there is further characterisation ... To say 'I *merely* want this' without any characterisation is to deprive the word of sense; if he insists on 'having' the thing, we want to know what 'having' amounts to.

Want claims then must be explicated with reference to an end or purpose to give that claim meaning and intelligibility. I can only make sense of a claim to want a saucer of mud or a twig of mountain ash if the claimant can also tell me why such objects are wanted, for example to use as a medicinal poultice or to prepare cuttings for my garden. If such reasons cannot be given or if ends cannot be specified then quite simply the claims make no sense. This applies even to the wants which assail us, the longings and cravings that are typical of addictions and compulsions, for though it may be difficult for the subjects of those experiences to specify what they want a piece of coal for or why they want to wash their hands compulsively, even these kind of wants require ends to which they refer and a context in which they can be explained. Although we may feel that we just want to eat coal or to obsessively wash our hands and we have no clearly formulated goal in mind when these feelings overwhelm us, such feelings do relate to ends and purposes at least in the sense that fulfilling the desire is in itself a way of overcoming that desire. The end to which the want relates is simply to stop wanting. Furthermore, even cravings, compulsions and obsessions are not given. They do not just arise, though often they feel as if they do. There are in these cases particular physical or psychological backgrounds which if explained can render those addictions or compulsions, intelligible.

For instance pregnant women often have cravings for certain objects and the desire for coal is one of these. If the desire for coal is explained in this context, given theories about physical changes in pregnant women, the claim to want to eat coal becomes intelligible. Without this or some other explanation for which evidence can be provided the claim to want to eat coal is senseless. Similarly the desire to wash compulsively, if it can be explained in terms of a psychoanalytic theory, becomes intelligible because of reference to this.

Consequently 'want' statements to be meaningful must specify ends and purposes and the context in which they arise is always appropriate to their sensible explanation. Similarly, needs claims are only made intelligible when the end or purpose for which they are needed is specified. This does not mean that all want or need claims are followed by an 'in order to Y or C' clause since what the wanted or needed object is wanted or needed for may be tacit, understood or obvious. However, it does mean that unless the 'in order Y or C' clause is implicit, tacit or understood it can be added. If not, the want or need claim is unintelligible.

The goals, ends or purposes for which things are wanted are called 'desirability characteristics' by Anscombe (1957). And, according to Richard Norman (1971) the 'desirability characteristics' of the end or goal themselves presuppose publicly acceptable standards or norms. He argues 'the intelligibility of a want is essentially a matter of its relationship to public, supra-individual standards or norms' (p. 55). Reference to the 'desirability characteristics' of the end or goal has to be made in order to make both want and need claims intelligible.

Both wants and needs then are parallel in that they require for their intelligibility an end for which they are wanted or needed. However, since there is good reason to suppose that the intelligibility, justification and value of wants and needs cannot exceed the intelligibility, justification and value of the end they serve, wants and needs differ where questions of justification and value arise precisely because the character of the ends they serve differ.

Wants can relate to any end. It is logically possible to want anything at all. Under certain conditions human beings can come to want things that are trivial, detrimental or harmful to them. Even with control over the formulation of desires with full knowledge of their consequences, people can be attracted to things that are bad for them. Hence the fact that something is wanted per se, does not guarantee its value or justify its pursuit or satisfaction. Though the concept of need as merely something necessary to achieve a goal suffers from the same justification problems, the concept of fundamental human need does not.

Fundamental human needs differ crucially from wants and simple non-objective instrumental accounts of need, in that they include the necessary conditions for attaining ends that all human beings by virtue of their nature must share if they have any other ends they want to pursue.

Fundamental human needs are the necessary conditions for doing anything at all. They are the needs for survival and health and as such they are objective goals any and all human beings have good (though not always conclusive) reason to pursue, desire or value if they are to act to achieve any ends. It is the importance of these ends of survival and health that justify action in pursuit of these goals and the means – the fundamental human needs these generate.

Hence, the intelligibility and justification of wants and needs lies not in the fact that they are wanted or needed per se, but whether the purposes to which they relate are intelligible or justified. For this reason,

2 *Needs are objectively valuable and wants are subjectively valuable*

Needs are valuable whether we know or experience them, choose them, want them, act upon them or appreciate their importance. This is because they are the practical means to attain the universally important goals of survival and health and as such are the means to any and other ends human beings may have. They are valuable whether or not they are valuable subjectively.

Wants are what *we* value; we know them, experience them, choose them, act upon them and believe them to be important to us. They are subjectively valued, even if they are not objectively valuable.

3 *Mind dependency*

Fundamental human needs may not be known to us or experienced by us in the direct way that felt needs, wants and preferences generally are. If needs are objective requirements then we may be in need of something without being aware that we need it, feel the need for it or want it. We may not know what we need. We may be ignorant or mistaken about what we need in order to survive and be healthy. In contrast to this, we do know what we feel our needs to be and our wants are subjectively experienced by us. Hence there is a difference in the evidence for the existence of needs and wants.

Needs can be ascribed independently of subjective avowals. Their existence can be verified by causal explanations which with reference to biological and psychological theories, demonstrate the effects on survival and health if needs are inadequately satisfied or not met.

Since felt needs and wants are subjectively experienced people know what they feel they need and/or what they want. Evidence for felt needs and wants comes from subjective avowals: what people say they need or want.

This aspect of the distinction between needs and wants holds in general terms, even though it is acknowledged that:

a) Not all desires are straightforwardly experienced or their objects easy to identify by the subject of experience. Desires can be unconscious or subconscious, and the focus of our desires is not always transparent. We all have had unspecified longings as well as general confusion about what it is we do actually want. In these senses of wanting subjective avowals are not evidence for what we want and in some cases wants might be externally ascribed with reference to psychoanalytic theory.

b) Needs of course can be felt. We can want what we need and we can feel that we need something. Feeling the need alone though is not sufficient evidence for fundamental needs since we may be mistaken that we do need x or that x will satisfy our need.

Although then we:

a) sometimes do not know what we want, and

b) we can experience needs as felt needs or wants,

the distinction here between needs and wants claims that generally speaking,

a) wants are characteristically something felt (even if only subconsciously, or confusedly). They are mind-dependent and attributable to subjects of experience. Thus wants can be inferred from intentional behaviour, from avowals or from observing what people do (see 6);

b) with needs, though they can be felt, feeling the need is not a criterion for having a need or part of what it means to need something.

Needs are not dependent on the subject experiencing them, therefore they cannot be inferred directly from what people say they need or from what people actually do. This does not mean that there is no behavioural or empirical evidence relevant to identifying needs. Empirical evidence about means to ends can be brought to bear on the question of needs. Behavioural evidence which charts the consequences of unmet or inadequately satisfied needs will be relevant to any claim that human beings have fundamental needs.

Though we cannot infer needs from intentional behaviour in the way we can with wants, behavioural evidence can be cited in support of the objective identification of needs. Having a need though, is not a motivational force in the way that having a want is (see 6). We might be unaware of our needs or mistaken about their objects of satisfaction and even if we do know what we need we may not want it. To become a motivational force needs must also coincide with wanting.

4 Felt needs and wants involve beliefs in a way that needs do not

Felt needs may correspond to fundamental human needs. We may feel we need what in fact we do need. There may though, be psychological states with no fundamental, objective need correlative. This is because they are dependent on subjective experience and beliefs about what we feel and think we need. While we cannot be mistaken about our experiences – if I feel I need x then I am not mistaken about that feeling – we can mistake our felt need for a fundamental need by believing that something is needed when it is not or by believing that it will satisfy a need when it will not. Because felt needs involve beliefs which are affected by how needs are construed in particular social contexts and what it is possible to demand and achieve, felt needs may not be what we fundamentally need. We may have mistaken beliefs about the latter.

Similarly, wants may correspond to fundamental human needs but we often want what we do not need. Apart from the wants which are not consciously formed: cravings, impulses and instinctive reactions, our desires and preferences cannot be described simply as brute psychological facts or mental states. They are intentional and require objects wanted. They are consequently dependent on beliefs about the desirability and availability of wanted objects which are conditioned by social contexts and circumstances within them.

If beliefs about the necessity of objects we feel the need for, or the desirability and availability of wanted objects, are shown to be mistaken or false, then there is no longer any rationale for pursuing the desire or feeling the need. We can then evaluate, criticise and alter our past felt needs and wants in the light of new information.

In contrast to this, fundamental human needs are independent of feelings and beliefs about what we need or want. What I feel I need and what I want may be the object of belief, what I do need is not. Because felt needs and wants are belief dependent, subjective experiences of need or want in conjunction with a particular belief can lead me to feeling I need or want almost anything. But I cannot really need 'just anything;' what I need is restricted by natural necessity. I need something because it is essential to survival and health whether I believe it to be, feel it to be or want it. If I need something because it is essential to survival and health it must be essential to survival and health. I can feel the need for x or want x without x satisfying the need or fulfilling the desire. If I fundamentally need x, I can only need it if x satisfies the fundamental need.

5 For this reason wants involve choice and needs do not

Choice and deliberation are involved in the formulation of many desires and preferences and there is a sense in which desiring and preferring are themselves acts of choice. To want or prefer x is to choose that x should come about. Having a need is not an act of choice. When A prefers x to y, A prefers that x should come about and in this sense chooses x rather than y. In some cases effectively desiring x involves an act of choosing x. We are not free to choose our needs because what our needs are is determined and limited by our biological and psychological constitutions. The range of our derived needs may alter and differ over time and place but our fundamental needs are unalterable. Likewise having a need is not an act of choice in the way having a want is, since it is possible to be aware of our fundamental needs and the means to satisfy them and to choose not to attach any importance to them or seek to satisfy them.

6 Desires are reasons for action in a way that needs are not

We might know what we need and not feel the need for it or be motivated to get it. 'Need' is not an intentional verb or connected with action in the way that 'desire' is. Need is not motivationally linked to action directly though (a) needs do tend to produce action when known and therefore produce a desire to act and (b) they provide reasons for action for the agent even when the agent has no desire to act. Though action may depend on desire, the fact that x is not wanted does not make it undesirable or not a reason to act. There may be good reasons for action and x may be desirable even though the agent does not either desire x or desire or act.

Conversely, though not every desire leads to action, desires in conjunction with relevant beliefs are part of the agent's own reasons for action. However the fact that x is wanted doesn't make it desirable in itself. A desire may be the agent's reason for action but may not provide an objective reason for action, simply because we can desire almost anything and our desires may rest on false or superficial beliefs about what is worth desiring. Consequently they can be irrational. Reasons for action are not provided by the fact that x is desired but by something in virtue of which x is worth desiring. In both needing and wanting, the desirability of action to satisfy or fulfil the need or want is independent of whether the desire for action itself is in fact present.

2 Facts and values

1 'Need' statements

The argument in Chapter 1 suggested that the differences between wants and needs and the subjective and objective ends they serve respectively are significant for questions of justification. 'Wants' explain what people do but do not necessarily justify their behaviour or justify providing them with what they want because 'wants' depend on particular ends and purposes. 'Needs' on the other hand both give people reasons for meeting them and justify activity aimed at their satisfaction, because they serve objective ends characteristic of human existence.

At the level of ordinary discourse this difference is well understood. Our normal everyday practices testify to the view that needs have strong links with obligations in a way that whims, tastes, preferences, pleasures and desires do not. And this assigning of moral priority to needs over desires stems from the deep rooted belief that meeting needs generally speaking matters more to our lives and is more important than desire satisfactions. The smallest child barely able to speak grasps and often exploits the different weight of the justifying force of wants and needs. Children present their desires and demands in the language of necessity precisely because they have understood that needs make a legitimate claim on others whereas wants are easily denied satisfaction. The language of wants frequently elicits the response 'but you ought not to have it'. But only when the 'need' claim is fraudulent is the appropriate response 'you ought not to have it'.

Our ordinary intuitions and actual practices thus suggest that needs have moral force. Are there, though, good reasons for supposing that needs deserve such treatment?

Is it possible to justify the nature of the connection between factual statements to the effect that 'x needs y' and moral conclusions that 'x ought to have y'?

Defenders of naturalism in ethics have claimed that to establish the fact that someone needs something, or that something is needed, is to establish a prima facie good reason or ceteris paribus claim to satisfaction (see for example Nielsen 1969, 1977, Charles Taylor 1967). Opponents of this view have argued that any such enterprise is misconceived (P. Taylor 1959, Ross Fitzgerald, 1977b). Paul Taylor illustrates the errors of this approach by identifying four types of 'need' statements and their variety of uses. These four types of statements are as follows:

1 Statements that refer to a rule or law.
2 Statements which refer to means to ends.
3 Statements which refer to human cognitive dispositions.
4 Purely normative statements.

Taylor claims that the first three types differ only insofar as they refer to states of affairs which would make them true. The fourth type differs from the others in not referring to states of affairs in this way. He elaborates his position thus:

1 'Need' statements of the first type refer to states of affairs in which something is needed, required or demanded by a prescriptive regulation, rule or law. The statements are true in virtue of the said regulation, rule or law. For example:

'One needs a licence to go fishing here' (Law of State)
'You need a membership card to enter the clubhouse' (Institutional regulation)
'He needs a jack of spades to have a straight flush' (Rule of a game)
'We need to draw this conclusion if we accept this premise' (Rule of inference)

Such statements could be asserted for a variety of purposes: to recommend that the act needed to be done or that the thing needed to be obtained, to guide conduct, to warn about the consequences of not obeying the rules, to teach someone to do something, or to explain an occurrence which resulted from disregarding the requirements.

2 The second type of 'need' statements imply that something is needed as a necessary means to an end, though the end is often presupposed rather than asserted. For example:

'I need a watch'
'He needs a doctor'
'There is a need for traffic lights at this intersection'
'People need clothing, food and shelter'

Taylor claims that what people need in this sense is always relative to what they want. The purposes for which these 'need' statements are used are to give information, to recommend action, to explain an action, or to make a suggestion or request.

3 The third type of 'need' statements refer to the cognitive dispositions of human beings or animals, by which their behaviour is motivated, consciously or unconsciously. Here 'need' is equivalent to 'drive', 'wish' or 'motive'. For example a mother's unconscious need to be compensated for the rejection of her child, a guilty man's need for punishment, would be examples of unconscious needs in this sense. An ambitious man's need for success, a drug addict's need for a drug, an artist's creative need, an outraged man's need for revenge, would fall into the category of unconscious needs. Within this type fall the needs of members of different groups: children's needs for love and affection, an adolescent's need for security, a racist's need to dominate, an American's need to buy a new car every year.

These types of 'need' statements are used to explain behaviour, guide behaviour, criticise behaviour and to recommend courses of action. Human needs then, according to Taylor can refer either to those things necessary to achieve human goals, or they can refer to the cognitive dispositions of human beings.

4 The fourth type of 'need' statement is purely normative. Taylor explains that to make a statement of this sort is simply to recommend a certain course of action. It always implies the speaker's value judgement that it is better to do what is necessary. Taylor points out that if we do not know the context in which a 'need' statement is used, it is impossible to know whether the statement is purely normative in which case 'need' could be replaced by 'ought', or whether the statement functions as a justification or an explanation, for example the statements:

'We need to make the highways safer'
'Slums need to be replaced by good housing'
'We need union leaders who cannot be bribed'

could function as pure recommendations that a certain course of action should be taken, could function as purely factual assertions of means to ends or could be justifications or explanations of actions depending on the context.

Having distinguished these four types and functions of 'need' statements, Taylor demonstrates that claims to establish a scientific ethic of human needs are misconceived because of two fundamental errors. The first of these is a failure to notice that need statements and their uses may be both (a) factual assertions which are empirically verifiable (senses 1–3) and (b) pure recommendations (sense 4). The second error is the failure to recognise that because something is a need in senses (1–3) – the only empirical senses, it does not follow that it is a need in sense 4 (the only normative one).

Kai Nielsen (1969) makes a counter argument to Taylor's position. Nielsen had argued that Taylor obscures the non-contingent relationships between facts about human needs and sound moral appraisals. Nielsen argued that in 'need' statements of type (1) 'must' can be substituted for 'needs'. This is so because the fact that it is reasonable or even desirable to act in accordance with rules of law provides good reasons for asserting that what is needed should or must be done. Here, what is reasonable has a directive, that is a normative force. Similarly, all statements of type (2) could be replaced by sentences which are normative. If a type (2) statement is asserted, then it can be concluded that what is needed should be done. In the cases of type (3), Nielsen argues, there is a more than contingent connection between saying 'x is needed' and saying this need ought to be met. He claims that it is 'logically odd' to say that 'human beings need security, but they ought not to have it'. Therefore, if it can be established that what is asserted is really needed, then it can be concluded that what is needed ought to be done, all things being equal. Thus all 'need' statements of types (1), (2) and (3) are themselves normative or state good reasons for claiming that what is needed ought to be done. According to Nielsen, then, to say 'x is needed' is always to claim that there is a good reason for having what is needed.

Fitzgerald (1977b), endorsing Taylor's position, argues that Nielsen has missed the point of Taylor's criticism, which related to three problems, the third of which is the subject of this section:

a) The problem of whether the term 'need' can be given unambiguous meaning. The discussion between Taylor and Nielsen illustrated that the term 'need' has both empirical and evaluative components in its various meanings and functions.

b) The problem of whether it is possible to identify empirically what 'human needs' are, and of achieving agreement on the proposed schedule.

c) Even if the problems in (a) and (b) could be overcome, the problem of whether any normative inference could be derived from a trouble free empirical list of human needs remains.

For Taylor (p. 111) had argued:

> ... even if it can empirically be shown that man has certain basic needs in senses (2) and (3), it is neither self-contradictory nor logically odd to refrain from recommending that such needs be satisfied, or to recommend that they be not satisfied. The purposes and goals to which needs in sense (2) are relative may, after all, be morally undesirable. And we may disapprove of certain human dispositions, needs in sense (3), however dominant they might be in some individuals or groups. That human beings have a need for love, or for freedom, or for knowledge (assuming

that assertions of this kind could be empirically confirmed) is not in itself a justification for, or even a good reason in support of, the recommendation that these needs be met. What human beings need might not be for their good. (They might have a need for destroying one another, for example). Whether human needs ought to be met must be established on grounds independent of the 'need' claims themselves. This follows from the principle that there is neither logical entailment nor contextual implication holding between statement of types (2) and (3) and any statement of type (4). And this principle is one of the lessons we have learned from Professor Moore's 'naturalistic fallacy.'

A The first of these problems, whether needs can be defined empirically, has been addressed in Chapter 1.

B How these needs can be identified will be the subject of later chapters.

C How 'ought' statements can be inferred from needs will be prefaced below by a general defence of the validity of inferences of this type, though it is conceded that the relationship between facts and values is not one of strict implication.

2 The naturalistic fallacy

Opponents of naturalism in ethics claim that value judgements cannot be logically derived from factual assertions.

Drawing on an amalgam of arguments offered by supporters of naturalism (for example MacIntyre 1969, Foot 1958, Hampshire 1949, and particularly Keekok Lee 1985), I shall argue the following:

1. that to assume the relation of logical derivability is the only legitimate, logical and hence rational relationship that may hold between two propositions is to interpret rational argument too narrowly. It leads to an arbitrary restriction on the justifiability of moral assertions;
2. that the non-naturalist position obscures the types of argument in which moral judgements occur;
3. that one kind of statement may be established or defended exclusively by reference to another kind without the first being deducible or logically derivable from the second.

1 Rational argument interpreted as strict implication is arbitrarily restrictive

I shall argue that to interpret rational argument as identical with logical justification, logical derivability, deductibility, strict proof or implication is arbitrarily restrictive. This is so, because since the inability to justify a conclusion unless it is entailed by its premises, to logically derive the conclusion from the premises (as in deriving an 'ought' from an 'is') is not a state of affairs peculiar to moral discourse.

To say that A strictly entails or implies B, is to say that it is not possible for A to be true and B to be false, or, that the truth of A is a sufficient condition for the truth of B, or, that the truth of B is a necessary condition for the truth of A. The inability to establish these kinds of entailment relations also occurs a) in discourse involving non-moral 'oughts' and b) in ordinary factual 'is' statements. If moral discourse is deemed irrational as a consequence of the absence of such a relationship, so too then must non-moral and ordinary factual discourse, otherwise the selection of moral 'oughts' as irrational is arbitrarily restrictive. The result of this would be to condemn as irrational much of non-moral and ordinary factual discourse normally regarded as rational and to consign them to logical limbo. Lee (1985) illustrated this point by showing that symmetry obtains between statements containing moral oughts (which she calls (A1), non-moral oughts (A2) and ordinary factual 'is' statements (A3). She argues that if it can be granted that propositions containing (A1s) (A2s) and (A3s) are and can be used to make assertions, then it is intuitively plausible that any of the three assertions require evidence or reasons to back them up. The corresponding evidence is called, (E1), (E2) and (E3) respectively.

For example the moral assertion, (A1) 'One ought not to kill' seems to require some kind of evidence or reference to reasons to back up that assertion, like, for instance, the evidence (E1) that killing causes pain.

Similarly, the non-moral assertion (A2) 'I ought to tidy my room' seems to require some kind of evidence or reference to reasons to back up the assertion, like, for instance, the reason (E2) 'I won't be given any pocket money if I don't'.

Again, the ordinary factual assertion (A3) 'The cat has given birth to three kittens' seems to require some kind of evidence or reference to reasons to back it up, like, for instance, (E3) 'I have just witnessed the birth'.

In each of these examples it is obvious that the relations between the evidence (or reasons) and the assertions is not one of strict implication or logical entailment as described above. It is possible for the evidence (E1, E2 and E3) in each case to be true and for the corresponding assertion (A1, A2 and A3) to be false. Likewise E1, E2 and E3 are not sufficient conditions for the truth of A1, A2 and A3 respectively, nor is the truth of A1, A2 and A3 a necessary condition for the truth of E1, E2 and E3. Therefore the inability to derive an 'ought' from an 'is' is not exclusively a problem for assertions characteristic of moral discourse.

The absence of strict implication obtaining between evidence and assertion occurs in all three forms of discourse.

Consequently, to place so much weight on the point that moral discourse and moral assertions cannot be rationally justified because they cannot be logically justified, derived, deduced, entailed or implied by factual statements is to be arbitrarily restrictive. It ignores the fact that such logical relationships do not hold in other forms of discourse either. Alternatively, to generalise the conclusions reached about moral assertions and thereby to condemn assertions made in non-moral and ordinary factual discourse as irrational because they are not logically derivable from any evidence, leads to a condemnation of many assertions generally thought to be rationally justifiable.

2 *The type of argument in which moral judgement occurs is obscured*

It might be conceded by opponents of naturalism that rational argument interpreted as strict implication is arbitrarily restrictive and not exclusively a problem for assertions characteristic of moral discourse while they still hold the view that facts about needs cannot rationally support moral recommendations.

It has been argued by supporters of naturalism that the types of argument in which moral judgements occur are situations where the moral agent is looking for an answer to a typical moral problem. This involves appraisal of the evidence and reasons for alternative courses of action in order for the agent to make practical choices and decisions. Such evidence or reasons must be relevant and do play a causal role in the making of the decision as to what ought to be done. Three possible objections to this view will be examined here:

a) That moral judgements are descriptions or expressions of emotional commitment. Facts about what is the case are therefore irrelevant to moral judgements.

b) Facts/evidence and reasoning are relevant to moral judgements but not to ultimate moral beliefs. Once the facts have been determined, no further argument is possible if moral disagreement remains.

c) Reasoning is important to moral judgements, and facts are relevant here, but not facts about human needs.

a) That moral judgements are descriptions or expressions of emotional commitment is the view of emotivists, who are concerned with the meaning and logical status of moral beliefs. They distinguish between descriptive and emotive meaning. Ethical judgements can describe or state facts about feelings, emotions and attitudes (individual or social), but the primary kind of meaning which ethical utterances have is not descriptive but emotive meaning. This emotive meaning has two functions – to express the speaker's feelings of approval/disapproval or/and to induce the same feelings in others. Moral judgements cannot be true or false since their function is not to state a fact but to express and evoke feelings.

However, it is misleading to present statements containing moral 'oughts' as mere exclamations or expressions of sincere feelings or to justify them simply in terms of the agent's choice or commitment to the oughts in question. This is because the agent would if pressed, have to defend his or her statement by a process of deliberation which would involve arguments and evidence being cited in support of the statement in question.

Morality cannot be simply a matter of emotion because moral judgements cannot be adequately explained either by replacing them by or supporting them with either descriptions or expressions of feelings.

Here, again, we might draw a parallel between moral oughts, non-moral oughts and ordinary factual 'is' statements.

Assertions like

A1) 'One ought not to kill' (a) cannot be replaced by descriptions or expressions or emotion, and (b) cannot be supported by them. They do not mean the same as, and require more evidence than the following:
'I am describing my feelings about killing',
'I happen to disapprove of killing', or,
'I am sincerely committed to the non-violent norm'.

Similarly, non-moral assertions and ordinary 'is' statements cannot be replaced or supported by emotional expressions.

A2) 'I ought to tidy my room' does not mean the same as 'I am describing my feelings about tidy rooms' and requires more evidence than, (E2)
'I happen to approve of tidy rooms' or
'I have sincerely chosen or committed myself to tidy up'.

Similarly,

A3) 'The cat has given birth to three kittens' does not mean the same as 'I feel that the cat has given birth to three kittens', and requires more evidence than

E3) 'I happen to approve of the belief that the cat has given birth to three kittens' or
'I have sincerely chosen or committed myself to the belief that the cat has given birth to three kittens'.

We do not think that (A2) and (A3) are descriptions or expressions of feelings or that (A2) and (A3) here, are sufficient or even appropriate justifications for those assertions. We are still entitled to press for further reasons and to ask 'WHY?' after the evidence (E2s) and (E3s) above have been given. So too then with moral assertions. Statements about feelings or commitments are just not sufficient justification to back up the moral assertions in question. If feelings and commitments alone are offered in justification for moral assertions it would be impossible to distinguish between moral judgements and expressions of feeling or commitment, such as, 'I like it' or 'I have chosen to accept a higher major premise beyond all reason'. Unless further reasons are produced to back up the claim, the assertion is nothing more than a personal preference. The distinction between feelings, commitments and moral judgements can only be made if we look for reasons beyond the former for the judgement.

b) Some philosophers would concede that we deliberate about the facts of the situation, but argue that once the facts have been determined, no further argument is possible if moral disagreement remains. At this point we are left with ultimate moral judgements which cannot be defended by further argument. Eventually the chain of reasons comes to an end and we reach a moral principle so general that no further reason can be given. At this point we choose between past basic values and choice must be an individual commitment.

Ultimate values are independent of reasons and are the fruits of pure choice. Hence that something is a reason for making a moral judgement depends ultimately on the values an agent has chosen. See, for example Richard Hare's position in *Freedom and Reason,* (Hare 1963).

This claim is usually illustrated by reference to some kind of example of a moral argument between two people where both agree on the facts of the situation (that is they agree on the evidence) but still draw different moral conclusions. It is claimed that once the facts have been determined there can be no further argument, since disagreement is not based on the facts of the situation but on the different ultimate moral beliefs of the agents involved. Phillips and Mounce (1969, p. 235) argue in this vein against Anscombe and Foot though they agree with the latter in holding that ultimate moral judgements are not matters of choice. They hold that moral judgements occur from within a framework of moral belief:

> that moral viewpoints determine what is and what is not to count as a relevant fact in reaching a moral decision ... If we believe that moral viewpoints can be justified by appeal to the facts; it is hard to see how one man can reject another man's reasons for his moral beliefs, since these reasons too, presumably refer to the facts. If, on the other hand, we hold that the notion of factual relevance is parasitic on moral beliefs, it is clear that deadlock in ethics will be a common occurrence, simply

> because of what some philosophers have unwisely regarded as contingent reasons, namely, the different moral views people hold.

To illustrate this, Phillips and Mounce argue that it is difficult to see how moral disagreement between a Roman Catholic housewife and scientific rationalist over abortion, could be resolved, even if both know and agreed upon the relevant facts 'about providing the good things in life for children' (p. 238). Moral agreement between them would amount to one of them renouncing their ultimate moral beliefs, for this is where the source of the disagreement lies, not in the facts themselves. The mother holds the moral opinions that 'submission to the will of God', the 'honour of motherhood' and the 'creation of new life' are of the greatest importance (p. 239).

Phillips and Mounce argue that we cannot regard such moral opinions as hypotheses which the facts will confirm or refute, for they consider that there could be no evidence which could be brought to bear on the question which would enable us to do so. Phillips and Mounce do not say that the housewife and the rationalist simply have chosen to regard different things as ultimately valuable, good or bad, but that these are given within the different moral traditions in which their judgements are made. They have different desires because they have different beliefs.

Philosophers who have argued against this position claim that the above conclusion is over-hasty, for it fails to consider other areas of factual disagreement. In the course of argument, after the facts of the immediate situation have been established, the contestants do not necessarily end the argument there, and agree to differ in their respective beliefs about what is morally good. They proceed to appeal to other facts and beliefs which are not strictly facts about the current dilemma but which inform or are presupposed by the contestants in their argument. Stuart Hampshire (1949, p. 475) argues:

> The point is that it does not follow from the fact that two people are in agreement about the facts of a particular situation, but disagree in their moral judgement, that their disagreement is ultimate and admits of no further rational argument; hence our disagreements about the moral or practical conclusions which is not a disagreement about the facts of the situation, is nevertheless a disagreement to which empirical arguments, beliefs about an indefinitely wide range of matters of fact are recognised to be relevant.

For example, relevant facts which could be brought to bear on the situation or which underpin the supposedly ultimate values involved could be psychological, historical, sociological or religious beliefs, such as whether there is life after death or whether Christian dogmas are true, or beliefs about human beings which in principle are based on empirical or corrigible beliefs. Hudson (1970, p. 28) argues against Phillips and Mounce's view that the difference between the housewife and the rationalist in their example is a difference in moral beliefs:

> But is it simply that the mother subscribes to the moral principles 'Obey the will of God!', 'Create new life!', or whatever, and the rationalist does not, as these authors appear to suggest? Or does the root difference lie in the belief, not about what is good for man, but about what man is. The mother believes him a child of God destined for eternal life, the rationalist takes an entirely material and terrestrial view of man's existence.

Hence, what is behind the disagreement are differing beliefs about the nature of human beings which can in principle be confirmed or refuted. That is disagreement concerns different beliefs as to what is the case, which entails the belief that certain things are true, and not merely based on different ultimate moral commitments which have no recourse to the citing of reasons or evidence which the proponents of the debate regard as justifiable in some way.

The R.C. housewife in the example, if pressed, would wish to make truth claims about the existence of God and the nature of human beings by the citing of reasons and evidence. If such evidence failed to establish her case, she may resort to defending her own beliefs via the notion of 'faith' which goes beyond the factual evidence originally put forward. However, her 'faith' is still a belief in an objective fact, the truth of the existence of God and hence the purpose and function of human beings. If she were to be convinced by counter arguments and evidence that God did not in fact exist, that He was merely a figment of her imagination or a consoling psychological prop in an otherwise purposeless world, then her continuing faith in God's existence and the nature and purposes of human beings would not be rationally supportable. Though she may heartily wish to continue to believe for psychological and emotional reasons, and such belief could be said to be a subjective necessity for her, continued belief nevertheless would be a rationalisation and not objectively necessary or rationally justifiable. In fact, she could only continue to believe at the expense of a massive denial of what she then knew to be the case.

Similarly, if the scientific rationalist's belief about the nature of human beings was shown to be based on false evidence, then he would no longer have any logical justifiable reason for adhering to his belief.

It is not my concern at this moment to justify either the R.C's or the rationalist's beliefs about human beings as regards their truth or falsity. It is, rather, my concern to show that their beliefs and moral commitments are based on the kind of evidence and reasons which could in principle be confirmed or refuted. I am not concerned with the empirical question as to whether the dispute between such protagonists could be resolved, but rather with the logical question as to whether it is possible to resolve it.

I am arguing against the view that assertions put forward in moral disagreements are ultimately based on different values which cannot be defended by further argument. Resolutions to moral disagreements are connected with evidence or reasons which can be offered in support of those assertions. The truth or falsity of that evidence will then support or defeat the moral assertion in question. That is:

a) moral beliefs and assertions are ultimately based on evidence which is cited in their support (and not on a commitment to ultimate values) which are believed by their proponents to be true; and

b) this evidence is in principle open to confirmation or refutation. If it were confirmed it would support the assertion, if it were falsified it would not support the assertion.

However, this is not to claim that all moral disagreements are logically or easily resolvable by appeal to empirical facts or that it is always possible in the end, to reach agreement by means of reasoning and the citing of evidence. In practice it is difficult for people with widely divergent moral beliefs to come to agreement on the facts in the first place, and what counts as reasons and evidence are themselves socially determined and influenced, and therefore maybe socially relative. Moreover, though psychological, historical and sociological beliefs, plus beliefs about the nature of human beings are in principle open to confirmation or refutation, our knowledge of them is not always sufficiently advanced to be able to confirm or refute them in any absolute or secure way.

Certain moral beliefs or assertions then, cannot be absolutely logically or conclusively supported by appeal to evidence for two reasons following from a) and b) above. In the case of a), though moral assertions and beliefs are ultimately supported by appeal to evidence which their proponents must believe to be true, these beliefs or assertions cannot be confirmed or refuted conclusively by appeal to evidence, in the sense that the truth or falsity of that evidence logically entails the truth or falsity of the assertion, and, b), though it is the case that the evidence cited in support of moral beliefs or assertions is in principle open to confirmation or refutation, it is not always possible to confirm or refute that evidence absolutely since all the facts may be unavailable or it may be difficult to establish the facts conclusively.

However, neither of these conclusions mean that moral beliefs or assertions cannot be defended or attacked by appeal to evidence.

In the case of a) because the truth or falsity of the evidence does not entail the truth or falsity of the assertion, this does not mean that there is nothing that can count as reasons for or against it. As has already been argued, this state of affairs is not peculiar to moral discourse. It also pertains in non-moral and ordinary factual discourse.

In the case of b) because it may sometimes be difficult to establish the absolute certain truth of the evidence (i.e. verify or falsify it absolutely) this does not mean that the assertion which it attempts to justify is entirely unsupported until knowledge of that evidence is absolutely certain and secure. As in a) this is not the case only in moral discourse, but pertains in non-moral, factual and scientific discourse. Whether we are dealing with evidence cited in competing scientific theories or competing moral claims, we prefer that theory or claim which gives the fullest possible explanation given the present state of our knowledge of the evidence. We choose Theory 1 over Theory 2, if the first can explain by the citing of evidence all the phenomena the second can explain, plus some additional phenomena the second cannot explain. This does not make the theory or the claim absolutely certain or secure; it merely, for the time being, by the citing and testing of evidence, allows us to regard this evidence as sufficient support for the truth of the theory or assertion. This epistemic relativity, leaves open the possibility of the revision, correction and modification of previous knowledge and assertions, as further developments in knowledge occur which yield new or further evidence. Evidence can support an assertion even when the status of that evidence is not absolutely secure and certain, and even though future evidence may be brought to light which could either defeat or corroborate it.

Consequently though moral disagreements are not easily resolvable in all cases, by appeal to evidence, it is evidence, upon which the justification of moral beliefs rest, and not upon any ultimate commitment to values beyond any attempt to support them in any other terms.

The criteria for the kind of evidence which can support or defeat an assertion will be elaborated in Section 3. Briefly, they include referential and causally relevant evidence, and the evidence must be both true and independent of a prior commitment to the assertion in question. If this is the case then the kinds of evidence that could be brought to bear in a moral situation could be agreed upon. For instance, physiological, psychological, historical, sociological and religious beliefs could count as evidence for determining how people ought to behave if they are causally relevant to the behaviour of human beings and if we have good grounds for believing them to be true. This means that we can agree upon what kind of evidence can be cited in support of moral assertions, i.e., any kind of evidence that is true and that determines, effects, influences, describes or explains what human beings are and can become. Therefore, if God exists and there is a causal connection between not obeying God and eternal damnation, then this will be important information directly relevant to how we ought to behave. If human beings are principally motivated by self-interest or they are capable of altruism, then we cannot overlook these motivations in determining what they can and should do. If human beings are robots manipulated by extra-terrestial computers, then this information would set limits to what they can and ought to do. Disputes will arise as to whether the evidence is true, but in principle, the criteria for what kind of evidence is relevant can be agreed upon. Evidence that is excluded will be any kind of evidence that is false or that has no bearing or is not causally related to the nature of human beings, human life, death or life after death.

What is being claimed is that facts about what is the case and what the nature of human beings consists of, are the main components of moral disagreements. This then suggests that there is a connection between certain facts about human beings and the intelligibility of moral assertions. Hudson's (1970, p. 29) observations vis-a-vis the housewife and the rationalist, he says, raise precisely this question:

> Can we say that there is a logical connection between what any man finds it intelligible to regard as a good man and what he believes man to be? If so, there would be that much connection between fact and value at least. And should we not be entitled to go on to say that, if we could settle what man is, we could demonstrate what he ought to do?

When arguing about a moral issue any kind of evidence which throws light on what human beings are, have become and can become, will if it fulfils the criteria, show us what it is rational to do and set the boundaries for 'oughts'.

If facts about human beings and moral assertions are connected in that the former provide reasons for the latter, this suggests that 'ought' cannot be used legitimately, nor can moral judgements be made legitimately, where there are no reasons or facts other than the person's choice of, or commitment to values, which are relevant to their application.

When we ask how to justify a moral assertion, expressions of feeling or sincere commitment are insufficient justification, for feelings and commitments have been seen to involve the citing of reasons and evidence, claims and beliefs as to their truth, and which are logically prior to that feeling or commitment.

c) Richard Hare (1952, 1963, 1981, 1988) agrees that moral language must be action guiding not by working on emotions but by being addressed to people as rational agents and telling them what to do. Reason has a role in making moral judgements in that reason derives moral judgements from more general judgements. He argues 'to do our moral thinking rationally is to seek opinions for which we can give reasons' (Hare 1988, p. 273). So, for Hare, reasons and evidence are important to the making of moral judgements. For Hare, the relevant kinds of facts are 'the inclinations or preferences of all parties' (Hare 1988 p. 212, see also 1981, p. 90). Hare (1988, p. 213) does though argue that moral conclusions are not derived or deduced from these facts about preferences of the agent and (via universalisability) of other people:

> My method of reasoning is not a derivation or deduction of moral conclusions from premises about people's preferences. The judgement it leads to is, rather, what all those who think rationally and are in possession of the facts will say, i.e. the moral prescription they will accept.

However Hare (1988, p. 213) argues that reference to facts about preferences is important:

> the whole point of prescriptivism is that it makes moral judgements equivalent to certain kind of prescriptions, and prescriptions are the expressions of preferences or desires in a broad sense.

He continues, (p. 214):

> that moral reasons are not the same as prudential reasons. The latter have, perhaps to be traced back exclusively to desires or preferences, present or future of the agent. But the former have also to take into account the preferences of others affected.

For Hare (pp. 214–215) both prudential and moral reasoning must in different ways take into account desires and preferences:

> It could be wished that moral philosophers would give up needs as a basis for their theories. They will not bear any weight. The word 'need' is etymologically connected in many languages with words for 'necessity' (e.g. the German 'Not' and 'notwendig'). If I need something, it is a necessary condition for the realisation of some end, to say that someone needs something is always to say something incomplete, unless we specify what he needs it for, or what it is a necessary condition for. Very often this does not have to be specified because it is so obvious, and that is what has misled these philosophers. But for completeness it has to be specified. This is apparent in the form of the objection here considered. We need food for survival, and survival for 'human flourishing'. We do not need 'human flourishing' (whatever that is) for anything, and therefore it is improper (as anybody who knows the language and can decipher that expression will recognise) to say we need it. We desire it. To call it a need would imply that it was instrumental to something else. What constitutes 'human flourishing' is another question - a question of value which cannot be settled by appealing to needs ...
>
> Settling on an end, like deciding what 'human flourishing' is, is answering an evaluative question. We cannot therefore without circularity answer all evaluative questions by appealing to a telos as given. The telos of actions is what we desire (boulometha) for its own sake; so there are no ends without desires.

Hare's position implies that we can choose our needs because we can reject the end or norm of 'flourishing' presupposed by the need claim and that such norms can never be discovered empirically. Such norms pertain to individual ends or desires like flourishing and this means we can choose our ends (since these are not given) and choose the nature of 'flourishing' or any other telos.

The value of our ends/desires or telos is plastic depending on whether we accept or reject a particular norm.

But, the argument of the first chapter showed that the notion of fundamental human needs avoids this problem. This is because there are some ends which we can take as 'given' in Hare's sense and they can be discovered empirically. These are the ends any human being, regardless of the norms they accept or reject, has good reason to value. These are the conditions necessary for successful human activity and for the pursuit of any goal. This view of needs as the means to achieving all wants and ends accommodates the claim that needs are fundamental and inescapable. While it is appropriate to say 'A desires x but x is not good, therefore A ought not to desire x' the same formulation is inappropriate for needs. If survival and health are indispensably necessary for the attainment of any ends, then at least there must be prudential reasons for acting to achieve survival and health needs.

In this section it has been conceded that value judgements cannot be logically derived from facts but can be supported by them. Specifically it has been shown that:

a) Moral judgements are not simply descriptions or expressions of emotion.

b) Even ultimate values in principle can be supported or undermined by appeal to reasons and evidence.

c) Needs are factual matters and are evidence for what people ought to do.

In Section (3) I will take up the problem of the criteria for reasons and evidence that can be given to establish and support moral assertions or commitments, and then apply this criteria to 'need' statements.

3 *There are kinds of statements which can be established or defended exclusively by reference to another kind, without the first being deducible or logically derivable from the second*

Though it is agreed that values are not logically derivable from factual statements, values can be established or rationally supported by arguments which appeal to factual evidence. Using Keekok Lee's (1985) theory, which seems to me to systematise other philosophers' suggestions on this matter, I shall argue that the kind of evidence which is capable of rationally supporting an assertion (either moral or non-moral) must fulfil the following criteria:

1 The evidence must be relevant from a referential point of view. The same object must be referred to in both the evidence and the assertion.

2 The evidence must be relevant from a causal point of view.

3 The evidence must be true.

4 The evidence must be causally independent of a prior commitment to the assertion.

I will illustrate this by applying the criteria firstly to ordinary factual assertions (A3) then to non-moral oughts (A2) and finally to moral oughts (A1).

Ordinary factual assertions (A3s) It is proposed that the ordinary factual assertion, 'This dog is ill' (A3) could be backed by the evidence, 'This dog has lost weight' (E3)

Can the evidence offered support the assertion?
Does it fulfil the criteria 1 – 4 outlined above?

It fulfils:

1 in that the evidence is relevant from a referential point of view. There is a shared term 'This dog' in both the assertion and the evidence. Compare this with the evidence like, 'I am committed to the view that this dog is ill', which is not referentially relevant. It is a subjective account which is not open to public scrutiny.

It fulfils:

2 in that the evidence is relevant to the assertion from a causal point of view. That is, the predicate variables 'is ill' and 'has lost weight' are causally related to each other. There is a causal relation between being ill and losing weight. Causal relations are empirically discovered. Once they have been established between two terms or processes, then a meaning link between them is also established via these causal connections for the meaning of being ill is partially explained in terms of such things as losing weight etc.

If the evidence for the assertion was not relevant from a causal point of view, for example, if the evidence offered in support of the assertion 'this dog is ill' was 'this dog has a black nose', the assertion would not be rationally justified as no empirical causal connection has been established as yet, between being ill and having black noses. However, evidence for 'this dog is ill' could be 'this dog has a hot nose', since causal connections have been established between hot noses in dogs and illness.

Since causal connections are empirically discovered this leaves open the possibility of discovering further causal connections and so of establishing meaning links as well as the possibility of disconfirming hitherto regarded sound causal connections. There does not however seem to be a causal connection between saying that 'this dog is ill' and 'I am sincerely committed to the view that this dog is ill'.

Does it fulfil criterion 3, that the evidence must be true?

If the evidence, 'This dog has lost weight' is also true, then it can be said to rationally support the assertion, 'This dog is ill'. If the evidence 'This dog has lost weight' (though it is referentially and causally relevant to the assertion, 'This dog is ill') is false, then it would not be rational to conclude that the assertion is justified or supported by appeal to such false evidence.

Does it fulfil criterion 4, that the evidence must be causally independent of a prior commitment to the assertion?

The evidence must be causally independent of a prior commitment to the assertion so that the evidence can be offered in support of the assertion and in justification for any commitment to that assertion. It is the evidence that the dog has lost weight (if it is true) which gives support to or justifies any commitment to the view that the dog is ill.

Non-moral oughts (A2s) It is proposed that the assertion, 'This object ought to be treated with extreme care' (A2) is backed by the evidence, 'This object is the last surviving art work of its kind' (E2).

Could the evidence fulfil criteria 1 – 4?

1 Referential relevance obtains – the assertion and the evidence contain reference to the same object, i.e. 'This object'.

2 Causal relevance obtains because there is an empirically discoverable causal connection between treating something with extreme care and preserving it. Consequently a meaning link exists between the predicate variable, 'extreme care' and the 'last surviving art work of its kind'.

3 Do truth criteria obtain? If it is true that the object is the last surviving art work of its kind, then this evidence would support the assertion that it ought to be preserved. If it were false, then it would not support the assertion, in the absence of other reasons.

4 Causal independence obtains since the evidence is causally independent of the assertion and hence justifies it. Commitment alone would not be sufficient or appropriate justification for the assertion.

Moral oughts (A1s) It is proposed that the assertion, 'torture is an activity which ought to be avoided' (A1) be supported by the evidence, 'torture is an activity which causes pain' (E1). The evidence fulfils:

1 Referential relevance. The same referent, 'torture', appears in the assertion and in the evidence.

2 Causal relevance obtains. A causal connection can be established. It is an empirical fact that something that causes pain is something that people tend to avoid. There is a further causal link between 'torture' and

'causing pain' which establishes the overlap in meaning between the two terms, for it is not possible to explain the meaning of 'torture' without referring to pain.

3 Truth criteria obtain, since it is true that torture causes pain and it is the truth of this which supports the assertion that this activity ought to be avoided.

4 Independence criteria obtain, for the assertion has been supported by evidence independent of a commitment to the assertion.

Given the foregoing discussion, it can be claimed that one kind of statement can be established or defended exclusively by reference to another kind without the first being deducible or logically derivable from the second. The way in which one kind of statement be it 'moral', 'non-moral' or an ordinary factual 'is' statement can be defended by another factual statement is termed 'epistemic implication' by Keekok Lee (1985). 'Epistemic implication' then, characterises the relationship between assertions and evidence in the three types of statement discussed. Therefore, 'epistemic implication' holds between values and facts when the facts are referential and causally relevant to the values, when the facts are true, and when the facts are established prior to a commitment to the values in question. When these conditions hold, then values can be supported rationally by appeal to the facts.

Objective facts then give grounds for assertions, factual, prescriptive, practical and moral, because of the nature of the facts themselves. It is indisputable that the facts cited in:

E3 This dog has lost weight.
E2 This is the last surviving art work of its kind.
E1 Torture is an activity that causes pain,

do not logically entail facts, practical or moral, prescriptions or assertions that:

A3 This dog is ill.
A2 This art work ought to be treated with extreme care.
A1 Torture is an activity which ought to be avoided,

but this does not obliterate the practical rationality (all things being equal) of doing so. The notion of 'epistemic implication' entails only that one proposition gives rational support to another without logically entailing it.

However, it might be argued that in the case of ordinary factual 'is' statements, we need only to establish the status of the evidence (E3) as referentially and causally relevant, true and causally independent and prior to the assertion (A3) in order to give rational support to the factual 'is' statement asserted in the conclusion, whereas in the cases of non-moral and moral assertions, establishing the status of the evidence in this way is a necessary but not a sufficient condition to rationally justify the conclusions asserted in A2 and A1.

That is, in order to rationally justify the assertions,

A2 This object ought to be treated with extreme care, and
A3 Torture is an activity which ought to be avoided

we need to establish, not only the status of the evidence, but also establish that the justifiability of the conclusion is dependent on acceptance of the beliefs, desires and intentions of the agent in question. That is, in A2 and E2, that art objects ought to be preserved or that the agent wants to preserve art objects, and in A3 and E3, that one ought not to cause pain or that the agent does not want to cause pain.

This suggests that the ought statements of the conclusion in A2 and A3 should be classified as hypothetical imperatives. The ought statement of the conclusions arise in answers to the agent's practical questions of what to do in order to achieve, or do something else, in a situation where the agent wants or intends to do something else and needs knowledge of what to do in order to get it.

'Want' occurs in the hypothetical imperative, where wanting or intending to do x practically or normatively requires doing y, where the doing of y is a causal, empirical or analytically necessary condition for the doing or achieving of x. The practical or normative force of the hypothetical imperative bears on the means in relation to the end in question. Thus, if the agent wants or intends to do x, he ought or must do y. Therefore in addition to the evidence and estimation of its status in E2 and E3, we also need some statement about the agent's desires or intentions in order to pass to the conclusions in A2 and A3, viz;

E2 This is the last surviving art work of its kind, *plus*
W2 If the agent wants or intends to preserve art works, then
A2 He must or ought to treat it with extreme care.

E3 Torture is an activity which causes pain.
W3 If the agent wants to avoid causing pain then,
A3 He must, or ought to, avoid torture.

That is, where the agent wants to know what to do in order to achieve or do something else, what to do in order to preserve art works or to avoid causing pain, in a situation where these ends are the object of the agent's desire or intention, then it follows that he ought to do whatever is the means of achieving these ends, where the doing of the means are necessary conditions for the doing or achieving of those ends.

This draws attention to the fact that when human agents are engaged in practical activity, as opposed to logical contemplation, they can and do derive validly technical imperatives from theoretical premises. The recognition that 'ought' cannot be logically derived from 'is' need not foreclose the possibility of a justification of a practical morality based on objectively valid hypothetical imperatives.

In the case of non-moral assertions cited in A2, the evidence E2 plus the condition W2, 'if A wants or intends to preserve art works' may be sufficient only to establish that A, as a particular agent ought to preserve the last surviving art work of its kind, since the desire, intention or end of preserving art works may be A's particular preference and not a desire, intention or end which is capable of universal assent. In the case of moral assertions, if there are universal desires, intentions or ends, then these, plus appeal to evidence could give good grounds for making moral assertions. I suggest that fundamental human needs are means to ends such as these.

What has been established here, in general terms is that appeal to facts and evidence, conditional on the desires, intentions or ends of the agent in question give grounds for making moral assertions. Though values cannot be derived logically from facts the notion of 'epistemic implication' together with the technical reasoning of the hypothetical imperative allows us to argue that values can be supported rationally by facts. This argument does not claim that the values that are thereby derived cannot be overridden by other values. However it is to claim that such overriding cannot consistently be argued to be either necessary or even normally warranted.

Facts, values and needs: application of this to 'needs' – a model

I shall now show how 'epistemic implication' holds between the principle 'human beings' fundamental needs ought to be met' and the factual evidence about human needs. Below is an abstract model of how this may be done.

In support of the principle 'human beings' fundamental needs ought to be met' the following evidence can be cited. Though this support does not amount to logical derivation, it does satisfy 'epistemic implication' between the principle and the factual premises:

i) Human beings, by virtue of being prospective, potential or actual human agents in possession of any ends at all, who have to act to achieve these ends, and who desire success in achieving them, have needs for survival and health, ('Fundamental Human Needs 1') which are empirically discoverable necessary conditions or means to these ends. They are objectively necessary rather than subjectively desirable.

ii) Human beings, as a matter of fact, seek to meet 'Fundamental Human Needs 1' as a result of their being means to any end.

iii) Since survival and health also can be described as objective ends pursued, desired and valued intrinsically as well as instrumentally, 'Fundamental Human Needs 2' are the empirically discoverable means to the achievement of survival and health, for the moment defined as 'Survival Needs i, ii, iii ...' and 'Health Needs i, ii, iii ...' Content will be given to these needs in Chapters 6–8. Human beings must meet FHN2 as a result of their biological and psychological constitutions, as well as a result of these needs being means to ends which FHN become.

The four criteria for 'epistemic implication' will hold if it can be shown that:

1 The assertion or the principle and the evidence share the same subject term. This is the case since both assertion and evidence refer to 'human beings' (meaning all human beings who are prospective, potential or actual human agents) therefore the condition of referential relevance is satisfied.

2 Causal relevance between the assertion and the evidence will obtain if it can be shown that

a) the meaning of the terms 'meeting needs' and 'needs being met' can be rationally explicated by reference to terms like survival, health and SNi, ii and iii, HNi, ii, and iii, and

b) if a meaning link exists because survival and health are things that human beings pursue given that they are agents in possession of ends, and

c) if a meaning link exists because the things SNi, ii and iii and HNi, ii and iii are things that human beings as a matter of fact must seek to achieve given the ends of survival and health and given their biological and psychological constitutions. If this can be done when the terms survival and health SNi, ii and iii, and HNi, ii and iii have been given empirical content, then causal relevance will be satisfied.

3 The truth condition will be satisfied if it can be shown through factual evidence

a) that human beings in order to act to achieve any ends necessarily have to have certain means, survival and health

b) that human beings have certain biological and psychological constitutions so that when SNi–iii and HNi–iii are obtained, the effect is the satisfaction of 'Fundamental Human Needs 1', survival and health.

4 Causal independence will obtain since it will be obvious that the causally relevant evidence cited is causally independent and prior to the commitment to the principle.

If the above criteria can be applied, then 'epistemic implication' obtains between values and facts, that is, it is possible for one proposition to give rational support to another without logically entailing it.

But, to fully justify the assertion 'Fundamental Human Needs 1 and 2 ought to be met', in addition to the status of the evidence, we must also establish the desires and intentions of the agent.

As has been argued, the 'ought' statement of the conclusion or assertion can be classified as a hypothetical imperative, in a situation where the agent wants or intends to do something else (achieve some end) and needs to know what to do in order to achieve it. But, these desires, intentions and ends are not subjective or peculiar to any particular human agent, but are objective in the sense that they are desires, intentions or ends which any human agent has good reason to pursue, desire or value (a) by virtue of being a human agent in possession of any ends at all ('Fundamental Human Needs 1') and (b) by virtue of these 'Fundamental Human Needs 1' being ends in themselves which any human agent has good reason to pursue, desire or value. Conditional on these as an antecedent, plus appeal to a theory which provided factual evidence regarding human ends and human needs and by establishing the status of the evidence cited in backing the assertion, it is possible to give rational and objective grounds for making moral assertions.

The hypothetical imperative plus 'epistemic implication' might be construed thus:

CONDITIONAL	If A, by virtue of being a human agent in possession of any end E wishes or intends to act to achieve any end E,
EVIDENCE	and survival and health are the necessary conditions ('Fundamental Human Needs 1') for the successful action for the attainment of any end E,
ASSERTION	survival and health ('Fundamental Human Needs 1') ought to be met.
CONDITIONAL	If A (any human agent) has good reason to pursue, desire or value ends survival and health (intrinsically and instrumentally)
EVIDENCE	and SNi–iii and HNi–iii are the empirical means ('Fundamental Human Needs 2') for the attainment of survival and health

ASSERTION SNi–iii and HNi–iii ('Fundamental Human Needs 2') ought to be met.

Prudential – moral obligations

So far, this argument has established that any human agent, by virtue of being an agent in possession of ends who must act to achieve them, prudentially ought to meet the fundamental human needs (for survival and health) which are means to these ends.

It has not been established that morally these needs ought to be met, that is, that there are moral obligations to meet other people's needs.

I think a relatively simple argument can show how prudential obligations to meet one's own needs can lead to moral obligations to meet other people's.

If A, by virtue of being a human agent in possession of ends, has survival and health needs that are practically necessary in order to achieve their ends, it follows that any and all human agents in possession of ends have these needs and have the same prudential obligation to meet them. They cannot fulfil their purposes unless these are met.

If A accepts that she has prudential obligations to meet her needs, then logically she must accept that all other agents have equally strong prudential reasons for meeting their own. Therefore she must acknowledge the obvious point that all persons ought prudentially to meet their needs.

Now, as a matter of empirical fact people cannot meet their needs if other people act to prevent them from being met or do not help them meet them when they cannot be met by individuals acting alone. This means that no agents can meet their needs unless other people refrain from interfering with them or in some cases offer assistance towards their satisfaction. Any agent then who accepts that she has a prudential obligation to meet her needs, and therefore that all other agents do, will then be committed to working towards the general satisfaction of needs.

If I deny my own needs ought to be met, I accept that others may interfere with my survival and health or refrain from promoting my survival and health and this contradicts the view that my survival and health are necessary conditions for any activity, for the pursuit of any goal. If I accept my own needs ought to be met, because they are the necessary conditions for achieving any goal, then I must accept all other agents' needs ought to be met. If I interfere with their needs or do not help them meet them, then I deny what before I have accepted: that fundamental human needs are necessary conditions of any activity and therefore necessary goods to all agents.

Accepting fundamental human needs as practically necessary conditions of any activity and therefore equally important to all agents, insofar as agents are the potential recipients of my actions, I ought to act in accordance with meeting other people's needs.

This argument starts with the practical interests each agent has in satisfying their needs and encompasses obligations to meet other peoples. These obligations are moral because the agent must take positive account of other people's interests when the agent acknowledges that all agents have practical interests in satisfying their needs.

The argument proceeds from an individual's self interest in meeting their own needs but is not an egoistic morality. I acknowledge other people's need claims not as a means to meeting my own but rather on the same grounds that I acknowledge that my own ought to be met. This commits me and every other agent to refraining from interfering with other people's attempts to meet their needs and assisting them in meeting them. If I do not do so, I deny what I cannot help but acknowledge.

If the reader finds the above argument too simplistic I refer them to a more rigorous argument provided by Alan Gewirth (1978, 1982, 1984a, 1984b, 1987) which aims to show that needs as the necessary condition of human action are the subject of human rights. This argument can be adapted to provide support for my contention that fundamental human needs ought to be met.

Gewirth's argument

Gewirth (1978, 1982, 1984a, b, 1987) argues that the concept of rights is central and indispensable to morality. He claims that morality and rights are connected with human action, which itself is the general context of all morality and practice. Gewirth (1987, pp. 59–60) argues that rights are crucial to all actions because human rights have as their object the necessary conditions of action and successful action in general:

> Human rights are justified requirements that all persons have as their due, as what they are entitled to, as what they can justifiably demand that all persons respect either by non-interference or, in certain circumstances by positive assistance. And the content of these goods are the necessary conditions of action and successful action in general. Thus, what human rights require is that the necessary goods not be removed or interfered with by any persons, or groups, and also, in certain circumstances, that the necessary goods be provided for all persons who cannot obtain them by their own efforts.

Gewirth argues that what is at issue here is the fulfilment of needs, the fulfilment of the needs of action which are the central concern of morality. Gewirth (1987, p. 61) identifies *freedom* and *well-being* as the generic features and necessary conditions of action. He explains that:

> Freedom is the procedural feature of action; it consists in controlling one's behaviour by one's unforced choice while having relevant knowledge of the circumstances.

and,

> Well-being ... is the substantive generic feature of action; it consists in having the purpose-related general abilities and conditions that are required either for being able to act at all or for having general chances of success in achieving the purposes for which one acts. The components of such well being thus fall into a hierarchy of goods, ranging from life and physical integrity to self-esteem and education.

Gewirth proposes that the concept of universal human rights is crucial to all action and therefore must be accepted in this context because they are the necessary conditions of successful action in general. Without them people either cannot act at all or cannot act with any general expectation of achieving their purposes.

In the argument that follows I have substituted survival and health for Gewirth's conditions of freedom and well-being. In my account freedom is not considered as a separate feature and need of action since the type of behaviour we call action is identified by the goal or end it was the agent's intention or purpose to bring about. Therefore the purposiveness which underlines well-being covers both features of action. No action that is purposive could be regarded as involuntary and no involuntary action could be regarded as purposive. Furthermore, freedom, as the ability to act and achieve ends and purposes, involves fulfilling the needs of survival and health which are means to those ends. Survival and health approximate Gewirth's conditions of well-being as the necessary conditions of any successful and purposive activity.

The argument proceeds as follows:

Any agent A, defined as an actual or prospective performer of actions, when s/he performs an action, s/he can be described as saying or thinking:

1 'I do x for end or purpose E'.

From A's standpoint, E is something s/he believes has sufficient value to merit action towards attaining E.
(1) therefore entails

2 'E is good'.

Now, in order to act for E, A must have the proximate necessary conditions of action (survival and health) Hence, from the agent's standpoint, from (2) there follows

3 'My survival and health are necessary goods'.

This may also be put as

4 'I must have survival and health'.

This 'must' is a practical-prescriptive requirement expressed by the agent. It signifies the agents advocacy of having what s/he needs. From (4) there follows

5 'I have rights to survival and health'.

(5) follows (4), because if the agent denied (5) because of the strict correlativity of rights and strict 'oughts', s/he would also have to deny

6 'All other persons ought at least to refrain from removing or interfering with my survival and health'.

By denying (6) s/he must accept

7 'It is not the case that all other persons ought at least to refrain from removing or interfering with my survival and health'.

By accepting (7), s/he must also accept

8 'Other persons may (i.e. it is permissible that other persons) remove or interfere with my survival and health'.

And by accepting (8), s/he must accept

9 'I may not (i.e. it is permissible that I not) have survival and health'.

But (9) contradicts (4), 'I must have survival and health'.
Since every agent must accept (4), s/he must reject (9).
And since (9) follows from a denial of (5),
'I have rights to survival and health', every agent must also reject the denial. Hence, every agent logically must accept (5). 'I have rights to survival and health'.

The concept of rights then, is logically involved in all action as a concept that signifies for every agent his claim and requirement that he have the necessary conditions of action.

The criterion of these rights is only prudential in that it consists for each agent in his or her own needs of agency in pursuit of his or her own purposes. Further steps show how this prudential right claim also becomes a moral right.

The reason every agent holds s/he has rights to survival and health is that s/he is a prospective purposive agent. Therefore s/he must accept

10 'I have rights to survival and health because I am a prospective purposive agent'.

If the agent rejected (10), and instead claimed s/he had rights on some more restrictive characteristic R, the agent would be saying

11 'I have rights to survival and health because I am R' where 'R' is something more restrictive than being a prospective purposive agent (for example being male or white).

The agent then would contradict himself because he would be saying that if he did not have R, he would not have the generic rights, so he would have to accept

12 'I do not have rights to survival and health'.

But, as an agent, he must hold that he has these rights.
Hence he must accept (10).
By virtue of accepting (10) the agent must accept

13 'All prospective purposive agents have rights to survival and health'.
(13) follows from (10) because of the principle of universalisation.

At this point rights become moral ones in two senses. One, because the practical requirements are categorically obligatory and two, because they involve taking favourable account of the interests of others.

When the agent says (13) s/he is logically committed to taking favourable account of other people having the necessary conditions of action. Since all other persons are actual or potential recipients of his or her action, every agent is logically committed to accepting

14 'I ought to act in accord with the generic rights of my recipients as well as myself'.

This requirement can also be expressed as the general moral Principle which Gewirth calls the 'Principle of Generic Consistency' (PGC):

15 'Act in accord with the generic rights of your recipients as well as of yourself'.

Gewirth then has argued that every agent must logically hold or accept that he has rights to the necessary conditions of his action, if he denies he has these rights, then he must accept that other people may remove or interfere with them. This contradicts his belief that he must have them. The agent also logically must accept all other prospective purposive agents have the same rights.

Objections

There have been many objections to Gewirth's attempt to derive universal human rights from the requirements of action. I shall examine some of the salient ones for the purposes of this book below:

1 *The Normative Structure of Action 1: Goods* (Adams 1984, pp. 8–23)

Adams questions the transition from
(1) 'I do x for end E' to
(2) 'E is good'

on the grounds that this agent-relative position doesn't indicate the features of objects that leads them to be desired or regarded as good. Adams' non-relativist position on judgements of good maintains that things are not good because they are desired, but desired because they are good.

Although Gewirth takes a relativist position on the goodness of the particular ends the agent wants to achieve, this relativism becomes universal and necessary with regard to the necessary conditions of action. These must be regarded as necessary goods by every agent because they are the proximate necessary condition of each agents acting to achieve any of his purposes. By accepting (2) 'E is good', every agent must also accept (3) 'My survival and health are necessary goods'.

Gewirth (1984, p. 205) writes, 'the fact that the necessary goodness of these conditions is relative to the cognitive standpoint of each agent does not militate against the necessity and universality of the envisaged conclusion'.

In terms of my analysis, it is precisely because survival and health are the means to any ends the agent wants to achieve, that they are universally necessary fundamental human needs.

2 *The Normative Structure of Action II: Right Claims* (Hare 1984, Raphael 1984, Nielsen 1984, Hudson 1984)

The above critics, in various ways, have criticised the crucial moves from

(3) 'My survival and health are necessary goods' to
(4) 'I must have survival and health'
(5) 'I have rights to survival and health'.

Hudson (1984, p. 127), for instance asks, 'How can the mere fact that anyone insists upon having something give him a right to it?' Gewirth's argument, though, does not proceed by ascribing a right to a person but by showing that he must hold or accept that he does have such a right on pain of contradiction between (4) and (9).

Nielsen (1984, p. 76) objects to the 'must' in (4) since it expresses the agent's 'firm resolve' and 'does not tell him or us what others are obligated to do'. Similarly Hare (1984) says that someone can want something without thinking they ought to have it. Because the agent must 'want' the necessary conditions of action it doesn't necessarily follow that the agent must 'therefore think that other persons ought to supply these necessary conditions by refraining from interfering' (p. 54) as step 6 suggests.

Other persons are 'bound to honour' this in the sense of recognising the rights of other prospective agents because these rights are based on the same justifying conditions on which the original agent based his own right claim. The generalisation (13) is a moral judgement because it requires the agent to take favourable account of the interests of other persons. Hare recognises that prudential judgements are universalisable, but only in the sense that they justify the transition from

(a) 'there is a prudential requirement on (an agent) to seek the necessary conditions for achieving *his* purposes' to

(b) 'there is a prudential requirement on other similar agents in similar situations to seek the necessary conditions for achieving *their* purposes' .

But, if an agent acknowledges (b) then he is endorsing other agents fulfilment of their agency needs; and this endorsement is a moral one, since the agent is taking a favourable account of the interests of other persons. By acknowledging (b) and endorsing others' fulfilment of their agency needs, he acknowledges that if his own effective help is a necessary condition of such fulfilment then he is logically committed to provide it, so satisfying what Hare suggests is a moral judgement (c) that 'there is a requirement on anyone, including the original agent, to seek the necessary conditions for achieving the purposes of anyone else who is similarly placed' (p. 55).

3 *The 'Amoralist'* (Nielsen 1984, Hare 1984)

Nielsen and Hare have focused on the gangster as an amoralist agent who disavows others' rights and obligations while doing all he can to protect his necessary goods of survival and health. But, Gewirth's argument repeatedly has shown that every person who is rational and cognitively normal, whether a gangster or amoralist, logically must use the concept of a prudential 'ought' both self and other directed and he must use the latter in a way that entails a correlative right claim. Every agent logically must generalise his own rights claims.

4 *Egoism* (Singer 1984, Kalin 1984)

Both Singer and Kalin object to Gewirth's ethical rationalism since it rules out all the varieties of egoism and other self-interested theories. Gewirth replies that universal ethical egoism is inconsistent and therefore cannot invalidate his theory. Ethical egoism logically requires the egoist to advocate two mutually inconsistent prescriptions for action: that his survival and health both ought and ought not to be interfered with by other people. As an agent he holds that his survival and health ought not to be interfered with by other people, and as a universal ethical egoist he holds that other people ought to interfere when it is conducive to their own self-interest.

5 *The Rights of Marginal Agents* (Hill, 1984)

On the question of whether 'marginal agents' such as children, mentally deficient persons, fetuses and animals have rights, Gewirth (1978, p. 22) says, 'members of these groups approach having the generic rights in varying degrees, depending on the degree to which they have the requisite abilities'.

In *Replies to My Critics*, Gewirth (1984b, p. 226) stressed the main point 'is that varying degrees of having the abilities justify varying degrees of having the rights, because of the way in which the having of the abilities bears on individuals' interest capacity for exercising the rights without harm to themselves or others'.

For Gewirth (1978, p. 123) established that the basis on which every agent logically can claim to have rights consists in 'actually being a prospective agent who has purposes he wants to fulfil'.

It is the having of purposes, and not the having of any practical abilities over and above the general abilities of agencies, that logically grounds for any agent his claim to have rights. Marginal agents are distinguished from prospective purposive agents according to the degree to which they have the practical abilities that make them capable of having and exercising their generic rights. Therefore individuals may have in varying degrees the practical abilities that entitle them to rights, but the basis on which they could rationally claim these rights for themselves does not vary in degree among different agents. Their rights might not necessarily be claimed by them but by others on their behalf.

6 *Positive Rights* (Narmeson 1984, Den Uyl and Machan 1984)

These critics raised questions about whether there are positive rights to wellbeing that is, whether there are rights to assistance in achieving survival and health as well as rights to not having survival and health interfered with or removed.

Gewirth claims the argument for positive rights is parallel to the argument for negative rights. That is, since survival and health are necessary conditions of action, every agent has a general need for its components. Hence, every agent has to accept

4a 'I must have survival and health'.
From 4a it follows
5a 'I have a positive right to survival and health'.

If he denies 5a, he has also to deny

6a 'Other persons ought to assist me to have survival and health when I cannot have it by my own efforts'.

By denying 6a. he must accept

7a 'It is not the case that all other persons ought to assist me to have survival and health when I cannot have it by my own efforts'.

But accepting 7a, he must also accept

8a 'Other persons may (i.e. it is permissible that other persons) refrain from helping me to have survival and health when I cannot have it by my own efforts'.

By accepting (8a) he must accept

9a 'I may not (i.e. it is permissible that I do not) have survival and health'.

But (9a) contradicts (4a) 'I must have survival and health'. Since every agent must accept (4a) he must reject (9a). And since (9a) follows from a denial of (5a) 'I have rights to survival and health', every agent must also reject the denial. Hence every agent logically must accept (5a), 'I have a positive right to survival and health'.

The argument for positive rights is parallel to, not derived from, the argument for negative rights. This then answers Narveson's objection that the right of non-interference in pursuit of purposes does not entail a right that others supply you with what you need to fulfil them. Both sets of rights are entailed by the same consideration, i.e, that they are needed as necessary conditions of action.

Conclusion

In this chapter, I have argued that in general terms facts can rationally support moral judgements, and that in particular, facts about needs provide grounds for both prudential and moral obligation. I have applied Gewirth's argument to put forward the strongest case of why this may be so.

3 Liberal theory

This book has defended a concept of need which argues that needs are objective requirements for survival and health. These are the means to ends any human being has good reason to pursue, desire or value. Such needs are universal and independent of any specific manifestations as wants, preferences, demands or satisfactions. It is these latter which differ according to the individual, time, place and circumstance. Wants, preferences, demands or satisfactions may be manifestations of fundamental human needs or they may not.

Chapter One established that there are fundamental human needs which differ from felt needs and desires. Chapter Two went on to argue that the satisfaction of fundamental human needs is both prudentially and morally obligatory. The argument so far suggests that the concept of fundamental human needs delineates the proper criterion for political policies aimed at the distribution of resources. However, liberal-democratic theorists by which I mean those who draw on aspects of the Utilitarians Hume, Bentham and Smith, orthodox non-Marxist economists, and many twentieth-century political scientists, regard attempts to define needs and calls for their satisfaction as deeply problematic. They stress instead the function of government and the effectiveness of the market system for the satisfaction of felt needs, expressed wants and demands.

The advantages claimed for policies and institutions based on felt needs and desires are:

1 That 'real' need theories are underpinned by ontological assumptions. They are metaphysical constructs and presuppose a metaphysic. Needs are not directly observable and their existence cannot be proved. Since wants are demonstrable dispositions to desire or prefer something, their identification

requires no metaphysical assumptions and raises no ontological issues. Felt needs and wants are the only real needs people have that can be said to exist.

2 Felt needs and wants are easier to know. Needs as objective requirements for some end such as survival and health may not be known to us or experienced as wants or demands. We may not know what we need nor want it. Since needs cannot be verified empirically from subjective avowals they have to be hypothetically constructed when not experienced. Wants are 'facts'. To establish the wants of the individual, it is not necessary to impute real needs which they may not feel, since people always know what they want. Wants can be identified by eliciting answers to questions about what individuals feel their needs to be or by observing their demands or by 'reading them off' from what they actually consume or use.

3 Needs, it is argued, are not simple matters of fact (Springborg 1981, Soper 1981, Ch.1, Fitzgerald 1977a, 1977b. Benn & Peters 1959, pp. 141–54, Taylor 1959, pp. 106–11). Any need theory which appeals to empirical data to substantiate its need claims must presume norms.

Need statements can only be made intelligible against a background of assumed ends, goals and purposes. Talk about human needs as empirical means to achieve certain human goals or human excellences presupposes a trouble free notion of human needs and ignores the different and competing models of 'man' which generate different catalogues of needs. Needs cannot be made empirical because empirical evidence can only be brought to bear on the question of needs after normative assumptions about the nature of human beings, their ends and purposes have been made.

No model of human nature is assumed and no normative judgements are made if political policies correspond to individual wants. Human beings simply have the desires they can demonstrably be seen to have and these are sovereign. Hence even if values are embedded in wants, we acknowledge and conform to these existing values: they are the values people actually have.

4 To emphasise needs in politics is often the hallmark of the authoritarian. (Flew 1977, Heller, 1980, McInnes, 1977, Fitzgerald, 1977b). Antony Flew (1977, p. 213) argues that:

> an emphasis on needs as opposed to wants, gives purchase to those who see themselves as experts, qualified both to determine what the needs of others are and to prescribe and enforce the means appropriate to the satisfaction of those needs.

Those who claim to know what real needs are will feel justified in imposing them on people's actual needs. Thus 'real need' theories threaten individual freedom. They are dangerous slides down the slippery slope at the end of which Flew (p. 220) fears:

there is the Platonic Guardian, whose absolute power is warranted by nothing else but a putative expertise consisting precisely and only in alleged privileged access to the objectives that everyone ought to have.

In contrast to this to emphasise wants avoids the dangers of coercion because political practices seek to satisfy the given wants people have.

5 Allocative priority based on planning to meet need leads to tyranny over wants. In the free market existing needs dictate the political institutions and economic processes. Actual needs are revealed ex.post through the experience of effective demand. Hence this form of political and economic organisation is conducive to the maximum and equitable satisfaction of needs.

It is not necessary for critics of the concept of need to hold all five objections detailed above. (1) – (3) argue that policies cannot be based on needs for epistemological reasons connected with the concept of need: because needs presuppose a metaphysic their existence cannot be proved, because they are hypothetical constructs they cannot be known, because they involve normative assumptions they cannot be made empirical. Objections (4) and (5) are empirical points that though policies could be based on need they lead to authoritarian and impositional planning, and that the market economy both avoids this danger and is more effective at meeting needs because it establishes ex.post through effective demand what they are.

Some of the alleged disadvantages of 'real' need theory have already been addressed in Chapter One. In relation to:

1 Fundamental human needs are what is necessary for survival and health. They are the empirically discoverable means to ends any human being has good reason to pursue, desire or value if they are to act to achieve any ends at all. They do not have to be felt to be said to exist. They persist and prevail whether or not their subject experiences them as wants, demands or fulfils them in consumption. They may correspond to wants, demands or actual consumption but are distinct from these.

2 Needs may not be known or experienced and cannot be always inferred from what people say they need or from what people actually do. However, their existence can be verified by causal explanation with reference to biological and psychological theories which demonstrate the effects on survival and health if needs are inadequately satisfied or not met.

3 Needs can be made empirical and are objectively valuable because they are the practical means necessary to act to achieve any other ends or values people may have. No matter what different ends, purposes or values people have there are some conditions necessary to attain these and therefore are goods any person has good reason to pursue, desire or value.

So, the liberal criticism of needs in relation to 1, 2 and 3 has been answered. The relationship between needs and freedom in 4 and 5 will be addressed here through a critique of the assumptions underlying the championing of wants.

I shall now proceed to show that the liberal theories' alleged advantages for the concept of wants are either invalid or can be outweighed by other considerations. Part of the argument I want to employ has already been presented in Chapter One. Contrary to liberal claims, it has already been shown that:

1 Felt needs and wants are not the only real needs that can be said to exist. Wants, demands and satisfactions are not the only objects of knowledge and these manifestations are not identical to, but distinct from, facts about our needs. Want theories only appear to raise no ontological issues because real needs are defined as equivalent to those which are felt, articulated or identified in consumption. Ontology is conflated with epistemology. What is has been identified with what we know. Thus assumptions are made about needs: the theory has not avoided metaphysics, but merely made different assumptions.

2 The idea that needs are unknowable because they are metaphysical or hypothetical constructs is held because it is assumed that what is directly known is what is knowable. However, even though this assumption can be challenged, it is not necessary to do so. It is enough to answer the epistemological problem about the unknowability of needs.

Needs can be known. In principle this is as 'easy' or as 'difficult' as the task of identifying the actual physiological and psychological effects of their dissatisfaction within a socio-historic specificity. Though wants can be known from subjective avowals, it is disputable whether this makes them 'easier' to know. Firstly, we may have unconscious and subconscious wants which are not articulated. Secondly, the idea of the general transparency of wants seems to me to be a myth. Most people experience an ambivalence and confusion about what they want and about what will satisfy the wants they do have. Even when we are sure that we want something, the advantages of this knowledge can be overridden by the fact that,

3 a) wants do presume norms, and
b) the fact that something is wanted and therefore subjectively valuable cannot by itself make it valuable, worth desiring or having.

a) Liberal theory identifies wants with psychological facts. The argument in Chapter 1 showed that wants cannot escape presumptions of norms. Wants involve reference to values and the liberal identification of needs with wants is neither factual nor neutral. They can only be so identified because the theorist adopts a particular definition of need which accepts current manifestations of need as the only real needs there are. This has the effect of positively evaluating and endorsing the existing patterns of wants and consumer satisfactions as appropriate and desirable.

b) The liberal may accept that wants presuppose values and still claim that we should accept existing values as facts, without endorsing them, if this happens to be what people want. But, if what people want is accepted simply because they want it, by virtue of the fact that it is desired, then the normative (though trivial and irrational) nature of this acceptance cannot be evaded. The unquestioned premise of the argument is that it is good for people to have what they want. Here, want is appealed to as an ultimate value. Since wants can relate to any end (good or bad) the fact that something is wanted per se does not guarantee or justify its value, pursuit or satisfaction.

What has been established so far in relation to 1–3 is the theoretical primacy of needs. Both wants and needs are empirically discoverable and there are difficulties involved in knowing either; hence no automatic advantage is gained for 'wants' in this respect. Given what has been established about objective values, it can be no longer assumed that it is in itself good for people to have what they want, whereas we can say that it is good for people to have what they need. The argument suggests that in principle policies for the allocation of resources ought to be based on needs rather than wants. Liberals may still make a case for wants based on the empirical claims:

4 that the free market is the most efficient institution for the maximum satisfaction of actual needs,
5 that want satisfaction enhances freedom.

This chapter will explore, in more detail and with additional arguments, how far the epistemic and empirical advantages claimed for the criterion of wants can be supported. I will do so by examining and criticising the liberal reduction of needs to either felt needs or wants, expressed demands or demands identified in consumption, this being the ground for claim 4.

Wants or felt needs

In championing the sovereignty of 'felt needs' liberals assume the existence of rational and autonomous individuals 'who are the sole generators of their own wants and preferences and the best judge of their own interests' (Lukes 1973, p. 79). The model of human nature underlying this notion is an abstract, general one where people's needs can be read off from observed features of the behaviour of individuals.

This model obscures the social, economic, political and commercial forces which determine the content of our felt needs. This is not to argue that there are no common biological or psychological determinants on needs, but only to insist that any explanation of the concrete forms in which such needs are expressed can only be understood fully when account has been taken of the social determinants on that expression. At least since the time of Marx, it has been a commonplace that the concept of the abstract individual used as the object of explanation is epistemologically inadequate, for Marx (1975) writes: 'man is no abstract being squatting outside the world. Man is the world of man, state, society'. Marx (p. 10), echoed Aristostle before him, who drew attention to the social, political nature of human beings. Aristotle (1962, p. 28) writes:

> ... man is by nature a political animal; it is his nature to live in a state. He who by his nature and not simply by ill-luck has no city, no state, is either too bad or too good, either sub-human or super-human – sub-human like the war-mad man condemned in Homer's words 'having no family, no morals, no home'; for such a person is by his nature mad on war, he is a non-co-operator like an isolated piece in a game of draughts. But it is not simply a matter of co-operation, for obviously man is a political animal in a sense in which a bee is not, or any gregarious animal. Nature, as we say, does nothing without some purpose; and for the purpose of making man a political animal she has endowed him alone among the animals with the power of reasoned speech.

In *The Grundisse*, Marx (1973, p. 84) re-iterates:

> The human being is in the most literal sense a *zoon politikon,* not merely a gregarious animal, but an animal which can individuate itself only in the midst of society. Production by an isolated individual outside society is a rare exception which may well occur when a civilised person in whom the social forces are already tyrannically present is cast by accident into the wilderness – is as much an absurdity as is the development of languages without individuals living together and talking to each other.

Real, living individuals always exist in some specific social context and it is to this that we must refer in order to understand the needs of people already formed in society.

To understand felt needs is not to understand what the abstract individual autonomously chooses, but to understand the socially determined nature of that choice at any particular time. This is so, Marx (1973, p. 92) argues, even with regard to the most obvious biological human needs, for:

> Hunger is hunger, but the hunger gratified by cooked meat eaten with a knife and fork is different hunger from that which bolts down raw meat with the aid of hand, nail and tooth.

That is, though it cannot be denied that there is an abstract need for food, or that this need is felt, even this uncontroversial need is socially mediated. The form and manner in which it is felt and satisfied always refers us to the social relations of production, distribution and exchange which operate in any given society.

Felt needs which are manifest cannot be seen as autonomous and unanalysable givens, nor does their lack of articulation imply no underlying needs. They are the effect of both anthropological and socio-economic determinants on their manifestations:

a) Most straightforwardly felt needs are the effects of what objects of satisfaction are actually around in society – what is produced, consumed and what is available to certain individuals.

The biological need for food may be manifest as the felt need for a bowl of rice or for three well balanced meals a day depending on what food is produced in a society and the distribution of wealth in that society. What is produced generates in two ways further felt needs which must be satisfied in order to have the original felt need satisfied. First, the perception of some products and the consumption of others give rise to new needs; and second, in order to meet our felt needs for food, the whole system of production of goods, employment and access to services, which distribute and deliver these goods, all become necessary.

b) Felt needs are not simply the effects of what is around in society but are influenced by people's perceptions of what is around, for instance:

i) people may be mistaken in their perceptions, their real needs may not be perceived through ignorance of what they are;
ii) their perceived felt needs may arise through ignorance;
iii) their perceptions of what their needs are may be directly manipulated;
iv) their perceptions may be limited to what is available within the system.

The existence of need thus cannot be identified with what people perceive their needs to be. People may be mistaken about or ignorant of what they need.

i) Real needs may not be perceived due to ignorance or lack of other resources; perception of needs may be affected by the level of distribution of intellectual and material resources.

Access to information and to objects of satisfaction can effect expectations so that though certain goods and services are produced in society some individuals will not feel the need for them. Several sociological studies confirm that an individual's social circumstances structure and restrict what they feel their needs to be. An attitude survey by Runciman (1960) revealed that the poorest sections of the population were hardly aware of their poverty. Coates and Silburn's (1967) study of poverty in Nottingham concluded that the lower a man's wages, the more deprived he appears to be, the less aggressively he will construe his needs and the less he seems likely to respond with vigorous complaints or even active discontent. Halsall and Lloyd's (1961) study of elderly patients admitted to hospital showed that more than two thirds claimed they had been ill so long that they had forgotten what it was like to feel well.

People may be unable to articulate what they need because they are not aware of their needs or their appropriate satisfiers. People may be ignorant that they need something because they have never experienced a deficiency of it or because they are unaware that a deficiency has occurred or will occur without the needed object. Deficiencies do not have to be experienced in a phenomenological sense. We cannot notice aluminium in the water supply or carbon monoxide in the air, yet these influence health. The need for clean air and water, though, will only appear in the need articulations of well-informed people.

ii) Felt needs may rest on people's mistaken perceptions of what will satisfy due to ignorance of what they really need. People may be aware that they need something but be ignorant or mistaken about what they need. A person will not know that they need fluoride if they do not know that fluoride is essential for dental care. A diabetic may crave sugar and be ignorant that what they need is insulin. In all these cases it can be assumed, all things being equal, that if information were available, such needs would be articulated. It cannot be assumed that the ill-informed have no respective health needs because they do not articulate them.

iii) What people perceive their needs to be is often the result of the conscious intention and deliberate manipulation of advertising and marketing policies which produce and stimulate new needs for particular objects of satisfaction (see also (c)).

iv) The socio-economic system also indirectly channels people's perceptions of what they need in certain ways. If people are to operate within the system, i.e. if they are to function as particular members of society or if they are to satisfy a natural biological or psychological need within it, they must have, in the sense that they are unable to do without, what the system offers or supplies as means of satisfaction. Thus needs are restricted to what is available within the system, unless people are aware of or are prepared to act upon the possibilities of changing the system (see also (c)).

c) In actual practice any socio-economic system must and does presuppose and recognise real unexpressed needs in order to determine their particular forms of expression as felt need. No economy can produce just anything. It must presuppose certain biological and psychological needs to exist whether or not their satisfaction is directly functional to the system and whether or not they are expressed. On one hand liberals subscribe to a deflationary ontology in confusing the existence of needs with their manifestations. Yet, on the other hand in actual practice they must presuppose real needs in order to channel their manifestations into a specific content that suits their purposes.

Under capitalist market relations the content of felt need is determined by the necessity for the reproduction of capitalist social relations. Meeting them is a means to the expansion of the capitalist system. The point here is not that in capitalist society real needs are determined, for any social production must both presuppose the existence of real natural need, and all natural needs are socially determined. What is significant is that under capitalism felt needs are moulded by class interests and power relations to suit the economic interests of the producing and owning classes and power holders whose interests are not identical to those of the people who feel the need. Hence the effect of moulding individuals' perceptions of what they need by shaping their preferences for alternatives and by shaping the alternatives themselves may be the inadequate and limited satisfaction of the underlying need.

The underlying needs that must be satisfied are those necessary for the reproduction of individuals in society. Society must produce food, clothing, shelter, recreation, education and all the means for survival and health in order to reproduce itself. These needs are acknowledged not only in taxation policies and state intervention in production but also are embodied in the material and non-material 'goods' that are produced in society. If 'products' do not correspond to real needs they will not 'sell'.

Advertising and marketing policies of large firms for consumer products are the most obvious example of how commercial institutions presuppose objective needs while intervening to mould the forms they take as consumer choices. They persuade people that needs will be met by the purchase of the products they promote. That is, despite their claims to the contrary, advertisers must impute real underlying needs in order for their products to be presented as symbolic objectifications of them, and so for anyone to want to buy them. The eight 'hidden' needs to which marketing theory is orientated have been classified by Vance Packard (1960, Ch.7) as the needs for emotional security, self esteem, ego gratification, recognition and status, creativity, love, sense of belonging, power and sense of immortality. Paradoxically, despite differences in terminology, these needs correspond to the lists of needs proposed by any 'real' need theorists.

For example Maslow's (1954) hierarchy of needs includes the needs for security, belongingness and love, esteem and self-actualisation. Fromm's (1956, pp. 30–66) list similarly includes the needs for relatedness, transcendence and creativity, rootedness and security, identity and a frame of orientation and devotion. These similarities are discussed further in Chapter 7.

Political institutions also presuppose real needs in order to influence their expression. Real need theorists claim that people have a need for security. Defenders of the felt need approach, of course, deny that we can have knowledge of real needs; yet they are only too aware of these needs in their manipulation of the forms of expression they may take. The content of the need for security is determined by the social and political theory which appeals to this need. Thus, in Thatcher's Britain the need for security becomes translated into the need for internal security in the form of law and order policies, more policing and tougher sentencing, and is reflected in volunteer schemes such as Neighbourhood Watch Committees and support for the victims of crime groups. Such policies have popular support precisely because they appeal to people's real security needs and touch on their concrete experience of rising crime and increasing violence. Yet since no alternative solutions are posed for the underlying causes of such threats, people's needs for security become identical with the felt needs for the authoritarian programme proposed.

Similarly the health, education, housing and welfare needs that people have are translated into advocating the entrepreneurial spirit, individual initiative, self reliance and personal responsibility which are thought to be requisites for satisfaction of such needs, and which the government policies on taxation, monetarism and the minimal welfare state are said to promote. The fact that such policies do correspond to real needs and experiences that people have accounts for the extent of their popular appeal. The very fact that they are located within the logic of an underlying acknowledgement of real need becomes a rationale and a justification for these policies.

From these examples it can be seen that the form our felt needs take is determined by the commercial and political institutions which appeal to the underlying need. They do not always provide satisfactory means of meeting them, due to the conflict between the function this conditioning serves and the goal of need satisfaction.

d) Though people's perceptions of their needs are the effects of social conditions, this is not to say that all economic and political institutions deliberately conspire to systematically dupe people into opting for forms of satisfaction which suit their purposes, nor to suggest that people are totally conditioned into accepting these forms of satisfaction. An economic system can create needs unintentionally and can inadvertently produce dysfunctional needs which arise as reactions to the prevailing channelled pattern of the manifestations of need. These needs may be felt in various forms, from general dissatisfactions to attempts to escape the dominant system of needs by seeking personal solutions and opting for an alternative life-style within the system, or to attempts to transform the system or transcend it. If needs were totally conditioned by the system all protest regarding their conditioning into those forms of satisfaction would be futile, if not impossible.

It is precisely because we can examine the conditioning process that our consciousness can cease to be determined by the inevitability of our felt needs. Andrew Collier (1973, p. 12) argues:

> precisely in order to serve our needs, cognition must attain a certain independence of them, ... we can study needs objectively and revise our account of external reality insofar as it was in the first place distorted by their influence ...

We can examine the evidence for the origin of our felt needs. It can be seen that the moulding of these needs into specific forms is not arbitrary, but serves a social use. Thus their function for the interests of those who determine them can be examined. It is possible then to question the causes of our felt needs and the function that channelling these needs into particular forms serve. That is, the fact that needs for security are felt as needs for law and order policies can be evaluated and examined in the light of political and economic considerations which require a strong state to establish the artificial conditions of the market order and to extend market criteria to other areas of social life. The fact that housing, education, health and welfare needs can find expression in government policies can be evaluated and examined in terms of the political interests served by such policies which foster attitudes essential for the development of a competitive economy and justify the current attack on collective welfare provision.

Summary and conclusion on the alleged advantages of felt needs or wants (1–5)

1 The liberal view that the notion of felt needs or wants requires no theory of need and raises no ontological issues is mistaken. They operate with an inadequate theory of need because they subscribe to a deflationary ontology. They conflate the existence of needs with their manifestations as felt needs or wants. Thus assumptions about needs are not avoided. Moreover, the assumptions are false, because, for the reasons given, what people say they need does not always correspond to what they do need.

Also, in spite of the theoretical conflation of needs with their manifestations, economic and political practice informed by such theories in actual fact must presuppose a more substantial theory of underlying need in order to channel their felt manifestations into specific contents to suit their purposes.

2 Identifying felt needs or wants may be relatively unproblematic in the sense that we can simply ask people to specify their wants, but felt needs are not the only needs people have, because:

a) Felt needs are the effects of what is produced, consumed and the availability of resources.

b) Felt needs are affected by people's perceptions, so that
   i) felt needs may not express real needs
   ii) felt needs may rest on mistaken beliefs about what will satisfy
   iii) felt needs may be the effects of deliberate manipulation
   iv) felt needs may be limited to what the system requires or provides.

c) Felt needs are channelled into certain directions by economic power-holders and political institutions.

   The overall result may be the inadequate satisfaction of need. If social policies are based on felt needs alone, then real needs that people have but which are not expressed because of the role of social forces on consciousness of them, will not be satisfied.

3 Liberal theory, in effect adopts a theory of need which has normative implications. Identifying current manifestations of need as the only needs people have is not factual or neutral. It suggests that felt needs are the proper criteria for allocation of resources and positively evaluates and endorses existing patterns of felt need. It makes value assumptions about the nature of existing wants. It ignores the fact that felt needs are not spontaneously given but are the effects of biological and social determinants.

Endorsing and accepting what people happen to want involves appealing to wants as ultimate values and has the added disadvantage that it:

a) overlooks the fact that the ends and purposes for which something is wanted may be bad or undesirable; and
b) disallows the allocation of resources for the meeting of unfelt needs and therefore devalues the needs that may not be expressed.

4/5 The view that want satisfaction through the market increases freedom cannot be defended without appeal to freedom as a value; but it cannot be maintained that want satisfaction does increase freedom.

The explanation of how felt needs are constrained and conditioned by social forces and of the social function this conditioning serves is an argument against the autonomously chosen and non-normative status of felt needs claimed for them by liberal theory. What people want results from power relations which determine the level and nature of social production and the individual's place within the reproduction of those relations. Hence satisfactions available and the availability of satisfactions are restricted in ways over which the individual has little control, and function to serve the interests of the power holders whose principal aim is not the satisfaction of need. If we have no knowledge or control over the formation and development of wants, then action motivated by them cannot be free activity even if we are free to pursue and satisfy the wants so formed and developed. Where individuals have little or no control over the determination of wants they are denied freedom, since action informed by them is insufficiently purposeful or intentional to be called freely chosen. Thus even if the market did deliver the goods people want, the wants themselves have not been freely formulated, therefore the notion that want satisfaction equals freedom cannot be defended.

Demands and actual consumption

The previous section argued against the alleged advantages of using 'felt needs' or 'wants' as a basis for the allocation of resources. This section will proceed to examine the advantages claimed by some liberals for using the criteria of expressed needs or demands and effective demand or actual consumption as indications of either what people want or need.

The liberal theories, to the extent that they identify needs with demands or with actual consumption, inadequately conceptualise needs and do not escape ontological or value assumptions. When political economists use actual consumption of commodities as the crucial criteria for empirically identifying needs, needs which are felt and expressed but which are not gratifiable in consumption are ignored. Even liberal theories which acknowledge that people have needs for goods other than commodities, if they still identify needs by demands or consumption alone have to ignore needs which are felt and expressed but which are not followed by consumption (either in the form of commodities or other forms). This latter point is a failing of liberal theory, whether or not people's needs are identified as needs for commodities.

C.P. Macpherson (1977, pp. 31–32) has argued that Millian ethical liberalism reacted against and rejected the Benthamite notion of man as infinite consumer, together with the lack of distinction between the qualitative and quantitative dimensions of wants and also replaced maximising the provision of material goods as the criterion of social good by the value of maximising man's development and use of his human capacities (moral, intellectual and aesthetic). Mill believed that the full development of capacities would generate these new higher wants and steer people away from material consumption. Macpherson argues that though Mill sees the possibility of wants changing qualitatively he pays little attention to how they have been developed and produced by capitalism. Since Mill believed in competitive private enterprise he was unable to see that the development of an individual's capacities and the satisfaction of needs could not come about under the present system.

Consequently, given the good reasons for not basing allocative policies on felt need, then because expressed needs or effective demands may not correspond even to felt needs, there is a double reason for not basing provision on them. This can be described as follows:

a) The reduction of need to effective demand for, or consumption of commodities

The reduction of need to effective demand or the actual consumption of commodities reduces need to need for what is quantifiable, what can be possessed, bought or sold. This identification is underpinned by a Benthamite liberal individualist model of man as an infinite desirer, appropriator and consumer of material utilities. Logically, on this view, scarcity is an eternal phenomenon for there can never be enough material goods to meet limitless wants. Although this theory claims that the only index of need is effective demand, the assumption of unlimited desires in relation to the amount of material goods supposedly desired automatically implies that there are needs which are not realised in consumption. That is, that consumption is not an accurate measure of felt need (or real need) even on this theory's own terms.

Despite the problems of unlimited desire and scarcity, neo-classical economists have claimed that the free market economy is the means by which the satisfaction of rational individual choices and demands and the consequent allocation of resources could be optimised. That is, in the perfect free market actual consumption would reflect real needs.

Yet, even if this were so, even if the market could deliver the commodities people demanded, the needs that were reflected in actual consumption would be, merely the needs appropriate to human beings *if* they can be identified as infinite consumers of material utilities. This model of human nature liberal theory takes as given and for all times and places. This is then, why they suppose that actual consumption in perfect market society would reflect real needs.

However, rather than showing that the capitalist market economy is fit for human beings given their nature, this view of human nature can be questioned. Macpherson (1973, pp. 26, 27, 31, 36, 37) argues that this supposed nature of human beings was introduced into Western theory and Western ideology in order to justify the capitalist market economy. In particular, the belief in the right to unlimited appropriation was necessary as an incentive to increase productivity. The notion of human beings as consumers was required to justify a society in which consumerism played a central role. The notion of human beings as possessing infinite desires was essential to establish and reproduce the capitalist economy.

The reproduction of the capitalist economy depends on the reproduction of labour power and the means of subsistence and production. That is, it depends on the reproduction of the set of relations which separate the direct producers from the ownership of the means of production. The needs and subjective preferences expressed in consumption are determined by the social function of the individual within the reproduction of these capitalist social relations. Simon Clarke (1982, pp. 177–78) argues that for the worker the reproduction of his place in these relations depends on the worker's need to have the commodities required for the historically and socially conditioned level of subsistence, and the need socially imposed on the worker to reproduce himself as a particular kind of worker. To ensure that the worker is so reproduced, (and his position within social relations reproduced) depends on the relation between these needs of the worker and his means of consumption being one of scarcity. This is achieved by reducing wages or expanding consumption both in terms of quantity and on the production of new types of commodity.

The reproduction of capitalist social relations reproduces private property and the division of labour. Through the creation of surplus value, material wealth is created. On the one hand this reproduces relations of relative wealth between the capitalist and his means of consumption, though it imposes on the capitalist the need to sustain the accumulation of capital. On the other hand in the long term relative scarcity is reproduced between the capitalist and his means of consumption in the sense that the capitalist's need becomes a need for possessions in increasing quantities.

Consequently, it is the individual's position within the reproduction of social relations which determines the different and unequal system of needs which individuals have and express in the market as effective demand. Though there is a difference and an inequality between the 'wealth' and 'poverty' of these needs, for *both* the worker and the capitalist the form these needs take is determined and limited to the need to have, to possess, to consume. Consumerism is seen by individuals as the route to personal satisfaction rather than the self expansion of the economic system involving the reproduction of individuals with a set of needs which society imputes to him or her. The consumption of commodities is seen as the means for satisfying needs; in the most extreme case the possession of the commodity is seen as itself constituting the satisfaction of the need.

An alternative tradition from Mill to Marx has challenged the Benthamite liberal individualist notion of quantitative needs by interposing qualitative needs. Writers as diverse as Fourier, Ruskin, Morris, Kropotkin, Fromm, Illich, Marcuse and Macpherson have contrasted the notion of human beings as consumers with human beings as doers and exerters; the needs to have with the need to be. It is often argued that these differentiations are not fruitful.

William Leiss (1976, p. 85) criticises Maslow for suggesting that commodity activity should be transcended in order to arrive at self-actualising activity not related to the exchange of goods. Leiss argues that needs for self-esteem and self-actualisation are expressed through the purchase of commodities which have a complex set of meanings associated with them. Leiss says that if people interpret and experience self-actualisation in relation to material goods, then Sunday sermons about the priority of spiritual matters are peripheral. Leiss (p. 58) concludes:

> One cannot divide the non-material and material dimensions of needs. In industrialised as well as in other societies the ensemble of needs constitute

a uniform sphere of activity, each segment of which mirror the common characteristics of the whole.

Katrin Lederer (1980) emphasises the interconnections between material/non-material qualitative/quantitative needs and their satisfaction. She argues that human beings often require a pair of satisfiers, both material and non-material. For example, food is a material satisfier but it fails in its role as satisfier without the culturally specific concomitant non-material satisfiers (ceremony, company etc). Self-realisation could be characterised as the need to be as opposed to the need to have. But, Lederer argues, how could self-realisation come about if certain material and non-material preconditions were not fulfilled?

The criticism of liberal identification of needs in consumption does not deny either the material or non-material aspects of needs or their interconnections. Rather it criticises the notion that allows people's needs to be identified with a limited range of material goods which are not autonomously chosen and which sees the possibility of satisfaction exclusively as a function of consumption. Merely to have, to purchase, to consume or to possess a material object itself does not constitute the satisfaction of either the non-material need with which it is associated or the non-material need to which its use may be a means of achieving.

Needs expressed in this manner are subject to constraint in the form they may take, since the individual can chose as an object of need only those forms which are imputed to him as consumer and only those which he may chose from within his position in social relationships.

b) Needs not converted into demand and demands not followed by consumption

In so far as liberal theory identifies need with demands it ignores those felt and unfelt needs not expressed as demand. People feel the need for certain goods and services, but because they have no access to resources such as money, wealth, time, energy, skill and information, they do not express such needs as demands. A person may be ill and feel the need for treatment, yet if medical care costs money, the possession of money becomes a necessary condition for treatment, rather than the need to be well itself. If the ill person has no access to money, his felt need for treatment may not be expressed as demand, since such a demand would be pointless, given the absence of the further necessary qualifying condition for receiving treatment (i.e. money).

People may not make demands because, if they have no access to information about the available supply, they will be discouraged from making a demand. The same applies to the case where the supply itself is limited or there is no supply. Here need cannot be identified with a 'demand' concept at all but rather as a 'quasi-supply' concept since in these cases needs exist only insofar as there is a supply of goods and services to meet them. Williams (1974, pp. 61–71) argues that though people may feel the need for medical treatment and even demand it, if there is no or limited supply, the implication is that they are not in need. In medical cases where there are no available drugs to treat the patient (or where the efficiency of existing treatment has become zero) it is implied that though the person is still sick, since there is nothing that can be done for them, they are no longer in need.

The failure to express need as demand can reflect not the absence of need, but the absence of conditions of access or the absence of, or limit to supply. These further conditions are necessary for the expression of need as demand and therefore of qualifying as need at all in liberal terms. For now feeling the need is not a sufficient condition for ascribing or acknowledging need. Rather to turn felt needs into demands and therefore to be worthy of acknowledgement, felt need PLUS money, time, energy and information are required. Felt need MINUS these conditions does not qualify as need. Needs which are acknowledged are those expressed as a result of access to resources which are unequally distributed and possessed. Hence, there arises a situation in which felt needs of people may be the same, but as only some people have access to their enabling conditions only they can express their needs as demands, thus leading to further inequalities in their acknowledgement and satisfaction.

To the extent that liberal theorists assume that needs can be identified in consumption alone, they have to deny that needs may be felt, and converted into demands, but not followed by consumption.

Market economists claim that the resulting patterns of actual consumption reflects people's needs and preferences by their willingness to pay for goods and services. It must seem a remarkable coincidence that those individuals with more income and resources have more 'real' needs than those whose felt needs lack the backing of money to make them register as effective demand. The differences in actual consumption can be explained as effects of initial structural inequalities of income and resources. The connection between existing need and products actually consumed is contingent.

To the extent that liberal theory assumes that needs can be equated with felt needs, demands or read off from consumption, they deny that felt needs may not correspond to what we do need, they deny the value and reality of felt needs not expressed as demand and those demands not reflected in consumption.

Freedom and the market

This still leaves the argument that policies based on effective demand and the market economy preserve freedom. It will now be argued that the market does not guarantee freedom.

The rationale for assuming the index of need to be demand for actual sale of goods or use of services is the claim that needs cannot be assessed a priori. To do so, and to plan to meet needs on that basis, is to endanger individual freedom of choice. The market economy which identifies need a posteriori in actual consumption can respond to changes in effective demand and is to be preferred as individual freedom is preserved. By instituting freedom of choice market society maximises utility and does so equitably.

This is, it is assumed that economic processes are the outcome of the free and rational choices of individuals, an assumption which has been criticised already.

It is also assumed that individuals are free and equal in the purchase of products in the market place to satisfy their needs (The view of Friedman, Hayek, laissez-faire liberalism and present day Conservatism). It is claimed that individuals are equal in their subjection to the impersonal laws of the market which apply to everyone, and are placed in a situation of equal opportunity before its laws. Individuals are equally free from impediments in the pursuit of their ends. The state regulation of industry and collective welfare provisions are to be minimised as they are seen as impediments to liberty. Public power is to be restricted to maintaining and expanding the framework of private property, free competition and trade which guarantee free scope to private enterprise and free choice. The implicit normative claim is that in an unfettered market these institutions guarantee equal freedom of choice, are self-adjusting leading to an equilibrium of supply and demand and are conducive to maximising satisfaction, that they are both efficient and equitable.

Economists claim that on the basis of the given distribution of income and resources, the perfect market economy would represent the realisation of individual rational choice for goods and services and would maximise this choice equitably and efficiently.

However, if the satisfaction of need is measured by the aggregate effective demand, those individuals with more wealth, income and resources (energy, skill, information etc) will have more and therefore an unequal say in determining the efficient allocation for the satisfactions of need. If there is more effective demand for certain goods and services, then efficiency, on this model, dictates that these demands be met rather than rival felt needs or demands which lack the money or resources to make them register as effective demand. As a result of the initial inequalities, effective demand is also unequal.

Market economists can only show at most that the market is the mechanism by which need is met in equal proportion to the money and resources an individual possesses or has access to. They cannot show that the market maximises equitably according to need.

Following from this, neither can it show that the capitalist market economy enables individuals to freely purchase products or use services to meet their needs. That defenders of the capitalist market economy can claim this results from their inadequate conception of freedom which allows only deliberate interference to count as an impediment to freedom. Consequently many 'unfreedoms' are ignored.

Firstly, as has been argued by many critics of this notion of freedom, the defining of freedom as the absence of deliberate interference is inadequate. It neglects the possibly unintended but nevertheless inevitable effects of social arrangements and capitalist property relations and removes these from critical scrutiny with respect to freedom. Secondly, it is still inadequate to construe freedom as simply the absence of interference. This is so, since it undermines the rationale, even according to this tradition's own standards, for valuing freedom in the first place. If the absence of interference to buy goods is valued at all it is because we value the ability to buy them. That is, it is not just a matter of whether we are free from interference, but whether we are free to do and have what we want. If capitalist property relations are not called into question it could be argued that the owners of wealth and resources are both free from interferences and free to do and buy what they want. But capitalist property relations can be called into question. The question is not whether the existing distribution of wealth and resources under capitalism maximises freedom for the owners to do or buy what they want. What is questionable is the distribution itself and whether this distribution maximises for people in general freedom to do and be able to buy what they want.

Since under capitalism there are owners of the means of production and direct producers, this initial unequal distribution of the means of production leads to inequalities in income. Inequalities in wealth and therefore in consumption follow from these unequal relations.

Both those who have the wealth and those who do not are equally free from interference to purchase products in the market place to satisfy needs, but this freedom is useless and merely formal for those who are unable to do so. Their ability to do so depends on their access to the means to do what they want (income and resources). If their income and resources are low, this liberty is pointless. Those with little income and resources are unfree in the sense of not having the ability to do what they want (purchase goods) because of a lack of access to the means of realising their ends. It is absurd even on this tradition's own terms to construe freedom only as the absence of interference, for if this is so, there is absolutely no point in upholding freedom as a value at all.

It can be concluded that the lack of conditions of access to the means of satisfying needs is an impediment to liberty.

The connection between freedom and needs

Two criticisms have been given of the liberal claim that want satisfaction and freedom are inextricably linked:

a) wants and preferences are coercively conditioned by power relations and social forces that shape and constrain them. Where individuals have little control over the determination of their wants, they are denied freedom since action informed by them is insufficiently purposeful and intentional to be called freely chosen;

b) the inability of specific classes of people to convert wants into effective demand is a limitation on freedom. If people cannot satisfy their wants because they have no access to the means to do so then they are not free.

These criticisms show that

a) even if capitalist society were to satisfy wants, want satisfaction in capitalist society could not be equated with freedom because of the lack of freedom involved in the formation of wants;

b) in any case, the claims made for the freedom to satisfy wants in capitalist society are false.

In different ways each criticism breaks the alleged link between freedom and wants claimed by liberals and defenders of the market economy. However, they do not break the link between wants and freedom per se. In (a) freedom includes the absence of coercion in determining wants. Therefore the wants of the hypothetical informed individual are still linked with freedom. In (b) freedom is extended to include the ability, opportunity and resources to satisfy actual wants. Therefore the actual wants capitalism has engendered are still linked to freedom. But in (a) no space is left for evaluation or criticism of the informed wants a hypothetical individual may choose. In (b) the wants themselves are not judged or criticised. Their frustration is seen as the only legitimate target.

I will argue that the recognition and satisfaction of needs are important for freedom though accepting the conditions for freedom in (a) and (b). Freedom involves both the absence of coercion, and the presence of positive conditions.

But freedom cannot just be the absence of coercion and the presence of positive conditions to do what we want because this overlooks the fact that the wants themselves may be sources of unfreedom:

1 Though wants are subjectively valuable (and may even be freely chosen by an informed individual) the fact that something is wanted does not make it valuable, worth desiring or having (see Chapter One).

2 Furthermore, the wants themselves may frustrate our basic ends and purposes and interfere with the exercise of future autonomy.

1 There is an immediate intuitive appeal to saying there is a necessary connection between freedom and doing or having what we want. But, simply being free to do what we want (even if we knowingly and freely choose this) is not the be all and end all of being free. If it were it would mean that all desires are important to freedom simply because they belong to me, because I choose the object of desire and this subjective feeling of mine, this act of choice itself, the fact that I desire a certain object dignifies the object of desire. If what makes the object of desire valuable is the brute fact of my desire, then the object of desire is given a value independent of its intrinsic desirability.

This assumes that all desires are equally valuable whether they are trivial, petty, cruel, vicious, stupid, harmful or dangerous. It values senseless desires, it supports irrational desires. Even with the proviso that want satisfaction can be equated with freedom when such satisfactions do not interfere with those of others it is still counter-intuitive to connect desire satisfaction as such with freedom, given the diversity and subjectivity of desires.

What makes something valuable or desirable are not facts about individuals' desires, but facts about the object of desire. What is important for freedom is not the informed individual's preferences, but the information itself. What makes a desire or choice objectively important is not whether an informed individual chooses or desires it, but whether what is desired is objectively important, whether the object of desire is valuable.

2 Charles Taylor (1979) writes that 'being free can't be doing what you want in an unproblematic sense. It must also be that what you want doesn't run against the grain of your basic purposes' (p. 180). Freedom is important to us because we are purposive beings, and since some purposes are more important than others any meaningful sense of being free must include in the conditions for freedom the absence of coercion and the presence of positive conditions – the ability to act on and fulfil our most important purposes. Any attribution of freedom only makes sense against a background of more or less significant purposes.

Since significant purposes can be frustrated by our desires, desire satisfaction alone cannot be equated with freedom. Our ends may be frustrated by our desires directly or indirectly. If we are subject to impulses, obsessions or compulsions we may be doing what we want and so be exercising autonomy in that sense, but we are constrained from achieving what we have set ourselves to do. We feel these desires as obstacles, as internal inhibitions to the fulfilment of our ends, even though they are unquestionably desires which are our own. They are obstacles to our purposes and hence to our freedom since their presence leaves our purposes unfulfilled and their absence would not only clear the way to their fulfilment, but also could be sustained without any regret or loss as to who we are. Often, we have occasion to 'force ourselves to be free' and do so by relinquishing some intense or pressing desire for the sake of achieving some end which could not otherwise be achieved. When we do so we do not feel a victim of our own authoritarian repression (though we may regret that we can't have our cake and eat it) but feel in control of more important aspects of our lives.

Similarly, if we are subject to indirect negative constraints of which we are unaware, such as unconscious forces, repression, false consciousness or self-deception, then again we may be acting on our desires without being free. Our behaviour is indirectly determined in ways we cannot control and action so motivated may serve to defeat our purposes.

Want satisfaction then cannot guarantee freedom because the desires themselves (even if freely chosen) may not be objectively valuable and the desires themselves (even if satisfied) may frustrate our most significant ends and purposes, and so though in the short term pursuing them may be an exercise of autonomy, in the long term this may be destructive of it.

The pursuit and satisfaction of wants then are not necessarily connected with freedom. I will now discuss how needs are necessarily connected with freedom and why a theory of need is necessary.

It would seem that needs are important for freedom since needs are objectively valuable and a means to the fulfilment both of any ends and purposes and our most significant ends and purposes. Needs are objectively important whether we desire them or not for we cannot function successfully to satisfy desires or achieve other ends if we lack what we need.

Exclusive concentration on wants (whether from a liberal perspective or from other perspectives which do stress their coercive conditioning or the inability to satisfy them but still treat want satisfaction as the appropriate criterion of value) ignores the fact that wants may be sources of unfreedom, that they may defeat our purposes and interfere with our future capacity for action, and that we can have needs which we do not express as wants. An explicit theory of objective need is required to expose the lack of freedom which results from social and economic forces which determine whether needs are felt or articulated at all and which limit how these needs are expressed, the forms of satisfactions available and who has access to them. Liberal theory and capitalist society can be criticised from the point of view of freedom for both the denial of the ability, opportunity and resources for people to articulate and recognise their needs as well as the coercive conditioning of them and the denial of the ability, opportunity and resources to meet them. If people cannot articulate their needs, whether through ignorance, false or incomplete information or mistaken beliefs concerning them, their freedom is diminished just as surely as it is by direct or indirect coercion, or imposed solutions to their problems. (the two main fears of liberal theorists).

Theory and practice informed by objective needs independent of experience is not a threat to freedom but necessary for freedom, for explanation and information regarding needs plus the means to realise them enhance the possibility of need satisfaction for those people most 'in need'.

Moreover a theory which provides knowledge of objective needs and policies which provide access to their satisfactions do not necessarily lead to imposition of these over felt needs, since the point and purpose of such a theory is that people informed by it can come to feel the needs themselves and be motivated to seek the means for their satisfaction.

If despite this, people do not experience their needs as desires, they will not be motivated to achieve them since desires and action are connected in ways that needs are not (see Chapter One). Action taken on their behalf will not only be impractical, counter-productive and self-defeating but will be freedom-diminishing. For though freedom includes knowledge of our needs, it also includes the absence of negative and positive constraints. Given that freedom includes the absence of coercion, to be truly free people must also desire to meet their needs. It is an inescapable conclusion that people can only emancipate themselves.

Freedom is not acting on desires per se (even informed ones) but acting on significant desires, which requires the ability to satisfy needs. What is needed is not a matter of choice, for what we need for survival and health is determined by the kind of creatures we are, and is objectively important whether we desire it or not; for we cannot function successfully to achieve our ends when we lack what we need. Part of freedom involves knowledge of necessity, knowing what we do need as well as the ability, opportunity and resources to achieve it. It is rational to suppose that, all things being equal, this knowledge will give reasons for action, that the provision of resources will give the abilities and opportunities for action, that once informed and empowered people will act to satisfy their needs. This is why a theory of objective needs is important as the first stage in the emancipatory process. This is how freedom and need are connected.

It has been established that want satisfaction does not necessarily lead to freedom and that freedom and need are necessarily connected. Policies based on needs do not by their very nature lead to authoritarianism. However there are occasions when the overriding of desires by needs is justified.

Overriding needs or desires

It is recognised that liberty is infringed if force is used to prevent someone from doing what they want to do or to make someone do what they do not want to do, even if the infringement also can be justified by appeal to other aspects of freedom. But sometimes desires and preferences can be justifiably overridden when doing so promotes (a) other people's freedom or (b) my own future freedom.

a) Non-interference on its own does not guarantee the non-violation of freedom. Freedom also crucially depends on the presence of positive conditions and the degree to which all human beings can be free depends on the extent to which those conditions are distributed equally. This is the case because as other writers have argued freedom and equality are complementary values (Tawney 1964, Carritt 1976, Walzer 1983, Nielsen 1985, Norman 1982, 1987). Carritt (1967, pp. 136–137) argues that:

> one man's freedom is apt to be inimical to his neighbours ... when therefore we say that men have a right to freedom or that freedom is good ... we can only mean equal freedom. Indeed if we use the language of natural right, the right to equality must be more fundamental than that to liberty or life or anything else, since men cannot have absolute rights to any of these things (for one man's possession of them may be incompatible with another's) but only *(ceteris paribus) equal claims* ... the amount of freedom a man has a right to, the amount we ought *prima facie* to secure him; is just so much as is compatible with an equal amount for others.

And Norman (1987, p. 133) argues:

> ... if we are to apply the epithet 'free' to a whole society, we have to consider how (the) positive conditions of freedom are distributed within that society, and the society will be a free society to the extent that these conditions are distributed equally rather than enjoyed disproportionately by particular sections of the society.

The idea argued for here is that everyone should have equal freedom to meet their needs. Equal freedom to meet needs is hindered by inequalities in access to the conditions that enable them to be met. When freedoms conflict they have to be weighed against each other. The pursuit of the positive conditions of freedom which promote the fulfilment of needs and other ends override the negative non-interference conditions of freedom when these give some people power over others and restrict the freedom of others to satisfy their needs. Wants and preferences sometimes should be overridden when doing so promotes an equal distribution of freedom, so that everyone should have as much freedom as is compatible with the same degree for everyone else.

b) Desires and preferences also can be overridden justifiably if doing so prevents an individual from depriving herself of what she needs for future action and promotes the ability to satisfy her needs. The idea that even if present desires conflict with future capacity for action and future goals because they are trivial, stupid or harmful, as long as the individual is over twenty one and not mad or misinformed she has a right to spoil her own life, so that restraint or compulsion for her own good cannot be justified, is firmly rejected here. A theory of freedom worth the name must respect the individual and therefore must protect people from whatever threatens their survival and health needs, from whatever demeans, debases or degrades them, and can make no exception for those sources of harm that are self-directed or self-inflicted. To think otherwise is to elevate the importance of desire and of freedom as the absence of constraints on this desire to a ludicrous position, which in championing the value of the individual ironically is prepared to let that individual go to perdition, as long as she does so by her own hands.

Interference to protect an individual from themselves is not necessarily always justified, (as pointed out above) but to say that it is never justified is to give insufficient attention to sources of unfreedom beyond the direct coercion of actual desires. It ignores the fact that desires are not simply given but are dependent on beliefs about the desirability and availability of the object of desire which may be mistaken; it also ignores the ways in which human beings can be enslaved by their own desires and gives no importance to the recognition and satisfaction of needs as a necessary condition of freedom.

Overriding the freedom of non-interference can be justified if doing so promotes the fulfilment of needs essential for survival and health, the conditions necessary for successful action to achieve other ends. This does not make decisions easy or obvious in practice, nor does it mean that whenever the conflict between desires and needs arises, needs or the means to their satisfaction should always be imposed, or that desires can never be more important than needs. It is often reasonable to take calculated risks involving danger to survival and health needs or even to sacrifice the satisfaction of these needs altogether for the sake of some other end. These cases may range from the relatively trivial and occasional, 'This is bad for me, but I like it', scenarios most of us are pretty familiar with, to the occasions when people lay down their lives for the sake of others or for some cause.

In the first type of case the lack of prudence can be justified since the degree of probability that serious harm to survival and health needs will result is slight. In the second the desires that are more important than survival and health may be justified when the subject of those desires has no other ends s/he wants to pursue (so that survival and health are not needs as means to them), or when the ends in question are of such fundamental value that the necessity of the risk to survival and health is justified. The ends which qualify here are usually satisfaction of other aspects of that individual's health or the survival and health of other people. The rational importance of these needs is not denied by the seemingly more fundamental importance of desires in these circumstances.

The dilemma of imposition arises when for A to continue to pursue her desires would be to entrench her unfreedom and endanger the positive conditions of freedom and her ability to satisfy her needs, but to force A to abandon her desires would be to offend against the negative conditions of freedom.

The justification for making needs override desires in these circumstances could be only in terms of whether or not such action diminished or enhanced survival and health, and the future capacity to attain ends.

Conflicting intra and interpersonal freedoms have to be weighed against each other and the imposition of needs over desires can sometimes be justified in theory. In practice, though, there should be caution about imposition, because of the empirical problems of imposing wrongly. Furthermore, the point of action and policies informed by theories of need is not to ride roughshod over the negative conditions of freedom repressing individual preferences but to call attention to the social, material and intellectual conditions which are conducive to all people meeting their needs so that they can be free to attain their ends.

Though people may sometimes justifiably be protected against themselves, the overall aim is still freedom. Gibbs (1967, p. 109) writes:

> A free society is not simply one that makes its people do what is right and good. It is a society that respects the human nature of its members, that makes them do what is right and good by making them desire to do it understanding that it is right and good.

Conclusion

This chapter has attempted to show that the criterion of wants does not have the advantages as a criterion for the distribution of resources that liberals claim for it.

1 Firstly, identifying needs as wants, demands or consumer satisfactions involves ontological assumptions about the essence of man and the reality of need. Ontology is conflated with epistemology. The manifestation of need is taken to be what is. This acknowledges the reality of need and is informed by value-laden conceptions of human nature abstracted from the social and economic circumstances which together with biology influence the expression and satisfaction of need. Further, insofar as needs are deliberately determined in their forms of expression, there must be an a priori supposition as to the nature of needs in order to determine the forms they take. Thus 'want' theory does not escape the charge of assuming an ontology of 'real' need.

In addition to this, unfelt needs, wants not converted into demands or satisfactions as a result of social circumstances are unacknowledged on this theory and hence are deemed unworthy of satisfaction. There is still an ontology, but one that is a) false and b) has harmful consequences.

2 The claim that 'wants' are easier to know than 'real' needs because we can simply ask people what they feel they need or want, observe their demands or what they consume or use has been challenged. Wants, demands and consumptions are not just facts about people's preferences. They are the effects of social determinants which influence the ways in which they are expressed and whether they are satisfied in consumption. They are also

dependent on subjective experience and beliefs about what we feel we need and what is thought to be desirable and available. They are conditioned in a particular social context and reflect the needs of human beings as defined by this context and their individual social position within it.

Hence an individual's wants, preferences and consumptions may rest on false beliefs about what they actually need, what is desirable and available and whether what they want will satisfy their needs. If this is the case, the ease in identifying 'wants' is outweighed by the lack of rationale for the individual in pursuing or satisfying a want resting on a false belief.

If whether wants are felt, expressed or explicit in consumption is determined by social conditions, then when we 'easily' identify these wants we should be clear about exactly what it is we have identified. We have identified the effects of those conditions. We have identified what people feel and believe they need as a result of their social circumstances. We have identified what people have the resources to consume given their social and economic circumstances. The advantage of simplicity of identification is overridden by the fact that we have in effect identified the wrong thing. We have identified only what people feel they need; we have missed unfelt needs. Because we have only identified wants satisfied in consumption, we have missed the needs not converted to demands, not satisfied or satisfiable in consumption.

3 The claim that emphasis on wants escapes value assumptions has been challenged. Value judgements about the desirability, appropriateness and satisfaction of wants are inescapable if wants as a criteria for resource allocation is to be justified. Normative judgements are made regarding which and whose needs should be satisfied and normative claims are made on behalf of a specific socio-economic system for meeting these needs efficiently and equitably. Even if liberals claim that this avoids assumption of values by taking as a starting point the values embedded in the wants people have, this claim can be overridden by other considerations. Because wants require for their intelligibility, justification and value ascription an end for which they are wanted, then their intelligibility, justification and value must relate to the intelligibility, justification and value of the ends in question. Wants can relate to any end. Hence the fact that something is wanted alone cannot guarantee its intelligibility, justification or value and therefore its claim to satisfaction.

4 The celebration of the market economy for its response to people's wants and preferences has been challenged. It has been established that in market society because of social conditioning and structural inequalities in access to resources, felt needs or wants may not correspond to real needs, felt needs may not be converted into demands and demands may be unfulfilled. Hence the market does not guarantee maximum satisfactions of actual needs.

5 The claim that emphasis on wants is freedom preserving has been challenged.

a) If conditions for freedom include the absence of negative constraints, wants and preferences are not expressions of rational and free choice because they are coercively conditioned as a result of power relations. Even if the market delivered the goods people wanted, these wants are not themselves free.

b) If freedom includes the absence of positive constraints and the presence of positive conditions, the market doesn't preserve freedom because the inability of specific classes of people to convert their actual wants into effective demand is a limitation on freedom.

c) If freedom includes the ability to achieve our most significant purposes wants cannot be equated with freedom. Wants may be sources of unfreedom, they may not be objectively valuable and may frustrate our most significant ends and purposes. Needs are important to freedom. Knowledge of these needs, the absence of coercion and the presence of positive conditions for the satisfaction of needs are necessary conditions for the ability to attain any other end. Emphasis on needs does not necessarily lead to imposition of these over wants, though on occasion wants may be overridden. On this view the market does not preserve freedom because it does not allow people to articulate, recognise and realise their needs and denies them the conditions which would enable them to do so.

It has been established that the criteria of felt needs, expressed needs or effective demand do not have the epistemological or empirical advantages claimed for them. The theoretical primacy and objective value of the concept of need has been established. There still remains the problem that even if theoretically the concept of need can be defended, in actual fact policies based on real needs will have difficulties empirically identifying needs which are unfelt or unexpressed. The rest of this book will answer these remaining objections. I will first examine the prior problem of the distinction between true and false needs, then look at how empirical indicators of real needs could be developed.

4 True and false needs

The preceding chapter criticised liberal theory, and the political economy informed by it, at a conceptual and epistemological level, for assuming 1) the identification of need with manifested wants and/or effective demand, as being all that can be known, and 2) that both identification and satisfaction of wants involve no normative claims. It also criticised the social policies and the socio-economic system informed by this theory, i.e. capitalism, at an empirical level for endangering freedom by coercively conditioning wants into specific avenues that suit its purposes, limiting the forms of satisfaction available, denying the satisfaction of unfelt need and denying people the ability to convert felt needs into demands and satisfactions.

But it was claimed that this argument did not depend on the notion that capitalism mysteriously has the ability to inculcate false needs into its subjects or that the grounds for its condemnation depend on this. That is, the argument does not depend on the division of needs into true and false, real and imaginary, natural and artificial. Rather, it rejects all the theories of true and false needs found in embryonic form in the Stoics, Rousseau, the Enlightenment Materialists and the early socialists and further developed in the works of Marcuse, Reich, Fromm and Sartre, whenever the arguments for them primarily depend on the critique of capitalism as a system which creates false needs, rather than a system which fails to meet need adequately, and/or the claim that the needs capitalism appeals to are not real or genuine, rather than that the forms genuine needs take are coerced, limited and channelled by the social relations of production, distribution and exchange which operate in capitalist society.

Rejecting the true and false dichotomy

Theories which demarcate true and false needs distinguish between them as a basis for ethics and as a criterion for the condemnation of a society which requires the creation and maintenance of false needs for its survival and reproduction. The characterisation 'true' usually corresponds to what are thought to be somehow 'natural', and 'false' to what are thought to be 'artificial' needs. 'True' needs are associated with the requirements of nature, and so personal virtue or good social arrangements are held to be concerned with acting in accordance with the natural. Evil social arrangements are associated with the creation and existence of artificial needs, which for the early socialists and Rousseau accompany technological progress and economic development, and for Sartre, Reich, Fromm and Marcuse result from social conditioning and manipulation which superimposes artificial needs on, or substitutes them for, the natural needs of individuals.

Rousseau, for example, believed that the concept of human nature undistorted by social and political institutions provided the basis for morality and a criterion by which to judge society. Patricia Springborg (1981, Ch.3) argues that the distinction Rousseau makes between 'amour-de-soi' and 'amour propre' is the major source for the distinction between true and false needs.

Amour de soi is thought by Rousseau to be a natural feeling functional to self-preservation. If directed by reason and modified by pity it produces humanity and virtue. Amour-propre is an artificial feeling which originates in society; it causes human beings to raise themselves above each other and is the source of all evil.

In *Emile,* Rousseau (1964, Vol.4, p. 493) states plainly:

> A self-love *(amour-de-soi*) which concerns itself only with ourselves is content when our true needs are satisfied, but selfishness (*amour-propre*), which is comparing self with others, is never satisfied and never can be; for this feeling, which prefers ourselves to others, requires that they should prefer us to themselves, which is impossible. Thus the tender and gentle passions spring from self-love, while the hateful and angry passions spring from selfishness. So it is the fewness of his needs, the narrow limits within which he can compare himself to others, that makes a man really good; what makes him really bad is the multiplicity of needs and dependence on the opinion of others.

Natural man, pursuing only natural authentic needs (that are limited by the natural environment which presents few objects of satisfaction) is basically good. Men become selfish as the result of social conditions which create a multiplicity of new and artificial needs, causing them to be acquisitive and competitive, and to come into conflict with one another as they attempt to satisfy their needs.

According to Rousseau, the transition from the good person with natural needs to the bad person with artificial needs results from social relations, the progress of ideas and the cultivation of the mind and are particular effects of the creation of private property, the growth of wealth, and the pursuit of luxury and ephemeral goods characterised by inequality, consumerism and corruption.

Rousseau condemns these specific social conditions, not society per se, for the creation of artificial needs. He recognised that society was necessary as a precondition for the perfectibility of human beings and that 'civilised' man could and should not return to the 'state of nature'. He advocated that in order to pursue authentic needs civilised man should, through the exercise of his reason and will 'live according to the principles of nature', thus re-establishing the harmony and tranquillity of natural man.

Even given the complexities of Rousseau's position, Springborg, (1981) argues that equations between good natural and true needs and bad artificial and false ones are implicit in all theories of true and false needs. For instance, the early socialists, the Babourvists, Owen, Cabet, Fourier, Dezamy and Gay believed that evil and conflict were artificial phenomena which arose with the growth of civilisation and so were not inherent in human nature. Sartre, (1976) argued that the alienation of man from his essence occurred when the needs of human beings were replaced by the needs of the social structure. Reich (1975) thought that as a result of sexual repression human beings sought alternative gratifications which emerged in the form of artificial needs. Fromm (1956, p. 20) holds that true needs are inherent in human nature and that our biological constitution is the source of norms for living:

> A sane society is that which corresponds to the needs of man, not necessarily to what he feels to be his needs, because even the most pathological aims can be felt subjectively as that which a person wants most; but to what his needs are objectively as they can be ascertained by the study of man.

For Fromm (pp. 62–3) continues:

> ... often man is only conscious of his false needs and unconscious of his real ones, the task of the analyst of society is precisely to awaken man so that he can become aware of the illusory false needs and the reality of his true needs.

True needs are for Marcuse (1964, pp. 21–22)) the vital biological needs and the specifically human needs for the optimal development of the individual and:

> False (needs) are those which are superimposed upon the individual by particular social interests in his repression: the needs which perpetuate toil, aggressiveness, misery and injustice. Their satisfaction may be

gratifying to the individual, but their happiness is not a condition which has to be maintained and protected if it serves to arrest the development of the ability (his own and others) to recognise the disease of the whole and grasp the chances of curing the disease.

Capitalism's social control is anchored in the creation and maintenance of these false needs by indoctrination and manipulation.

For Reich, Sartre and Marcuse, the conditioning process is so successful that in one sense it becomes difficult for them to deny that these conditioned artificial needs in fact do become a person's real needs. Reich (1975) claimed that sexual repression results in individuals feeling the artificial needs to be their own even though they are contrary to their genuine interests. For Sartre (1976) the ultimate alienation occurs when existence and essence coincide in this way. Marcuse (1964, p. 26) goes a step further:

> When the individuals identify themselves with the existence which is imposed on them and have in it their own development and satisfaction this identification is not illusion but reality. However, the reality constitutes a more progressive stage of alienation. The latter has become entirely objective; the subject which is alienated is swallowed up by its alienated existence. There is only one dimension, and it is everywhere and in all forms. The achievements of progress defy ideological indictment as well as justification; before their tribunal, the 'false consciousness' of their rationality becomes the true consciousness.

Though false needs are 'real' because individuals feel them to be their own, they are 'false' because they are the result of social manipulation and indoctrination which transplants social needs into the natural needs of individuals. Individuals are alienated when they identify natural needs with imposed needs. Human liberation, happiness and social justice depend on correct consciousness and the consequent replacement of socially conditioned false needs by true ones.

The problems of the division of needs into true and false arise firstly from the fact that the basis of the distinction seems to be reducible to a contrast between the natural and the social, and secondly from the fact that false needs are thought to be produced primarily by social manipulation and indoctrination. The first is a problem, since even the most incontestable biological needs are always socially mediated and expressed. The second arises from the over-emphasis on the role of consciousness, both in the supposition that consciousness can be manipulated to such an extent, and in the supposition that the manipulation and inculcation of false needs is totally conscious and deliberate. Both these points overlook the significance of the fact that all needs are socially determined, so that the division into social and natural does not justify on its own criteria the denotations 'true' and 'false'. Moreover if people were totally victims of manipulated consciousness, no criteria for the distinction between true and false would be available to consciousness anyway.

The problem in Marcuse's case, which I shall discuss here since Marcuse is the main contemporary writer to distinguish true and false needs, can be traced to an over-simple account of how needs are actually produced in a society. Needs are not produced first and foremost by the deliberate intention on the part of the ruling class to deceive its subjects into accepting forms of expression of needs which suit its interests.

The societal needs of the capitalist mode of production for the reproduction of social relations, which require the reproduction of agents with a certain set of needs, are met largely, to the extent that the system is successful, without the conscious inculcation of societal needs in place of the individual's natural or true needs. Nor do people come to accept these ideas as their own through a process of deficient perception or crude self-deception which systematically blinds them into taking on board societal needs antagonistic to their natural needs, resulting in their being rather pathetic dupes of the system and victims of an unsubtle brain-washing.

This kind of approach is accurate to the extent that it is an explanation of the requirements of the capitalist mode of production for the reproduction of agents with a certain set of needs, and to the extent that it is an observation of the fact that the expression of needs in capitalist society is in part deliberately manipulated. However, this explanation, on its own, offers a limited account of how needs are actually produced as well as why they are accepted. It offers no account at all, and could offer no account, of the existence of dysfunctional needs which, though they are produced by the system, cannot be satisfied within it.

We may refer back to previous arguments, and re-assert that fundamental human needs for survival and health are biologically determined, but the form they take results from the social relations operating in society.

Felt or expressed needs are produced in the following ways:

a) They are the effects of what is produced, consumed and available to individuals given their resources in a particular social context. What is produced, the consumption of others, what is available stimulates felt needs and generates further needs as means to meeting the original need.

b) They are the effects of people's perceptions of what is around in society:
i) felt needs may not be produced, due to ignorance or deprivation;
ii) felt needs may be the product of ignorance;
iii) felt needs may be produced deliberately (e.g. advertising);
iv) felt needs may be produced as an indirect result of the organisation of production, social relations and political policies which have the affect of channelling needs into what is required to function within the system or to fulfil biological need within it. They are relative to and defined by

the individual's position within the reproduction of social relations and restricted to what is available within the system;

c) they are the effects of social, economic and political policies which must presume and to some extent satisfy natural needs in order to reproduce the system of production with a particular set of social relations and individuals within it;

d) they are the effects of a reaction to the system which inadvertently produces dysfunctional needs.

In addition to these:

e) felt needs, expressed needs and actual consumption are the effects of social conditions in that access to the abilities and resources necessary to experience, express and satisfy needs stem from social arrangements which cause the abilities and resources to be distributed unequally.

The above illustrates the fact that the distinction between true and false needs cannot rest on the 'natural versus social' criterion advocated by Marcuse. All needs are socially produced and are a mix of both natural and social factors. Although some needs in society are produced by conscious manipulation and the manipulation of consciousness, in the main they are not the products of social conditioning but the effects of social conditions. Even the needs that are produced by deliberate deception can be consciously rejected, as any attempt to escape or reject the prevailing patterns of needs testifies. Felt needs in society are the indirect effects of the system of social relations, the organisation of production and consumption and the social and economic policies which reproduce these. Social conditions can influence individuals' perceptions and access to resources which affect their experience of their needs and their ability to satisfy them. People are not victims of manipulated false needs. Social conditions may restrict their choice of objects to meet their needs, these objects may not meet the requirements of needs, and needs may be left unsatisfied; but these needs are not false. They are socialised experiences of needs; they represent genuine attempts to satisfy them.

Distinguishing the natural and social

The argument that all needs are socially produced, which has been used here to attack the equations 'natural = true', 'social = false', has been used by many critics of 'false' need theories. However, in the course of their argument they suggest that the reason the equations do not balance is because the natural and social should not and cannot be distinguished themselves.

William Leiss (1976) for example rejects the distinction between true/false, natural/artificial needs for similar reasons to those presented here, that is that such distinctions ignore the fact that all needs are a mix of both natural and cultural factors. However, he goes on to imply that these factors cannot and should not be separated. To do so presupposes the existence of needs in pure forms uncorrupted by socialisation. When natural needs are abstracted from their social mediations, the socio-economic reality in which they are formulated and satisfied, a false objectivity is claimed for needs as physiological requirements for survival. Leiss (p. 62) argues:

> The real problem about the satisfaction of human needs arises only when we abandon the abstract category of food ... All the most important issues arise when we study how the objective necessities of human existence are filtered through symbolic processes of culture and individuals' perceptions. In short all the most important issues arise just in that nebulous zone where the so called objective and subjective dimensions meet.

The separation of natural needs and socialised wants, the claim that the former can be abstracted from their social context and can be objectively determined, has the danger of leading to an inadequate and primitive egalitarianism, to policies which legislate the form that needs can legitimately take and to regarding the satisfaction of needs as a purely quantitative problem. Leiss (p. 62–3) goes on:

> It is trivial to calculate the need for food in terms of minimum nutritional requirements, for example. The real issues are: what kinds of food? In what forms? With what quantities? And how does the perceived need for certain kinds of food stand in relation to other perceived needs? If we attempt to answer these questions, the distinction between needs as objective requirements and wants as subjective states of feeling breaks down. It is important to understand this point because what is at stake is not only a theoretical or conceptual approach, but also practical issues of social policy. What is detrimental about the attempted demarcation between needs and wants is that it encourages us to regard the sphere of needs largely as a quantitative problem: each person needs a certain amount of nutrients, shelter, space, social services. The practical outcome of this statement of basic need is reflected in some of the social policies of the existing welfare state: bulk foodstuffs for the poor, the drab uniformity of public housing projects, and the stereotyped responses of bureaucracies. The qualitative aspects of needs are suppressed in these policies, just as the qualitative aspects of needs are suppressed for society's more fortunate members in the quantitative expansion of the realm of commodities.

Agnes Heller (1980, p. 215) highlights the totalitarian dangers of equating the natural and social with the true and false:

> Dividing needs into 'true' and 'false' not only involves denying acknowledgement of needs considered to be unreal, but means too that the demand for their satisfaction is irrelevant. Advocates of the 'true' and 'false' needs concept believe that unreal needs should not be satisfied. It is precisely this type of argumentation that founds every dictatorship of deciding people's needs.

My position concurs with that of these critics insofar as it is acknowledged that the crude separation of the natural and social, plus the simplistic account of the social production of needs, must be rejected. So too must the claim that socially produced needs are unreal or false. But, if the distinction between natural and social cannot be made at all, then the valid point that all felt needs are both socially mediated and real leads to a false conclusion which identifies the social with the natural and maintains that felt needs are the only real needs people have.

To insist that all felt needs are the effect of social determinations and never exist in a purely natural form does not entail that needs can be explained without reference to the determinations that result from the biological and social nature of human beings. If we regard the natural and social neither as equivalent to different sets of needs, true and false (as 'false' need theorists do) nor as inextricably mixed (as some critics of the true/false dichotomy do) but as an analytic distinction between abstract general needs and their socially determined manifestations as historically and socially specific instances, then,

a) we can elucidate the insights and avoid the problems of 'false' need theories, and
b) we can avoid being subject to Leiss and Heller's criticisms of 'false' need theories while overcoming the shortcomings of positions which do not distinguish the natural and social.

a) When we take Rousseau's distinction between 'amour-de-soi' and 'amour-propre' we do not have to regard these as different needs, natural and social, true and false, but rather we can see that selfishness or vanity are the manifestations self-love takes when particular social conditions are conducive to its expression taking these forms. When Marcuse (1964) calls false the needs to relax, have fun, behave and consume in accordance with the adverts, to love and hate what others love and hate, we do not have to assume that the needs to relax, have fun and have a social identity are not 'real' needs. We can, though, note that Marcuse draws our attention to the fact that the avenues for the expression of such general needs are limited or distorted by the effects of social conditions. Springborg (1981), a virulent critic of true/false need theories, claims that Marcuse overlooks the fact that capitalism's success is due precisely to the fact that it appeals to genuine and deep seated needs. Springborg argues that, as the sociologists on whom Marcuse draws heavily have shown, advertising succeeds where it appeals to well established, not culturally specific, needs which are played out in the realm of consumption.

Though Springborg's argument on this point contradicts her own position that we cannot have knowledge of 'genuine', 'deep seated' or 'well established' needs, we can agree with her that capitalism does not depend on the creation of false needs. The needs it appeals to are genuine, and people are motivated by their real needs. What we can rescue from Marcuse's argument, though, is that the ways these needs are manifest and satisfied are effects of social conditions which may prevent free determination and cause impoverished satisfactions. This leads to a criticism of these conditions, if they are not inevitable and if other possibilities and objects of satisfaction are historically available.

The distinction between abstract general needs and their historically specific manifestations, which should replace the true/false need dichotomy, is implicit in Fromm's distinction (1956) between the instincts or organic drives rooted in physiological needs, and what he calls the 'character rooted or human passions' which are substitutes for poorly developed instincts, rooted in character. While instincts are answers to physiological needs, character-rooted passions are answers to existential needs which are specifically human and rooted in the conditions of human existence. While existential needs are the same for all human beings, individuals differ with regard to their dominant passion. Whether an individual's dominant passion is to love or hate, each is an attempt to satisfy an existential need and varies depending on that individual's social circumstances. The details of Fromm's theory do not concern us here; the point that his theory can illustrate is that true and false need theorists do not have to assume that natural needs are true, while social needs are false (and different from natural needs) but rather that socially produced needs are instances of natural needs. Criticism does not have to rely on calling socially produced needs 'false' as they are indeed felt and real expressions of needs and it is this which is their motivating force.

b) Leiss argued that true and false need theories presuppose that needs can be abstracted from their social mediations. This leads to viewing needs as objective requirements and so aiming social policies at quantitative satisfactions calculated in terms of minimum requirements without heed to the qualitative aspects of needs. However my argument does not fall prey to this criticism, since it does not deny the socially mediated character of needs; it merely asserts that this does not entail a denial of their natural determinants. Hence, if we take the need for food, it does not necessarily involve us in quantitative calculations as to the minimum requirements for the satisfaction of this need, as Leiss suggested (though this in itself would be a great advance for the world's hungry peoples in terms of the satisfaction of their needs, a point Leiss seems to overlook). We can refer to the given historical possibilities which exist to satisfy this abstract need in particular social circumstances.

And to be fair to Marcuse, this is the point he consistently makes in *One Dimensional Man* (1964). He argues here that the 'vital' needs should be satisfied at the attainable level of culture under optimal utilisation of the material and intellectual resources available. For Marcuse the question is posed in terms of the truth and falsity of needs, which he claims are historically objective. Apart from the disagreement with Marcuse on this issue already aired, the point that is being made regarding the historical standards that apply to the satisfaction of needs refutes Leiss' argument that the separation of natural and social leads to regarding needs as a quantitative problem. Marcuse (p. 22) says:

> 'Truth' and 'falsehood' of need designate objective conditions to the extent to which the universal satisfaction of vital needs, and beyond it, the progressive alleviation of toil and poverty are universally valid standards. But as historical standards, they do not vary according to area, stage of development they also can be defined only in (greater or lesser) *contradiction* to the prevailing order.

The argument advanced by Heller, that to divide needs into true and false and equate them with real and unreal needs involves the denial of the satisfaction of needs considered to be unreal, has been avoided here. This is so since it has been argued that all needs that are felt are real. The criticisms of the content of such needs are not based on their unreality but on the social conditions which generate them and lead to limited satisfactions and failure to satisfy them. Criticism of the content of felt needs does not entail calls for denying them satisfaction. In fact, quite the reverse; for one of the most fundamental criticisms of capitalism has been precisely that it generates needs which it cannot satisfy, given the unequal distribution of resources it depends on.

As for the felt needs that are inadequately satisfied, criticism is not based on the mere fact that they are derived from social arrangements, since all needs are. Criticism is directed towards those coercive social arrangements which serve to reproduce class interests, leading people to acquire needs they would not otherwise have had, limiting the forms of satisfactions available and providing objects of satisfaction which do not adequately meet needs. This criticism does not entail that these felt needs should not be met. In the short term and from within the system, once a person has a felt need, there is reason for them to regard it as important and to pursue its satisfaction. The felt need may be so deeply ingrained that they cannot function without its satisfaction, or at least they would feel frustrated and resentful if it is not satisfied. From this perspective it is irrelevant how these needs were acquired, and to deny them would be counter-productive, possibly inhumane and paternalistic. However, from within a broader perspective, facts about how needs were acquired become relevant as a critical tool against social forces that generate them. The long term solution here is to change the social arrangements and so the needs derived from them.

Against false need theorists and with Leiss and Heller, it has been argued that felt needs are both natural and social. However, this does not mean that we cannot distinguish analytically between abstract general needs that are naturally determined and the socially determined historically and socially specific instances of them. Such a distinction preserves the insights of false need theorists elucidating that felt needs are the effects of social conditions which prevent free determinations and cause impoverished satisfactions; while avoiding the problems arising from labelling natural needs true and socially determined needs false. The distinction also avoids Leiss' objection that abstracting needs from their socialised expressions involves viewing needs as a quantitative problem. Since needs are seen in their social context, policies for their satisfaction refer to historical possibilities and social arrangements. Because all felt needs are acknowledged as real, the danger that 'unreal', 'false' or 'artificial" needs ought not to be satisfied is overcome.

The distinction between abstract general needs and their social instances has the added advantage of

a) retaining the distinction between the natural and the social and not reducing the biological to the social or mistaking the latter for the former
b) not reducing real needs to felt needs, which is done if it is insisted that socially expressed needs are the only real needs there are.

Avoiding essentialism and reductionism

Attempts to explain needs as conditioned by both nature and society even when such explanation does not entail denoting such needs true and false respectively, are often viewed with unease. It is thought that to emphasise the natural component of needs is to veer dangerously between the Syclla and Charibdys of essentialism and biological reductionism. I will refer to Timpanaro's argument for acknowledging nature's role as a determinant, and then examine Soper's objections, to show that both types of conditioning, natural and social work together to produce needs.

The view that needs cannot be explained fully without reference to the determinations which result from the biological and psychological nature of human beings, is avoided by some Marxists, both to avoid the charges of essentialism in their own position and to challenge the view expressed in that facile phrase, 'You can't change human nature' which attempts to describe what is socially produced as natural and is generally said apropos some example of selfish, aggressive, individualistic, sexist or racist behaviour abstracted from its social context and for which universality is claimed. This criticism, admittedly valid as it stands, does not entail that it is invalid or impossible at least in principle to examine common features of human behaviour in their social context, which is what many socialist theorists imply when they substitute a socio-economic reductionism for biological reductionism. As Timpanaro (1975) argued, those Marxists who argue for the 'decisive primacy' of economic and social structures in the conditioning of cultural factors, put themselves in a scientifically and polemically weak position if they then deny the conditioning which nature exercises on human beings. He illustrates the absurdity of such a position by way of a metaphor. Such a position Timpanaro (p. 44) argues is:

> ... like that of a person living on the first floor of a house, who turns to the tenant on the second floor and says: 'you think you're independent, that you support yourself by yourself? You're wrong! Your apartment stands only because it is supported on me, and if mine collapses, yours will too', and on the other hand to the ground floor tenant that 'What are you saying? That you support and condition me? What a wretched illusion! The ground floor only exists in so far as it is the ground floor to the first floor. Or rather, strictly speaking, the ground floor is the first floor, and your apartment is only a sort of cellar, to which no real existence can be assigned'.

Timpanaro (p. 45) goes on to argue that:

> ... the historicist polemic against 'man in general' which is completely correct as long as it denies that certain historical and social forms such as private property or class divisions are inherent in man in general, overlooks the fact that man as a biological being, endowed with a certain (not unlimited) adaptability to his external environment and with certain impulses towards activity and the pursuit of happiness, subject to old age and death is not an abstract construction, but, one of our pre-historical ancestors, a species of pithecanthropus now superseded by social and historical man, but still exists in each of us and in all probability will exist in the future. It is certainly true that the development of society changes ways of feeling pain, pleasure and other elementary psycho-physical reactions, and that there is hardly anything that is 'purely natural' left in contemporary man, that has not been enriched and remoulded by the social and cultural environment. But the general aspects of the 'human condition' still remain, and the specific characteristics introduced into it by the various forms of associated life have not been such as to overthrow them completely. To maintain that, since the 'biological' is always presented to us as mediated by the 'social', the 'biological' is nothing and the 'social' is everything, would once again be idealist sophistry.

Timpanaro (1975, pp. 51-52) does not argue for a metaphysical, essentialist or metahistorical account of biological determinism or of human nature. He accepts that the biological is socially mediated while not denying that the biological partly determines. He recognises that our nature is not that of 'eternal man' but is subject to evolutionary processes, though this transformation occurs at a slower rate than that of historical or social institutions.

Kate Soper (1979) has challenged Timpanaro's position. She claims that his zeal to emphasise the determination by biological givens leads to an almost Feuerbachian position of the abstract generality of human nature. She argues that because the effects of determinations never exist in pure form, biological determinations cannot be contrasted with the effects of social relations, as Timpanaro supposes, because culture is an effect of their interaction. She argues that Timpanaro presents the biological and the social as if they were different kinds of existence that mix together while retaining their separate status within the mix, rather than recognising that the effect produced is a compound different in kind from the ingredients. Soper continues by arguing that this does not mean that the 'natural determinants disappear' or that the biological is reduced to social relations, but, since the biological is always socially mediated, 'these social features in a real and important sense render the natural a cultural product' (p. 78). This argument is pretty confusing; it seems that Soper cannot have it both ways. She argues for biological determinism while seemingly denying biological nature; she implies that because the biological is socially mediated it becomes a social fact, which would seem to preclude it also retaining any status as biological fact.

She offers many examples which are designed to reinforce the idea that even the most indisputable biological facts have the concrete manifestations they do as a result of their social determinations. For example she has argued that human beings are biologically determined by virtue of their common biological structure, certain levels of physical strength, sex and somatic instincts, physiognomy and role in reproduction. But it is how these instincts are satisfied, the value conferred on physical attributes, the forms in which sex divisions are lived and experienced, which are central to any understanding of the concrete effects of these determinations (p. 78). She argues that our subjection to old age, illness and death themselves are not given, as she assumes Timpanaro supposes, in the sense that their significance and the experience of them differ according to the time and society we live in, as well as our place within it (p. 95).

She charges Timpanaro with conflating the effects of biological determination with the determinations themselves, since even brute biological facts cannot be given a purely biological explanation. But Soper's own view veers dangerously towards the opposite mistake, of conflating the effects of the social determinations with the determinations themselves; for if the biological and the social determinations are so interwoven we can have access only to the socialised instantiation of that compound. This point can be highlighted by her apparently innocuous remark that one must differentiate between the universal biological instinct of hunger and 'this hunger for this kind of food, consumed in this kind of way' (p. 93). This instance of hunger she adds 'can only be explained as a materialisation of particular historical relations; it is not a mere *form* of abstract hunger and cannot therefore be conceptualised in the same terms' (p. 93).

However this comes perilously close to saying that because there are only specific social instances of hunger, we cannot say that human beings need to eat; we can only refer to specific instances of human beings feeling hungry. In this context her observation that 'Even death ... comes in a thousand different ways, and its advent is regretted and welcomed and mythologised and celebrated not in the annals of biology but in those of society' (p. 95) apparently overlooks the fact that it is because we are biologically determined that we do die at all, and that all the socially specific ways of experiencing and meeting death have ultimately less relevance than this.

Soper (p. 95-96) is aware of the possibility of this kind of challenge when she asks, 'What is wrong with saying that human beings are biologically determined in the very general sense of being subject to illness and death?' She answers that to do so may lead to a situation where it could be said of a specific human society:

> that is the human condition; and thereby to naturalise it, to collapse the difference between natural and social determinants operating within the social order and thus to relate to the latter as a form of the given.

The logic of her argument seems to be that to avoid the dangers of labelling socially determined characteristics 'natural' we should deny that nature determines. In the long run this has the further consequences Soper hoped to avoid: the 'social' is mistaken for the 'natural', since we are left with no way of being able to distinguish the one from the other.

And this does seem to be Soper's conclusion in her later work, *On Human Needs* (1981), which she reaches via an argument which potentially could avoid this. In Chapter 6 of this book she discusses Marx's distinction between historically natural and wholly historical needs. The former include, for example, the natural need for food and the forms it takes historically, and the latter include socially produced needs like the need for money. She argues that the need for food is always a historically specific need for a particular object; in this sense it is no different from any non-natural need like money. However 'non-natural' needs can be viewed also as a historically developed form of basic needs. She views money as the specific need for a specific object of wealth and as a manifestation of a general drive which she identifies as 'greed' or 'the mania for possessions'. That is, all needs are non-natural from one standpoint and all are historically natural from another. Soper (p. 123) argues:

> It is a distinction between a need viewed as a content, where it is its specificity that counts, and whose explanation can never refer us to an anthropological history, but only to the nature of the individuals and socio-economic relations contemporaneous with its existence, and the

same need viewed as historical development - a conception in which it is the form of which the need is the development which counts, whose explanation will precisely refer us to the historical development of human beings, and therefore leads us into the consideration of the abstract biological and psychological needs that are the element common to all our specific needs, and by reference to which we are alone enabled to view them as particular developments.

But, having said that specific needs are historical forms of general needs, Soper (p. 123) then immediately goes on to say that it is because of this that a theory of needs is doomed as a theory:

> if by theory is meant conceptual resolution, homogeneity of concepts, coherent systematisation. For this is a theory, if it deserves the name, whose theoretical statement is to the effect that all theorisation about needs must necessarily lie in the field of forces created by the antithetical poles of relativism and essentialism.

This view denies that it is conceptually possible to abstract from the specifically social content or manifestation of a relative experience of a need, the common general and natural elements of it.

If we can identify the common, general and natural elements of needs we can isolate the features of the concrete specific instance of a need which are not common and general and which are the effects of other determinants. In fact in other arguments Soper herself suggests this approach. Furthermore, if we can isolate the common and general needs we can then deduce that, where there are no individual concrete social instances of such needs, the lack of such instantiation is due to the lack of enabling conditions rather than a lack of need.

Exclusive emphasis on the fact that how people experience their need is socially determined can turn this harmless incontestable fact into one with harmful, contestable implications, viz:

either

1 That because there are ONLY socially specific concrete experiences and instances of need, there is NO natural need.

or

2 That if there are NO individual socially specific experiences and instances of need, there is NO natural need.

The absurdity of (1) is apparent and has been discussed. The definition of need in Chapter 1 showed that (2) cannot be true. Fundamental human needs were defined as the objectively necessary conditions for achieving any end and were identified as what is necessary for survival and health. For this reason there are many ways in which it is possible for there to be a need without there being any socially specific experiences of them as felt need and/ or instance of them in particular consumptions. They might be formulated in the following way:

a) When there is no experience but there is an instantiation.
b) When there is no experience or instantiation.
c) When there is experience but no instantiation.

a) denotes the simple sense in which survival and health needs persist even when not experienced or felt as a deficiency but which nevertheless have some instantiation. We may never have lacked what we need, but those needs are manifest in particular satisfactions, consumptions and states of affairs.

b) denotes the more complicated sense in which though people may not experience a need, a need can be imputed. Because needs are objective means to ends they are not dependent on feelings, experiences or beliefs about their necessity or desirability. We might be ignorant, unaware or mistaken about what we need in order to survive and be healthy, or we may lack the resources and opportunities to attain these goods. Consequently there are no experiences of them as felt need or want, and no specific instances of them manifest in satisfactions. They can though, be imputed via empirical evidence about means to ends and by causal explanations of the effects on survival and health of unmet or inadequately satisfied needs.

c) denotes needs which are concretely experienced but are not socially instantiated:

i) when people are aware of their needs but are not motivated to satisfy them, needs cannot be inferred from intentional behaviour;

and

ii) when people are aware of their needs as deficiencies but are unable either to express them as demands or fulfil them because they are not aware of the satisfiable character of the need or because they have limited access to the necessary resources.

In one sense a need only exists as a socially determined need where there is a specific concrete instance of this need, and this is important to the argument against true and false need theorists who want to deny the reality and the truth of some such needs, for all such needs exist and are real. However, this is not an argument against the reality or the existence of natural, biological and psychological determinants which have real effects, or the reality of needs which have no concrete manifestations.

I have rejected the argument that natural needs are true authentic needs and socially produced needs are false, while retaining a distinction between the natural and social determinants on needs. The natural components of needs are those general elements common to all our specific needs which are socialised, particular developments and expressions of them. It is acknowledged that the biological is always socially mediated without denying that biology in part determines. Because natural needs are understood as being always socially mediated, emphasising biological givens does not lead to an essentialist position which supposes the abstract generality of human nature (as Soper argues). Because socially experienced needs are understood as particular expressions of natural needs, the danger of naturalising the social can be avoided. If the natural and social components of needs cannot be contrasted or separated then this leads to a reductionist position which has the consequence of explaining the social in terms of the natural or vice versa, (since there is no criterion for the distinction) and implies that socially felt needs are the only real needs there are.

Ways in which people can be mistaken about their needs

It has been argued that needs must be explained by reference to both biology and society. Socialised expressions of needs are real needs. However, just because all needs that are felt are real this does not mean that (1) people may not have mistaken perceptions about their felt needs, and (2) because a need is not felt it is not real. These two points I will now go on to discuss.

1 Felt needs

Felt needs are what we feel, experience and believe our needs to be. They are constructed in particular social contexts.

a) They may not correspond to fundamental human needs.

b) They may correspond to fundamental human needs and so be the phenomenal form, the socio-historical manifestation of an underlying natural need.

Whether or not they are the socio-historical manifestation of fundamental need they are determined, albeit often indirectly, in the form they take by social conditions, by the social structure and the social relations of production, distribution and exchange and so by the social function of the individual within the reproduction of those relations.

Now because feeling a need is mind and belief dependent, felt needs are not criteria for fundamental human needs or part of what it means to need something. Hence,

a) If an agent feels a need for x that does not correspond to a fundamental need, then that agent will be mistaken in feeling, believing or valuing x as a need when it is not, or by believing x will satisfy a need when it will not. Because these felt needs are socially produced, social conditions then produce mistaken conceptions of needs. Although it follows that if the agent's felt need does not correspond to a fundamental need the agent is mistaken in feeling, believing or valuing it as a need, this is only significant if the felt need or want in question is destructive or harmful to the satisfaction of the fundamental human need.

b) If an agent feels this need and if the felt need is a socialised expression of a natural need, in pursuing it the agent is correct in thinking that this is 'a' way of meeting this need, the agent may have mistaken beliefs about the socio-historic character of the need. He may think that this form of expression is inevitable or the only expression of that need, and so may be ignorant of what is possible.

Again, facts about the acquisition of needs are only significant if the result is inadequate expression and satisfaction of needs.

Whether or not felt needs correspond to fundamental human needs, the agent may be mistaken as to the determination of the need (the causes and conditions for its expression), the social function this determination serves and the consequences which when they coercively determine and thwart the development, expression and satisfaction of the need become significant mistakes.

It is possible to explain the origin of the forms that felt needs take by an examination of the social, political and economic structures which generate them and the social relations which necessitate them being expressed in these forms. It follows that a person may not adequately conceptualise these social structures and social relations.

Therefore an individual may not be aware of the social conditions and their place within the system of social relations which generate and coercively determine felt needs and their possibilities of satisfaction. They may be unaware that these conditions, and the social form needs take, are not inevitable and may be subject to the possibility of historical transformation. That is, the agent may be ignorant and/or hold mistaken beliefs about what social arrangements are historically possible, what other forms of manifestation of need are possible, and what alternative objects of satisfaction could be available, and therefore as a result be unaware of the limitations which are placed on the developments of alternative expressions of need, objects of satisfaction and ability to satisfy them.

As a corollary to this, they may be unaware that this determination has the social function of reproducing social structures and relations which give rise to these manifestations in the first place, the principal aim and actual consequence of which is not the optimal satisfaction of the agent's need.

Whilst recognising that an agent's beliefs about their needs are informed by their own reasons and intentions, and that these felt needs are 'really' their own, it is still possible to re-describe an agent's beliefs about their needs (their determination, nature, forms of expression, manner and objects of satisfaction and ability to satisfy them), in terms of:

1 The social conditions and causes for their holding these beliefs, i.e. their origin

and

2 The social function of these beliefs

which explains how and why felt needs are experienced and perceived in certain ways. If these beliefs are false, then this redescription and subsequent argument assumes that a belief would not be held if the agent was not ignorant of the conditions and causes of the belief and the social function (as well as the consequences) of the belief.

The explanation of (1) engenders a conflict between the expressions of need people currently have and those they could have if other manifestations were humanly possible and if wider forms of satisfaction were historically possible. This explanation also gives rise to a critical account of felt needs and of the social structures and relations which condition them, if neither the manifestation, nor the forms of social relations which currently exist are inevitable. This account, too, provides people with reasons to change the system where the above is possible and where change is possible.

The explanation of (2) undermines the rationale for the agent's belief by showing that the belief is both mistaken and also necessary for the reproduction of social relations. This reproduction is an unintended result of the beliefs that people have about their needs and the action they engage in to pursue them, even though it may actively thwart the satisfaction of their needs. This explanation can provide the agent with reasons for both criticising and changing the system which requires for its reproduction the efficacy of mistaken beliefs. Furthermore, if this explanation can show that people unconsciously reproduce social relations which are ultimately detrimental to the satisfaction of their needs, it also on these grounds provides the agent with reasons to transform it and to create a society in which satisfaction of need is the primary aim.

So though needs are not produced by conscious intention and all felt needs are real, social conditions can generate mistaken beliefs about them.

2 *Unfelt needs are real – the ways people may be mistaken about them*

People have needs of which they may be unaware, and in this sense too they can be said to have mistaken beliefs about their needs.

Fundamental human needs may not be known or experienced even though they are objective requirements for survival and health. Need dispositions endure when not manifest or felt and are only felt or expressed under certain conditions. Their identification is independent of any corresponding desire or felt need and their social expression is dependent on social conditions, just as the form felt needs take is dependent on them.

Survival and health needs persist when not felt, as the absurdity of saying 'I have no general need to eat or sleep', just because I do not feel hungry or tired, illustrates. It is normally only on condition that I am deprived of food or sleep, or when I am at present pursuing some temporarily overriding need, that I will feel the need for either. So, I would be mistaken if I claimed that I have no need for food or rest just because at the moment I have no desire or do not feel these needs.

If I am a starving Ethiopian, deprived of food, I will feel a need for food which will be overwhelming. But this does not imply that I have no other needs which would be activated under certain conditions (in this case the condition being if the present need were met) even if the felt need or desire for food is at the moment overriding all other needs for which I have no present desire, and I would be mistaken if I supposed this to be the case.

People at certain times may *choose* to deny themselves the expression or the satisfaction of a need in order to concentrate on the satisfaction of others which are more important to them at that particular time, or to enjoy the effects of delayed gratification of the original need they suppressed.

There is, though, no evidence to suggest that people who are starving with no prospect of this need for food being satisfied would choose their situation or that they do not have this need per se. People who choose to deny their needs do so temporarily and it would be absurd to suggest that, because at certain times they did not manifest the need or feel any desire to fulfil it, this is the case in general: we would be mistaken if we concluded that they did not have these needs.

There are other ways in which we can be said to have unfelt needs. When I do not know that something is essential for what I want or desire to do, that is that x is needed to achieve my present ends. I may have a need for x which I do not feel (since I do not know it is useful). When I am mistaken about the need for x in order to achieve what I want, or to achieve my present ends, the mistake can be factual and due to lack of information and resources.

There seems to be no problem in saying that, given my present desires, ends or purposes, though I am unaware of the need and the need is not felt, it exists. This highlights the fact that if we know the ends or desires people in general must pursue (identified in this book as survival and health), there is no problem in claiming that though needs as the means to them may not be felt, they nevertheless exist. And this is surely why we persist in feeding our babies when they spit out food and put them to bed when they do not feel tired. We do so because we do not want them to feel the need, to get to the stage where their needs are so pressing that they demand to eat or sleep. We pre-empt the deprivation by satisfying the need before the experience of it and the demand occurs. It is why, when we consider relief for starving people, we are not so naive as to think that delivering grain meets all their needs. We do not have to wait for them to be fed and make further demands before recognising that they also need other things, e.g. clothing, homes, medicine and work, etc. It is also why social policies often are aimed at what people need in order to retain their health, in terms of directives to clean up the water or air supply, because it can be assumed, all things being equal, that the people want to be well, since this is a desire that most people do have, even if it is not expressed.

Where people themselves experience need negatively as a deficiency there is no problem in claiming that the need exists. Though the need itself is not imputed, it is felt negatively though not expressed positively. The person, though, may be mistaken about, or unaware of, the satisfiable character of the need and the forms of satisfaction which are available or which could be available. Hence they do not articulate or pursue their needs as desires, demands or activity aimed at their satisfaction. The reason why they are unable to do so is that the material causes and conditions necessary for the person to act, with regard to need articulation and satisfaction, are not present.

Even when the need is not perceived by the individual as a deficiency it is possible to discover empirical indicators of the presence of a need by identifying the physical and psychological effects, frustrations and behavioural patterns which occur when needs which have existed are not satisfied. (see chapters 6, 7 and 8 for discussion on how this can be done and the problems and issues it raises). We do not have to wait in each and every case until a deficiency has occurred before being able to infer the existence of a need.

Thus, though a person may not recognise what they do need and may not experience their needs as deficiencies, and therefore in this sense be mistaken about the needs they do have, their demonstrable behaviour and the presence of observable effects indicate that a need exists.

Conclusion

In this chapter it has been argued that the division of needs into true and false, where this correlates with the distinction between naturally and socially determined needs, has to be rejected, as has the account of the production of needs by conscious social conditioning. Rather, it has been argued that needs are produced by social conditions, not social conditioning. Natural needs are those which arise in any society and are always manifest in some social form, therefore true and false cannot be equated with natural and social. Consequently there is no question of disputing the truth or the reality of needs that are felt. However, this explanation does not preclude the existence of natural determinants. Socially produced needs are instances of natural needs which are socially determined into particular forms and it is this social determination which affects how and if needs are felt, expressed or satisfied.

This argument:

a) retains some of the insights of 'false' need theories;
b) avoids the dangers indicated by Leiss and Heller;
c) overcomes the dangers of naturalising the social (Soper's concern) or conversely socialising the natural;
d) claims that there are no 'false' needs but socially produced misconceptions about needs.

That is:

a) It claims that social conditions determine how and if needs are expressed and satisfied, thus allowing criticism of inadequately expressed and unsatisfied needs to be directed towards those conditions.

b) Because it acknowledges that all needs are socially determined the satisfaction of needs is not regarded as a quantitative abstract problem, but one which refers to historical standards and social possibilities in calls for their satisfaction (Leiss).

   Because all needs are considered to be real, socially conditioned needs are not regarded as false, and criticism of them is therefore not based on their unreality, thus denying them claims to satisfaction, but on how and why they are conditioned in certain ways and the negative effect this may have for satisfaction (Heller).

c) Because socially produced needs are explained as instances of natural, universal needs, this does not lead to the danger of naturalising the social (Soper).

   Furthermore, because the natural and social are distinguished, the opposite problem of socio-economic reductionism is avoided. This view, and any view which advocates an inextricable mix between the natural and the social has the same consequences, the inability to distinguish the natural from the effects of the social. Only if this is done, can it be shown (a) how and why needs are socially produced in particular manifestations and the consequences of this, (b) that the view that needs can be identified with people's social experience of them can be challenged and (c) that social conditions contribute to the inadequate satisfaction of and failure to meet need.

d) All needs that are felt are real. Unfelt needs are real too. As a result of social circumstances people may have mistaken perceptions of their needs in that they may be unaware of what they need or that they need something. They may have mistaken perceptions about their felt needs. They may be unaware of how and why their felt needs come about, their transformability and the consequences which may be the inadequate or non-satisfaction of fundamental human needs.

The kind of approach I have outlined in this chapter provides a criticism of capitalism but not from the point of view of its sinister power to manipulate and create false needs, since the needs it gives rise to are genuine needs. It rather criticises capitalism from the point of view of the limitations, reductions and frustrations it places on the formation of needs and their satisfactions. It thus provides a critique of the social structure and the social relations which condition these manifestations, and criticises the social function and social consequences of the beliefs it engenders about needs. It further provides a critique of the social conditions which prevent people from articulating, expressing or satisfying these needs.

5 Definition of health

I have consistently argued that survival and health are fundamental human needs. Survival is a need in the sense that if human beings have any ends at all or are to act to achieve them, they need to survive physically. Thus survival becomes an end in itself that any human being with ends has reason to aim at, desire or value. The means to survival which are instrumental human needs (SN2) are empirically discoverable and explained by reference to our biological nature in given social contexts. Whatever our overall and differing goals, our ability to achieve them is non-existent if survival as a goal is not achieved, or is diminished to the extent that SN2 are not met. The end of survival (SN1) and the means to survival (SN2) are then objectively important and objectively ascribable to all human agents who are in possession of ends.

However, though survival is a necessary pre-condition for goal achievement, survival alone is not a sufficient condition for purposive and successful action to achieve ends. Consequently it is proposed that physical and mental health are the necessary conditions for successful and purposive action, and these include survival needs. All are objective needs, as they are pre-requisites for such action, and objective ends which any human being has good reason to aim at.

In this chapter I will define 'Health' and defend this definition against objections. I will further address the objection that, as survival and health are not always necessary conditions for the achievement of other ends, they cannot be either fundamental human needs nor universally pursued, desired or valued as means to ends or as ends in themselves.

Definition

Health is to be understood as the natural functioning of the human organism. This notion of health draws on a series of articles by Christian Boorse (1975, 1976a, 1977) and conforms to the so called 'biomedical model'. Basically health is defined as the absence of disease. Disease is a technical term which belongs to medical theory in a textbook sense and includes all unhealthy conditions:

> infectious syndromes, deformities and disabilities that result from trauma, birth defects, growth disorders, functional impairments, symptomatic and asymptomatic disorders and all injuries and causes of death.

'Disease' as a theoretical term is distinct from 'illness' which is a practical normative term. Illnesses are diseases with incapacitating effects and which have certain normative features reflected in the institutions of medical practice. A disease is an illness only if it is undesirable to its bearer, is recognised as deserving treatment or is an excuse for undesirable behaviour.

Diseases are deviations from natural functional organisation. Calling X a disease means that it is not in the nature of the species. It is unnatural because it interferes with the performance of a natural function.

Here, the absence of health is not a deviation from a statistical norm. There are many deviations from the average, such as the possession of great strength or ability, which cannot be classified as signs or examples of dysfunctions. Nor does deviance of behaviour, motivation or having minority tastes alone qualify for such classification. Moreover, the frequency of dysfunctions could be endemic or universal as when whole populations are infected with diseases. Statistical normality is not a necessary or sufficient condition of health.

Rather, the account of health here as natural functioning distinguishes genetic and individual variation, social deviancy and environmentally caused dysfunction from disease, by drawing on a theoretical account of the goals to which the human organism is directed, given the design of that organism.

An organism is theoretically healthy if its functioning conforms to the natural design of that kind of organism. Deficiencies in functional efficiency are diseases when they are unnatural, they may be atypical, or if typical attributable to a hostile environment. If this is correct, the functional account avoids the pitfalls of statistical normality and normative assumptions. It might be conceded that a normative element is involved in practically determining the level of interference that counts as disease. However health never requires 'ideal' functioning but only an impeded functioning of each internal part.

Functions are to be thought of as causal contributions to goals pursued by the organism. According to Christopher Boorse (1976b, p. 78) 'organisms are goal directed in a sense that they are disposed to adjust their behaviour to environmental change in ways appropriate to a constant result, the goal'. And, 'to say that an action or process A is directed to the goal G is to say not only that A is what is required for G, but that within some range of environmental variation, A *would have been modified* in whatever way was required for G'. When an action or process is directed towards a goal it is necessary for the achievement of that goal. Hence, when natural functions are impaired, goal realisations, whatever they may be, are similarly impaired.

This is not to declare any goals as natural or unnatural. What goals an organism pursues, what goals natural functions promote, must be judged independently of the value of achieving, maintaining or restoring natural functions. Natural functions contribute to all goals neutrally. The heart pumping blood, the cells eliminating waste are necessary functions whatever one wants to do.

In order to achieve success in attaining any ends human beings may have contingently, human beings need the means to survival and physical health. These instrumental survival and physical health needs are what is necessary to achieve, maintain or restore actual or potential natural human functioning, and what is necessary to avoid risks or other factors which will ultimately interfere with natural human functioning.

Any deficiency with respect to these needs will endanger the functioning of a human being, as a member of a natural species *and* will endanger the successful action directed towards the achievement of any other ends the individual may have. Where natural functioning is impaired, goal realisation is similarly impaired, for whatever our goals we need to survive and to function effectively and the achievement of these goals is diminished if our natural physical functioning is impaired.

Mental health

Szasz (61, 63, 70a, 70b), Sarbin (1967, 1969) and the behaviour modification theorists question whether the notion of mental health is legitimate at all. Those who believe in mental health disagree about what it is and how to find out. Boorse (1976a) claims that the concept of mental health must be a faithful analogue of the concept of physical health. The functional idea of health in physical medicine applies to mind and body. Boorse (p. 64) argues:

> If certain types of mental processes perform standard functions in human behaviour, it is hard to see any obstacles to calling unnatural obstructions to these functions mental diseases, exactly as in the physiological sense.

Problems occur in this domain as opposed to the physical domain, as there is a less well developed theory of species-typical mental functioning and mental organisation. Natural psychological functions are less specific than physiological ones. As Jahoda notes at present, 'knowledge about deviations, illness and malfunctioning far exceeds knowledge of healthy functioning' (1958, p. 6).

Furthermore, there is the problem identified by Szasz and Sarbin that ascriptions of mental health based on deviance or malfunctioning can result in improper descriptions, stigmatizations, and social control of people who behave in disturbing or improper ways as mentally ill. Causal explanations of such behaviour by 'rule-following', 'communication', or 'social system' models are ruled out.

However, in spite of these problems, Boorse believes it would be a mistake for the clinical disciplines to follow Szasz et al in dismissing the idea of mental health. Just because there is an illegitimate use of the term 'mental illness' does not mean there cannot be a legitimate use of the term 'mental health'. The biomedical model clearly presupposes that the missing account of natural mental functioning can be developed and that there is such a thing as a failure to function. This neither involves labelling social deviances, nonconforming or maladaptive behaviour per se as illness, pathology or unhealthy, nor equating conforming adaptive behaviour with health, for deviance in itself does not define the health concept.

Boorse (1976a, p. 64) suggests that, even without appeal to any controversial psychological theory, it is easy to draw out some of the outlines of natural mental functioning and this can help distinguish the mental diseases which are currently classed as psychopathologies:

> Perceptual processing, intelligence and memory clearly serve to provide information about the world that can guide effective action. Drives serve to motivate it. Anxiety and pain function as signals of danger, language as a device for cultural cooperation and cognitive enrichment and so on. If these and other mental processes play standard functional roles throughout the species, we seem to have everything requisite for the possibility of mental health.

From elementary non-controversial functional assumptions it can be suggested that certain conditions are unhealthy. We can assume that the main function of perceptual and intellectual processes is to give us knowledge of the world. Though it would be wrong to judge every false belief as a functional abnormality, given both the limits to human intelligence and the evidence on which it works, where cognitive functions are disrupted to an unusually high degree by our wishes, such conditions seem unnatural dysfunctions. 'By this standard schizophrenia and all other psychoses look objectively unhealthy' (p. 77).

Similarly very limited functional assumptions will suffice to construe serious neurosis as a disease if traditional analytic descriptions of the neurotic process are accepted. Boorse (p. 77) writes:

> Since opposite desires are common in human beings, there must be some normal mechanisms for resolving them without permanent and paralysing conflict. If some of the neurotic's strongest desires remain locked in combat without freely realising their motivational force in behaviour, it

is not an implausible hypotheses that the conflict resolution mechanism is functioning incorrectly.

Moreover, Boorse (p. 78) argues that:

> It would not be difficult to construe psychoanalytic theory as a set of theses about biological functions of the mind. On this view the id might emerge as a reservoir of motivation, the ego as an instrument of rational integration and cognitive competence and the super ego as a device for socialisation. One could then give a straightforward argument that neurosis is a disease by appealing to its disturbance of the integrative and motivational function of the ego and the id.

This is not to argue that every neurosis is a defect of health. Neuroses could be what biologists call facultative adaptions to life circumstances or typical development stages. A neurosis is only unhealthy if we know the mind is not supposed to work in that particular way. However, even without confirmation of these elementary functional assumptions or a plausible theory of functional behaviour we can sometimes infer internal malfunction. This is because there are some mental conditions, states and symptoms which interfere with a person's ability to do various things and with their general capacity for action to achieve any other end or aim. These relate not to their choice of goal but to any goals a person may have.

These can be construed as interferences with natural functioning. Mental conditions classed as pathological – delusions, hallucinations, phobias, compulsions and obsessions and mental states such as depression and anxiety are all included here since they clearly interfere with and limit capacity for successful and purposive action. In addition to this, symptoms of emotional distress such as difficulties in interpersonal relations, feelings of insecurity, negative self image, identity confusion, frustration, boredom and generalised unhappiness (cf. Szasz's (1961) 'problems of living'), though not pathological in themselves and therefore not classed as diseases, are variables that could be included as symptoms relevant to mental health. They interfere with the general capacity for action and are known to be causally related to susceptibility to illness of all kinds.

These mental conditions, states and symptoms can indicate, though not prove (see 1c), both disturbances in mental functioning and the inadequate satisfaction of mental health needs – that is whatever is necessary to achieve, maintain or restore natural mental functioning.

Mental health is analogous to physical health in the sense that it is natural mental functioning. The goal of mental health is an objective and important need (MHN1) which any human being has good reason to pursue, desire or value as it is a means to the achievement of other goals. Any deficiency in mental health endangers natural mental functioning and limits action directed towards other goals whatever they may be. It is theoretically possible to be in robust physical health yet suffer deficiencies in mental functioning. In practice deficiencies in mental functioning are likely to affect the maintenance of physical health and vice versa, for mind and body do not function independently of each other. For an organism to function effectively, then, both PHN1 and MHN1 are necessary.

It follows from the above that any human being has good reason to pursue, desire or value the means to mental health (instrumental health or MHN2). These means are whatever is necessary to achieve, maintain or restore the equivalent of natural mental functioning and the avoidance of risks and other factors which would or could interfere with natural functioning. MHN2 then includes mental and emotional states as well as people, physical objects, states of affairs, personal and social relations, goods and services, institutions, living, working and environmental conditions, and socio-economic factors known to be conducive to achieving, maintaining or restoring health.

So far, in this chapter two broad claims have been made:

1 Both the notions of physical and mental health conform to the biomedical model. Health is the absence of disease, of deviation from natural functional organisation. Health is thus the natural functioning of the human organism.

2 Both survival and health are means and ends any human being must have if they are to act successfully and purposively. The means to survival and health (instrumental needs) are therefore also objectively important and objectively ascribable to all human agents.

The remainder of this chapter will address objections to both these claims.

The biomedical model: objections to the definition of health

a) The biomedical definition of health has been objected to on the grounds that it is too narrow a definition. Health , it is claimed, involves more than not being ill or diseased, and is something positive and enhancing. The World Health Organisation defined heath in its constitution of 1946:

> Health is a state of complete, physical, mental and social well-being and not merely the absence of disease and infirmity.

Menniger (1930, p. 2) argues:

> Let us define mental health as the adjustment of human beings to the world and to each other with a maximum of effectiveness and happiness.

Positive conceptions of health are particularly prevalent in discussions of criteria for mental health born of a scepticism about the concept of mental

Positive conceptions of health are particularly prevalent in discussions of criteria for mental health born of a scepticism about the concept of mental disease and the fear that genuine mental illness is too severe a category to be relevant to most psychotherapy patients. Positive mental health concepts emphasise a maximum quality of life, the idea of self-actualisation and personal development. Jahoda (1958) lists 6 different but related and overlapping criteria that have been used in different conceptions of positive mental health:

1. Attitudes to self – self-acceptance, self-esteem, self-confidence, self-reliance.
2. Growth, development, self-realisation, self-actualisation.
3. Integration – the balance of psychic forces in the individual, a unifying outlook on life, resistance to stress.
4. Autonomy – the regulation of behaviour from within, independent development.
5. Perception of reality – perception free from need distortions – empathy or social sensitivity.
6. Environmental mastery –
   the ability to love
   adequacy in love, work and play
   adjustment in interpersonal relationships
   efficiency in meeting situational requirements
   capacity for adaption and adjustment
   efficiency in problem solving.

These broad definitions of health, though, suffer from several problems. One is that they suggest that health is an absolute ideal state and insofar as they do so demand that only a perfect human being would qualify for the status of a healthy person. The second is that they tend to equate health with happiness without specifying what happiness may consist of. Thirdly, they overlook the fact that one can be unhappy and still be healthy, or be unhealthy and happy so that health cannot be equated with happiness. Fourthly, while drawing attention to the connection between social circumstances and health, the WHO definition falsely assumes that people cannot be healthy if they have social problems. People can be unhappy, poor and otherwise socially deprived without being unhealthy. Fifthly, there are controversies about what is meant by 'well-being'. The selection of these states as criteria for positive health depends on value-judgements about what qualities or attributes the people offering them admire or value. What the healthy mind and body are like are empirical questions as to how human beings are constituted, not judgements on how we would like them to be.

If health is defined as natural functioning and disease as interference with these functions, then the category of instrumental health (PHN2 + MHN2) can accommodate the states or qualities advocated by positive health theorists. Self-confidence, self-esteem, self-realisation etc. are only part of the concept of positive health if it can be maintained that these states are healthy in themselves and not just in virtue of their contribution to the avoidance of impairments in functioning. Being healthy is not the same as being confident, self-realised, happy or satisfied. The presence of these positive conditions, though, can be thought of as conducive to health and their absence to risk of ill health, insofar as there is a causal connection between certain mental states, happiness and health.

b) It is often thought that to emphasise health as the absence of disease encourages some to concentrate on acute care and curative medicine and to obscure the socio-economic causes of ill health.

However, the bias of the health care system towards acute care and the neglect of preventative and holistic approaches results from social and economic forces not erroneous concepts of disease. Furthermore the 'biomedical' model of disease does not entail ignoring its social etiology.

These fears are particularly prevalent with regard to defining mental health in terms of malfunctioning underlying certain behaviours and symptoms. It is thought that such a definition, in pre-supposing physical causes for mental ill health analogous to the causes of physical disease, leads to the following undesirable consequences. Firstly, the idea that appropriate treatment for mental conditions is the same as for physical conditions. The emphasis is on curative medicine with surgical, chemical and electrical intervention to restore natural functioning. Secondly, the view that the final source of discord is biological and located within the individual obscures the social and economic causes of ill health. The emphasis is on individuals who become sick – rather than the social, economic or environmental factors which cause them to be ill with the consequence that it is the individual who is 'blamed' for their illness and the individual who is treated rather than the circumstances.

However, none of these consequences are entailed by the definition of mental health as natural mental functioning. The judgement that a certain state, behaviour or condition is a symptom of malfunctioning does not entail any therapeutic judgement that the appropriate forms of treatment are physical – the surgeon's knife, drugs or electric shocks or that what is required is medical intervention of any kind. And this is the case with both physical and mental conditions, though critics implicitly assume that curative physical treatment and acute care are appropriate to physical illness when they complain of their inapplicability to mental health problems. The fact that the health care system in general is orientated towards acute care rather than preventative measures or holistic modes of treatment can be explained more plausibly by reference to the preservation and expansion of existing economic and professional interests rather than by claiming such measures are the result of misconceptions of health and illness. Curative medicine carried out by experts using complex technology ensures the fragmentation and commodification of health care needs which directly profits the health care industry and indirectly protects the economic interests threatened if preventative measures were to be put into practice. There is no incompatibility between a conception of ill health as interference with natural functioning and the need for alternative forms of treatment and approaches to the person who is ill. It does not preclude the importance of holistic approaches or preventative measures.

The charge that the conception of health as natural functioning emphasises the individual who becomes sick rather than the economic forces that make them sick, itself fails to distinguish between the individual who becomes sick and what will make them sick; what is ill health and what will produce it. There is no contradiction between saying that illness is located within the individual as the subject of illness (and this involves interferences with natural functioning) and saying that many physical and mental illnesses have socio-economic and environmental causes. From the claim that 'disease is located within the individual' it does not follow that diseases are caused by the individual (who can then take the blame) or that disease is cured by treating the individual in particular ways or in isolation from other factors. Confusion arises regarding the individual and the social from not distinguishing mental ill health – the mental conditions, states and symptoms which indicate disturbances in mental functioning and the multivariant causes of ill health and solutions to health.

Insofar as diseases are caused by socio-economic factors then preventative and remedial socio-economic measures are what are necessary to prevent disease and restore health. However, though disease may be environmentally caused and cured, the subject of ill health may still require treatment either because irreversible damage has been done to them or as an emergency interim measure.

Once again, the category of instrumental health (PHN2 and MHN2) as what is necessary to achieve, maintain or restore actual or potential natural functions and the avoidance of risks and other factors which will ultimately interfere with natural human functioning, can accommodate the different ways and methods of achieving health other than emphasis on acute care and can point to the socio-economic causes and cures for ill health and the conditions conducive to health.

c) It is often argued that the absence of mental disease is an inadequate definition of mental health. Since mental disease in many cases cannot be inferred from physiological changes in the functioning organism, it has to be inferred from the presence of behavioural conditions, states or symptoms. These do not prove mental dysfunction since many mentally ill people do not show such symptoms and there are apparently healthy people who do. Furthermore anthropological studies show that what is generally regarded as acceptable behaviour in some cultures is regarded as symptomatic of mental disease in others. Jahoda (1958, p. 13) argues that:

> evaluation of actions as sick, or normal or extraordinary in a positive sense often largely depends on accepted social conventions.

However, to argue that certain conditions, states, behaviours or symptoms can indicate a mental dysfunction does not entail proof of dysfunction nor that the presence of these makes a condition a disease. This position is to be distinguished from those positions which provide criteria for mental health in terms of normal or socially accepted behaviour. For example, Redlich and Freedman (1966, p. 2) argue that:

> In older texts and in current lay parlance psychiatry is often defined as the science dealing with mental diseases and illness of the mind or psyche. Since these are terms reminiscent of the metaphysical concepts of soul and spirit, we prefer to speak of behaviour disorder. Behaviour refers to objective data that are accessible to observation, plausible inference, hypothesis-making, and experimentation. The term disorder, although vague, is descriptive of malfunctioning behaviour without specifying etiology or underlying mechanism.

In contrast to this I have argued that health is primarily a function of the internal state of the organism rather than its behaviour. Though it is possible to call behaviour healthy or unhealthy as it is biologically functional or dysfunctional, 'behaviour' alone cannot distinguish the domain of physical health from mental health (Macklin 1972, p. 342).

Biologically dysfunctional behaviour such as pain, hallucinations, delirium and depression can result from psychosis and can occur in physical disease (for example multiple sclerosis, epilepsy, blindness) and are acceptable in some cultures. To distinguish the 'behaviour' disorders which fall into the province of psychiatry it must be shown that psychological disorders are produced by dysfunctional mental processes. The proper domain of psychiatry is disorders of the mind rather than behaviour.

If psychiatry deals just with dysfunctional behaviour, then there is a danger of abandoning biological dysfunction in favour of social deviance. Psychiatry deals with behaviours deemed deviant by society which are not physiologically explicable. Redlich and Freedman (1966, p. 1) suggest this:

> Defying easy definitions, the term ('behaviour disorders') refers to the presence of certain behavioural patterns – variously described as abnormal, subnormal, undesirable, inadequate, inappropriate, maladaptive, or maladjusted – that are not compatible with the norms and expectations of the patient's social and cultural system.

However, just as lung cancer and muscular dystrophy are diseases not because society believes them to be or disvalues them, but because they are cases of biological malfunction, neither is masturbation, homosexuality or feminism a mental disease because society at various times has disapproved of these practices.

The behaviour modifiers, Redlich and Freedman and others who take the social deviance route in contrast to the view here, abandon the idea of health as natural functioning in favour of 'normal' behaviour for at least behaviour is observable and can be changed. However, in so doing they are unable to distinguish anti-social and deviant behaviour from malfunctioning behaviour.

However, this view does hold that the presence of certain mental conditions, states, symptoms or behaviour are important in that they can in certain circumstances indicate a disturbance in mental functioning.

The fact that in some cultures what is regarded as acceptable behaviour is in others regarded as a symptom of mental illness does not discredit the claims made about the negative indicators of natural functioning. The superficial similarity in symptoms between a Buddhist mystic's meditation and the schizophrenic's catatonic trance do not indicate similar disturbances in mental functioning. The significance of patterns of behaviour is considered in conjunction with what is known about the individual and the society in question, the social role of that individual as well as their intentions and purposes, their ability to choose and control their behaviour and its unintended interference with the achievement of other ends. Clearly 'even' in a Buddhist culture the catatonic trance would be regarded as an interference in functioning just as 'even' in the West a Buddhist meditating would not.

d) Some critics insist that the concept of health is not a descriptive term as in the 'biological model' but a normative one. Health judgements are reducible to value judgements. Diseases on this account are deviations from some social or cultural norm and health is a set of physical or psychological characteristics valued by some theorist or culture.

But, as noted earlier when arguing against the social deviance view of health, it is not society, culture or theory that determines what is and what is not natural functioning. Though Jahoda notes 'evaluation of actions as sick or normal or extraordinary in a positive sense depends largely on accepted social conventions' this 'need not imply that the functional disturbance itself varies from culture to culture' (1958, p. 13). Flew (1973) argues that where there is a difference in belief about the evaluation of actions as healthy or unhealthy, someone has to be wrong on a point of fact. Flew (p. 42) goes on to argue that:

> It is also a fact that given sufficient data biologists generally find little difficulty in agreeing on what the function or functions of any particular organ are, or whether these functions are in fact being discharged efficiently; and in harmony with the discharging by other organs in the organism of their functions.

It may be that in practice we are unable to prove the point of fact which will render explanations of certain socially undesirable practices invalid if based on incorrect assessments of them as deviations from natural functioning. However this does not negate the theoretical point that it is in principle possible to describe biological and psychological functions in a non-evaluative way. Where the factual evidence is insufficient or ambiguous giving rise to competing theories, we opt for the theory which has the greatest explanatory power as we do in any scientific discourse.

Statements about biological and psychological functioning are descriptive rather than normative claims, in that they are statements about the causal conditions for goals pursued by the human organism. What goals the organism pursues can be described and confirmed empirically independently of the value a society or culture places on pursuing them, and so can the physical and mental conditions for their successful pursuit.

The health of the body and mind is not the same as its worth. What the human body and mind are like is an empirical question – a description of how we are constituted, not of what we value. Consequently, the notion of health as natural functioning is not an evaluative notion.

We do, however, and this account allows us to make value judgements about health, and one has been implicit in the arguments given in this chapter. It has been argued that health as natural functioning is something that any human being has good reason to pursue, desire or value. If people want to act successfully to achieve their goals effective physical and mental functioning are necessary means to doing so. Effective functioning contributes to all activities neutrally whatever other goals we have. This is not to suppose that health is the only desirable thing, nor that all undesirable things are unhealthy. It is only to claim their health is something which any person if they have any ends at all that they wish to achieve, has good reason to desire or value.

Objections to viewing survival and health as universally desired or valued

This seems an appropriate point to take up the objection that since survival and health are not always essential means to other ends, they cannot then be said to be universally desired or valued, or to be ends that all human beings have good reason to pursue. I shall answer this objection by using examples in the following categories:

1 The deliberate use or pursuit of death, injury, disability etc. as means to other ends.

2 The inadvertent use of illness, injury or disability etc., as means to other ends.

1 The deliberate use or pursuit of death, injury, disability etc. as means to other ends

a) When people deliberately sacrifice their life or health as means to other ends – for a cause or another person

It is the case that people may and do sacrifice not just their physical health but even life itself as a means of achieving some other end: for the sake of another person or persons or for a cause. For example, so that another person or persons might live or escape harm people in concentration camps have substituted themselves for fellow prisoners facing extermination; and I.R.A. prisoners were prepared to face death by starvation as a means of furthering their political cause.

However, these kind of supposed counter examples do not discredit the notion that survival or health are ends that human beings have good reason to pursue, desire or value. The existence of other goals does not deny that what is being sacrificed is something of great value both to the subject of the sacrifice and to others who benefit from it or who even merely have knowledge of it. The sacrificer makes use of the fact that survival and health are causal contributions to any goals, and therefore something of fundamental value, in making the sacrifice have any real significance or impact in the first place. Furthermore, the fact that people often sacrifice their lives or physical health for the sake of avoiding death or harm to others testifies to the value the sacrificer places on survival and health in general for those others, even if their own survival or health must be relinquished for the sake of others' survival or group survival and health.

b) When an agent uses or pursues physical ill health to attain psychological ends

An agent may sometimes forgo physical gratification of survival and health needs in order to achieve psychological ends. The most extreme cases of deprivation of this sort are exemplified by anorexics and insomniacs. People will at times forgo immediate satisfaction of physical needs in order to accomplish something they consider to be more pressing at the time, though these may be comparatively trivial as when people do without food or sleep to get something done, to continue with the activity they are presently engaged in. These examples would seem to illustrate that psychological and other immediate ends can, in some cases be more important than the end of physical health.

However, the deprivations which the agent uses can only be temporary, for if there is prolonged abstinence from food or sleep he will not survive, and so the possibility of satisfying other ends will be foreclosed. The extreme states of anorexia and insomnia could be viewed as symptoms of the organism still trying to achieve psychological integration or health, which is necessary for successful and purposive action to achieve other goals, even if by doing so they will ultimately thwart those ends and any others they may have. Furthermore, the fact that an agent may use or pursue physical ill health as a means to psychological ends illustrates the interdependence of physical and mental health as ends the agent has good reason to pursue if he has any other ends at all. The lack of gratification of psychological needs can lead to a deterioration in physical health which makes the agent less able to pursue his ends, and the deprivation of physical needs affects both natural physical and psychological functioning and so effects the achievement of other ends.

c) *The deliberate use of illness or injury to achieve the need of avoiding something*

There are cases when it would seem that the agent uses physical injury or ill health as a means to an end of avoiding something and that therefore health and the avoidance of injury cannot be a need in the sense that they are necessary for the achievement of other ends, nor can they be ends that people always have good reason to pursue, desire or value. Examples of these cases are when conscripts deliberately mutilate themselves in order to escape military service, the reputed instances of Vietnamese cutting off children's arms in order to avoid inoculation by the Americans, and conversely when people seek inoculation and so some form of illness to avoid contracting a disease at a later date.

However, it can be argued that the agent who acts in these ways is using physical injury in order to avoid the likelihood of what he or she considers to be a greater injury, harm or threat to health. The agent views conscription, inoculation or lack of it as a greater risk or danger to their health than the injury they inflict upon themselves. Their ultimate rational and desired end is still the avoidance of injury and the attainment of health as an end in itself and as a means to the achievement of other ends that they wish to set for themselves. If some lesser injury or impairment of health is a means to do this, this is unfortunate, but does not discredit the idea that the agents' overall aims are the preservation of health and with it the means to achieve other ends. Flew (1973, p. 45) agrees that health is something that an agent has good reason to value when he says apropos a similar example:

> insofar as the malfunctionings either cause, or partly or wholly consist in, incapacities; then they must surely be rated as, presumptively and in themselves, bad for the people concerned ... your tuberculosis must still be allowed to be presumptively and in itself bad for you; even though it is entirely due to the fact that you have this disease that you owe your exemption from military conscription, and all which that may involve. It must be: since clearly it would be better still for you if you could both

retain that exemption and recover your health; and since, equally clearly, your qualified satisfaction with your diseased condition can be made intelligible to the mean sensual man only by reference to particular present circumstances.

d) Deliberate uses or seeking of injury or illness as means to achieving the end of being accepted into an institution, group, society or way of life

Similar to the examples in (c) it would seem that there are cases in category (d) which show that physical health or avoidance of injury cannot be a need in the sense of necessary means to the achievement of other ends, as the absence of them can be used as means to other ends.

People deliberately undergo physical pain or mutilation in order to achieve acceptance into an institution, group, society or way of life or to adapt to some social role. Tribal initiation tests, female circumcision, footbinding in Imperial China and the castration of male opera singers exemplify this. However, these phenomena do not undermine the objective importance of health, since these practices rely on the importance of health to establish the participants' suitability to belong to the group in question and their commitment to it. They also underline the fact that the agents may consider aspects of their mental health, (the fulfilment of the psychological need to be socially accepted) as a more important end than the avoidance of physical injury. Their physical injury makes them fit for their own way of life (though it may make them unfit for another). An aspect of health is still the end that is being pursued – physical injury is accepted to avoid what is considered to be a greater harm to their overall mental health. Finally these phenomena do not suggest that health is not intrinsically something to be aimed for, for as in (c) we can reasonably assume that none of the practices described would be engaged in by the participants if there were any other accepted means available to demonstrate their commitment or prove their suitability to belong to their society or way of life.

e) Deliberate risk of injury

It seems that on occasion some people will deliberately risk injury or physical harm in a sense not covered by the categories and examples above. I will take the phenomena of Russian roulette as a paradigm case of this use of the deliberate risk of injury and examine whether in fact the participants in the 'game' use this risk as a means to an end, and so whether this provides a counter example to the view that health is an objectively important means to an end and therefore a need.

Graham Greene (1971, pp 127–8) explains that White Russian officers invented Russian roulette as a hazard by which to escape the boredom they faced due to inaction at the end of the counter revolutionary war. He also claims that he himself played Russian roulette, thereby risking injury and death, as a means to the same end, that of avoiding boredom. After five such 'risks', that is shots of the gun with the chances five to one in favour of life, he 'stumbled on the perfect cure' for boredom. Are we to view his action as the use of the risk of death and injury as a means to an end (avoiding boredom) and thus as a counter example to the argument that survival and health are means to other ends people may have? If we view the fact that Greene played Russian roulette because he was bored, we can see that this is not so. For being bored to this degree indicates a profound lack of interest in life, an absence of the existence of ends in the first place. Viewed in this way, playing Russian roulette was, for Greene, a symptom of his having no ends at all. If by playing the game, he inadvertently regained an interest in life, reclaimed himself as a person with ends to pursue, then their further pursuit would require his continuing health.

Similarly, we might view the American soldiers in Vietnam fictionalised in the film, 'The Deerhunter', who reputedly played Russian roulette as displaying symptoms of the same malady. It was precisely because their experience in that war had destroyed their sense of purpose, their desire to live at all and thus to have any other ends, that they were prepared to risk death and injury. The pursuit of other ends no longer had any significance for them as a motivating force. Consequently survival and health could not be seen by them as a means to other ends. In a television documentary about the effects of the Vietnam War on American soldiers, one veteran claimed that he played Russian roulette because in doing so he had a 1:6 chance of survival compared with the considerably lower chance of survival he felt he had when fighting in the jungle. We may regard this act, too, as a symptom of the relinquishing of ends. Fighting in the jungle was an imposed end which no longer had any significance for the veteran. The experience of fighting had caused him to lose the desire to survive, and so to have other ends. It may be that playing Russian roulette in these circumstances was a limited attempt to reclaim his own ends even though this end, if achieved, would have put paid to the achievement of others. 'At least I had a 1:6 chance', he claimed.

In the film 'The Deerhunter', the Vietnamese forced American soldiers to choose between participating in a game of Russian roulette or immediate death, though it has been claimed that in actual fact it was the Americans who forced the Vietnamese to do this. People who are forced to play Russian roulette as a form of torture do so precisely because they want to survive. They are prepared to risk death, as, in these circumstances, risk is the only way to avoid certain death. This is a case of using the risk of injury or death as a means of avoiding a greater injury (certain death) and so fails as a counter example according to the arguments outlined in (c).

2 *The inadvertent use of injury or illness as a means to an end*

There are instances when people use or even welcome illness, injury, or disabilities they have not deliberately chosen or sought but which inadvertently serves some other end they have, which they otherwise would have found difficulty in achieving.

Phillips and Mounce (1969, p. 237) give two examples of these instances in their objections to Phillipa Foot's view (1969, p. 207) that injury is necessarily bad. I will use their examples here to suggest that they do not discredit the idea that illness or injury are in principle to be avoided and that health is a means to other ends.

Phillips and Mounce quote the examples of St. Paul and Brentano to illustrate their claim that injury is not necessarily bad. According to Phillips and Mounce, St. Paul eventually does not consider the 'thorn in the flesh' from which he suffered to be a bad thing. He even thanks God for his disability as it is a reminder to him that he is not sufficient unto himself. His attitude to his injury is part of his conception of man's relationship to God, and the notions of insufficiency, dependence, and divine succour involved in this relationship. Similarly, they argue that Brentano's blindness at the end of his life was not regarded by him as a bad thing since it enabled him to concentrate on philosophy and avoid the pursuit of diverse interests which previously had prevented him from doing the former. Brentano's attitude to his blindness is explained by his dedication to enquiry and the virtues such dedication demands.

Phillips and Mounce claim, that in these contexts, it is dedication to God and to enquiry which determine whether injury or disability constitute goodness or badness. That is, in our terms of reference here, given the ends of dedication to God or to enquiry, in these cases, physical health is not a means to them or something to be pursued, but is in fact, quite the reverse. The absence of health and the presence of disability rather, is a means to these ends.

However, despite what Phillips and Mounce say, these disabilities are things which happen to be useful in the circumstances, for achieving the ends of the people involved. We could not suppose that either St. Paul or Brentano would have sought or chosen such means to their ends. They rationalised them after the event and made them serve their ultimate purposes. If other means had been available, it seems reasonable to believe that they would have opted for them. It is also reasonable to assume that if other means had been available which did not involve physical disability, that they could have been more successful in achieving their ends. For, even if, in one sense, their injuries aided them in concentrating on their purposes, in another sense they must have been a handicap too.

SUMMARY of the case against counterexamples to the view that survival and health are necessary means to other ends. If the counterexamples hold, then, survival and health cannot be objective needs or ends that any human being has good reason to pursue, desire or value.

a) When people deliberately sacrifice their lives or health for the sake of another person or cause, this does not deny and in fact, makes use of the objective fact that what is being sacrificed is something of objective value and objective necessity in that survival and health are causal contributions to any other goals (for that agent and for the others on behalf of whom he makes the sacrifice).

b) When people deliberately forgo physical health as a means to achieving psychological ends (or fulfilling psychological needs) this merely testifies to the importance of mental health and to the interdependence of both physical and mental health. Neither does it discredit physical health viewed as a means or as an end, because it can only be deliberately undervalued for a temporary period, otherwise any physical or psychological end will become unattainable.

c) When people deliberately use illness or injury as a means of avoiding something, their end itself is still physical and mental health, though a lesser injury may be seen as an unavoidable means to it.

d) When people use illness or injury as a means to achieving success in or acceptance into a group, society or institution or way of life, as in (a) this does not discredit the objective importance of physical health, but makes use of it as a yardstick to measure dedication and commitment, and, as in (c) it may be an unavoidable means to avoiding a greater injury or harm, and, in this case, the end is still some aspect of health.

e) When people deliberately risk injury, this can be seen as a symptom of the abandonment of ends and therefore does not discredit the idea of health as an objective need, since the way health has been defined, it is *only* a need when people do have ends, whatever they may be.

f) When people welcome illness, injury or disabilities which they have not deliberately chosen, but which inadvertently serve their ends, we cannot assume that they would have willingly chosen these means or would have had the same attitude towards them if they had other choices. Moreover, the means themselves are ambivalently advantageous for the successful achievement of their ends.

As we have seen, even if it is the case that some goals are not undermined by failing health, and that failing health may even contribute to the attainment of these goals, health is still objectively important in relation to their attainment. Even in cases where people have deliberately chosen illness or injury, we can reasonably assume that people would not have chosen these means if any others were available. Hence it could not be argued that there are cases where death, ill health, injury or disability is a need in the sense of a necessary means to an end. It illustrates rather the lack of choice of means to achieving them. Death or impairments of health would not be chosen as means to ends if there were other options.

It may be conceded that, strictly speaking, survival and health are not absolutely necessary means to any end while insisting on their objective importance as means to the achievement of ends in general and that they are objective ends themselves that any human agent has good reason to pursue, desire or value, for at the very least impairments in health reduce the range of choices and ends open to the agent.

Daniels (1985) argues that it is not strictly true that we need health whatever our goals, for some goals are not undermined by failing health and we can adjust our goals to fit our disability. However, he also argues that impairments of functioning reduce the range of opportunities open to the individual in which he may construct his 'plan of life' or 'conception of the good'. That is, his choice of goals is limited by impairments in natural functioning. Therefore, the kind of needs which are picked out by reference to functioning in the way natural to the species are objectively important because they meet the fundamental interest people have in maintaining the normal range of opportunities.

6 Instrumental health: Physical health needs

The last chapter defined and defended the concept of health as the natural functioning of the human organism. Physical and mental health are ends any human being has good reason to pursue, desire or value. The means to physical health (which include survival needs) and mental health are empirically discoverable by reference to the nature of these needs as means to ends and to facts about the biological and psychological constitutions of human beings in given social contexts. These instrumental needs are what is necessary to achieve, maintain or restore natural human functioning.

This chapter will suggest what the empirical content of physical health needs (PHN2) might be and address the question of how these needs might best be identified in order to facilitate meeting them.

A) Identifying physical health needs

SN2 and PHN2 as conditions for individual survival and individual health are determined biologically with differences according to age, sex, climatic conditions and physical and mental constitution.

SN2 at an abstract level of generality are the needs for air, (to live in a safe and unpolluted environment) the need for food, water, sleep, rest, reproduction and protection against the environment and climate (clothing and shelter) and against any physical harm which endangers obtaining these conditions. PHN2 include the above and in addition the needs for recreation and exercise and protection from any physical harm which endangers natural physiological functioning. We can postulate the existence of abstract general survival and health needs because we have the biological and physiological knowledge of what is necessary for survival and for the natural functioning of the human organism. And, it is precisely because we have knowledge of the human organism that we can deduce that all human beings have these needs, that they persist and prevail whether or not they are at any specific time manifest as felt wants, experienced as deficiencies, expressed as demands for goods and services or fulfilled in consumption.

However, the identification of SN2 and PHN2 at an abstract level of generality cannot provide sufficient information to identify actual needs. The specific content of SN2 and PHN2 and any choice of object to meet them (where 'objects' are people, social relations, states of affairs, physical objects, consumer goods and public services) is always determined socially. Therefore SN2 and PHN2 will include the social and material objects and conditions conducive to the successful attainment of survival and health. The identification of the content of needs and how they may be satisfied must be investigated in their social context.

SN2 and PHN2 at an abstract level of generality can be identified with reference to our biological constitutions. At a specific socio-historical level the manner in which they are experienced, whether they are experienced and satisfied can be identified with reference to social and economic determinants on their manifestations and fulfilment.

The social expression of the biological needs for survival and health is determined by the level and nature of material production and consumption, the organisation of distribution and the structure of social relations in the society in which they are experienced. Felt needs, demands and satisfactions or absence of these will reflect the individual's place in the social relations of production, consumption and distribution.

To illustrate this view of needs, their manifestations and possibilities of satisfactions, see Figure 6.1.

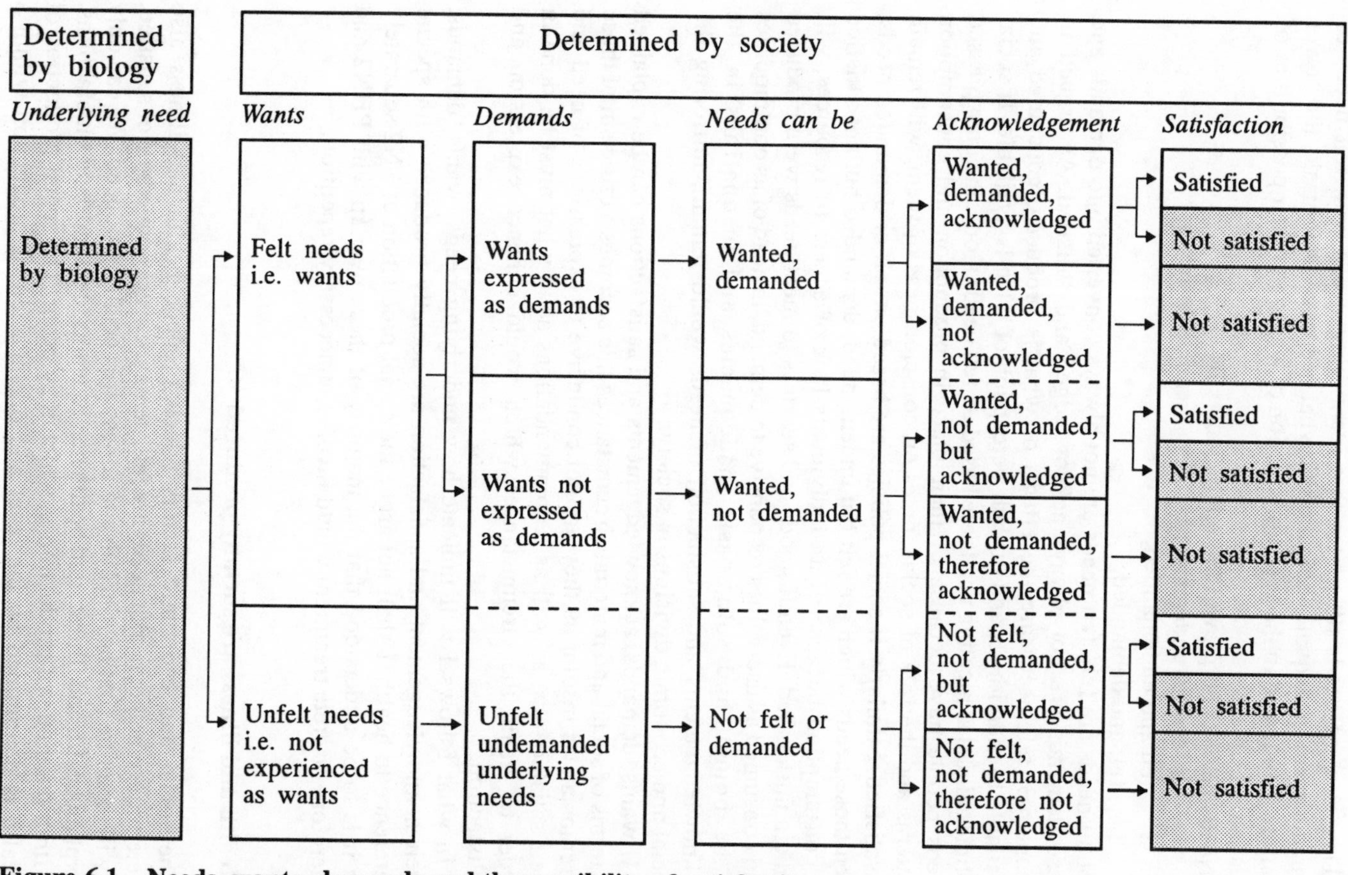

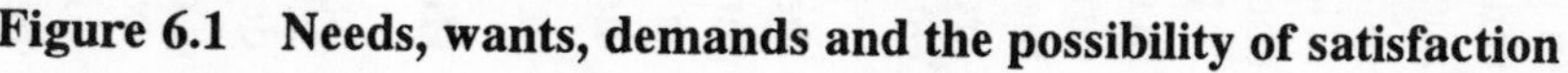
Figure 6.1 Needs, wants, demands and the possibility of satisfaction

This view of needs illustrates that identifying needs with felt needs or demands is an inadequate indication of what needs are as it masks the power relations implicated in the social production of wants and their possibilities of satisfaction.

Needs persist and prevail though they may be

1 unfelt and undemanded;
2 felt and undemanded;
3 felt and demanded.

Not all needs are felt, felt needs are not always converted into demands and these demands are not always acknowledged and satisfied. As argued in Chapter 3, felt needs are the effects of what is produced, consumed and available to individuals and of their perception of what is available. If social policies aimed at meeting needs are based on felt needs alone, the unexpressed needs people have because of their place in production and consumption patterns and the role of social forces on consciousness of them, will remain unsatisfied. Similarly if social policies are based on felt or demanded needs, then those needs which are felt but undemanded, demanded but not satisfied in consumption because of an individuals lack of access to resources, will remain unsatisfied. Even if goods and services to meet needs were produced and consumed as use-values responsive to demand, instead of as commodities to be bought and sold, basic inadequacies and inequalities in the acknowledgements and satisfaction of needs would remain, mirroring the social and economic divisions in society.

If wants, demands, acknowledgements and satisfactions can be explained in terms of social and material circumstances this becomes a criticism of those circumstances insofar as they are not conducive to expressions of need and their satisfactions, as well as recommendations as to what must be done in order to create the circumstances which would enhance expression and satisfaction.

In what follows I will indicate how underlying needs, wants, demands, their acknowledgement and satisfaction are socially produced with special reference to health. I shall not argue the social production of SN2 separately as it is to be understood that the majority of these overlap with PHN2 and therefore discrete treatment would involve unnecessary repetition.

Health and illness are socially produced

The social and economic factors which produce health and illness also determine whether health needs are felt, demanded, acknowledged or satisfied. I will examine first how health and illness are socially produced. We can only explain health and illness, and health needs, wants, demands and satisfactions, within the mode of production in which they occur. The social production of health is determined by the level and organisation of production within a society, what is produced, how it is produced, and what is available for consumption, as well as how goods and services are distributed and the individuals' access to them.

It is widely accepted that in underdeveloped, non-industrial countries the major causes of premature death and of disease involve the combination of biological causes with the material and social conditions which produce poverty. Diseases, some fatal, are contracted through the spread of human waste and airborne infections and exacerbated by malnutrition. Where such killer diseases as cholera, typhoid, TB and malaria have declined or disappeared, such success is largely attributable to improvements in working, living and eating conditions and the introduction of purified piped drinking water, sewers and the drainage of swamps. It is clear that in relation to these countries, death and disease are both caused and alleviated by social and economic factors and measures.

With reference to industrial societies, the major killers and disabling conditions are heart and cerebrovascular disease, cancer, bronchitis, emphysema, asthma, arthritis, diabetes and accidents. The causes of these are closely related to lifestyle and environmental factors which are not independent of socio-economic conditions, for example, industrial pollution, working conditions, diet, smoking, stress and lack of exercise. This would suggest that, as in underdeveloped countries, any substantial reduction of the instances of these diseases would come about through environmental, socio-economic and educational measures rather than medical intervention. There are, though, aspects of medicine which have been genuinely successful at preventing and curing disease and providing symptom relief, for example, antiseptics, vaccinations, anaesthetics and antibiotics. It is often claimed that the killer diseases and conditions in developed countries are diseases of affluence and so not as readily attributable to the socio-economic conditions of poverty as are diseases in the third world. However, though it might be said that such diseases accompany industrial development and improved material advantage, the actual pattern of illness, disease and health within industrial populations is not evenly distributed between social and occupational classes.

Townsend and Davidson (1982) showed that class differences in mortality rates (Standardised Mortality Ratios) are a constant feature throughout all age groups under 65. For a diagrammatic representation of this, see Figure 6.2.

The Standardised Mortality Ratio (SMR) is a measure designed to correct for differences in the age structure of the population, so that the actual number of deaths is expressed as a percentage of that number that would be expected if the age structure had remained unchanged from a base year.

At birth and during the first year of life social class gradients in SMR's are the most dramatic, but there remains significant differentials throughout childhood, adolescence and adulthood. Members of occupational class V have a two and a half times greater chance of dying before they reach retirement age than Class I.

The diseases which cause the most striking class differences in mortality are lung diseases, cancer, TB, bronchitis, pneumonia and deaths from accidents, poisoning and violence. The former are those which have been traditionally associated with poverty, the latter reflect occupational and environmental hazards more likely to be associated with the working and living conditions of the lower social classes. For diagrams representing mortality by social class and cause of death see Figure 6.3.

The same class differentials also apply in morbidity rates. Sickness absence data from the *General Household Survey* (1978, see Table 6.1) shows that semi-skilled and unskilled workers of all age groups report significantly higher rates of acute and chronic sickness than do members of the professional classes. Similarly a national survey conducted in 1979 showed pronounced inequalities in health between classes (see Table 6.2).

This data supports the general argument that social and economic factors influence health and the particular claim that the individual's position in the class structure is a significant determinant on that individual's health. The way in which class determines health however is complex and multi-causal.

Class influences on health

In order to explain class differences in health it is necessary to look at aspects of capitalist social and economic relations: the distribution of resources, patterns of work and the physical process of commodity production and consumption.

i) Access to resources

Class influences health because it determines other factors which exert a causal influence on health.

Townsend and Davidson (1982) attribute class differentials in mortality and morbidity in birth and infancy to differential access to material and non-material advantages between the classes. In the former, levels of income, maternal nutrition, type of housing (safe, unpolluted, uncrowded homes) warmth, hygiene, the possession of means of transport and communication (car and phone) are regarded as being among the factors which, when present, greatly improve the chances of early survival. Non-material advantage or deprivation also plays a role in increasing or decreasing mortality rates, for example, knowledge, skills and resources in verbal communication and parental motivation to provide adequate care for their children affect their survival chances.

In the age group 1–14, the majority of the differences in mortality ratios between class I and class V are due to accidents and respiratory diseases. In the case of accidents, the risk of being hit by a motor vehicle is five to seven times greater from Class I–IV. For deaths resulting from fire, falls or drowning the differences between the classes is even greater. Responsibility for such differences is attributed to material factors such as parental resources, environmental hazards and cultural factors such as levels of stress experienced. Differences in material resources constrain the level of care parents give their children, i.e. whether they supervise their play, and the kind and comparative safety of fixtures and fittings, appliances and heating that are in the home.

Respiratory disease, the other principal killer responsible for death differentials in the 1–14 group, is linked both to environmental factors prevailing in area of residence and parental history of occupation-related lung disease.

ii) Commodity production: patterns of work

The way commodity production is organised affects health. Townsend and Davidson (1982) show that differences in adult mortality between occupational classes is connected to the nature of work itself. Similarly the patterns of mortality by class in old age were associated with differential financial remuneration from previous work and the individual's place in the productive process during working life. Ill health, disability and death can be a direct consequence of being at work. Those people (generally the working classes) who are in dangerous occupations (mining, the construction industry, railway workers) face great life and health risks from industrial accident, injury and disease.

More generally, work and health are related in that the conditions under which some people have to work cause stress, which is increasingly recognised as a pre-disposing factor in psychosomatic problems and many physical illnesses (see Chapter 8). The demands of commodity production and the imperatives of capitalist accumulation which condition the nature of the labour process require many people to be engaged in monotonous, repetitive work with little job satisfaction, status or intrinsic interest. To meet production targets and to supplement low wages with bonus and overtime earnings, work often has to be performed at high speed and for long and unsocial hours.

Finally, lack of work also undermines health. Unemployment is a constant and endemic feature of capitalist society. For many people it is stressful and demoralising. It decreases their feelings of self-worth and social status and increases their material worries. Women, 'unemployed' in the home in non-wage labour, notoriously suffer from depressive and anxiety-related illnesses (see Chapter 8).

iii) Commodity production: effects beyond the workplace

The dangerous effects of highly industrialised commodity production extend beyond the workplace into the wider environment, causing pollution problems which are responsible both for impairing the quality of individuals' lives and for specific diseases. Workers transport toxic substances into their homes, factory wastes overspill into the immediate environment and industrial production generally produces pollution which affects the whole urban environment. Those who live in or near such areas are obviously more at risk than those who do not. These effects may appear to be the unintended but inevitable consequences of industrial production. They occur in so-called 'socialist' countries as well as capitalist countries. However, to the extent to which such techniques of production have been developed within a socio-economic system which is impelled to accumulate capital or which is primarily dedicated to the pursuit of private profit, the prospect of changing these techniques or counteracting their effects within the system is limited as long as capital accumulation and profit rather than public health remains the predominant driving force.

The risks and dangers which result from commodity production not only determine health but also determine class differences in health.

iv) Consumption patterns

Health hazards also result from the consumption of commodities whose nature is determined by their selling and profit potential. I will take two examples of commodities – tobacco and food to illustrate the point.

The consumption of tobacco is a major factor in the incidence of death and disability due to lung cancer, heart complaints, bronchitis and chronic chest ailments. The prevalence of cigarette smoking is largely confined to the working class, particularly women, and it is this class which suffer and die most from the associated diseases.

However, the phenomenon of cigarette smoking can only be understood within the context of a society which creates such dependency as a source of quick and easy relief from its various pressures, and within the context of a system which is constrained by certain economic interests from radically alleviating that pressure or from introducing measures to combat its consequences. The State makes limited attempts to curb tobacco consumption through educating the public to its dangers. While such moralising has some impact especially amongst the middle classes, educative measures alone will be insufficient to eradicate drug abuse. Many people will continue to smoke until some other readily available gratification is substituted or until the social causes of their habit are ameliorated. The Government is prohibited by financial constraints resulting from its policy on public spending from implementing measures which would satisfy either of these criteria. Furthermore lost revenue from tobacco taxes, the social security costs of paying pensions to those who would survive if they did not smoke, and of paying unemployment benefit to those who would lose their jobs in the tobacco and other industries dependent on cigarette advertising (newspapers) and sponsorships (sport), all militate against the probability that any significant action will be aimed at changing the pattern of tobacco consumption.

Food is indisputably a fundamental human need for both survival and health. Under capitalism, the mechanisation and concentration of food production and its consequences for diet and health are a result of the socio-economic development of capitalism and are determined by the need for capitalism to accumulate private profit.

Food in its final form is largely produced by giant multinational companies whose financial interests concur with less labour intensive farming (and therefore loss of jobs) and profits for themselves and the chemical industry through widespread use of agri-chemicals, fertilisers, insecticides, herbicides and fungicides. The result for the consumer is health damaging products. Industrial and technological development associated with capitalism also leads to new techniques of food processing, refinement and storage. Food products are artificially flavoured, coloured and preserved with additives often harmful to the health of the consumer. In general terms the result for health has been that the consumer eats an increasingly refined diet, high in sugar and fats, and low in vitamins, minerals and fibre, thus leading to associated cancers, heart disease, diabetes and tooth decay. The response of sections of the food industry has been to introduce expensive alternative health foods. The response of the Government has been to educate people into better eating habits rather than tackling the cause of poor diet and therefore poor health at source.

It is of course to be admitted that capitalism has led to improvements in the quality and quantity of food available to most people in industrial societies. However, given our knowledge of the benefits and dangers of certain types of food, it is still the case that consumption patterns express the same class inequalities as patterns of their related diseases (see Table 6.3). Patterns of health and illness, then, are socially and economically determined.

To be healthy we need access to certain standards of the following: income, diet, housing, heating, hygiene, transport, communication, rest, exercise and to the goods and services which promote those. We need safe work, living and environmental conditions and the education, information, skills, attitudes and beliefs conducive to maintaining or restoring health.

The quality and quantity of these, and therefore the quality and quantity of health, are dependent on social and economic arrangements whose principal interests conflict with the maintenance and provision of health and its objects.

Meeting health needs, then, depends on access to material and non-material resources, the nature of the production process and the pattern of consumption, not only on access to health care of a formal kind.

Felt needs, demands and satisfactions are socially produced

1 Unfelt, undemanded needs

It has been established that social and economic factors determine health and illness. These also determine whether health needs are felt, demanded, acknowledged or satisfied.

Needs may not be felt as a result of ignorance or lack of other material and non-material resources and concomitant attitudes and beliefs. If someone does not know the essential elements of a healthy diet or that exercise is essential to health or is sceptical about their merits, they are unlikely to experience the desire for them. If someone does not realise that certain symptoms require attention or is suffering from an asymptomatic disorder they will not feel the need to seek treatment. If someone does not know of the availability of certain services or believes that their condition does not merit help they will not feel the need for it or demand it.

As the people who are most likely to suffer from ignorance are the less educated it can be said that the social conditions which breed ignorance are responsible for this class of need being unmet. For example Townsend and Davidson (1982) illustrate how differences in attitudes between occupational classes leads to unfelt and unmet needs in relation to the percentage of old people who were receiving public or private domestic help, or who said help was needed (see Table 6.4). 90% of Class V neither receive domestic help nor feel the need for it. 50% of Class I and II had help and 50% of the others felt the need, but only one sixth of Class V who were severely incapacitated had help and only a third of the remainder felt the need for it.

2 Felt, undemanded needs

Not all the wants people feel are expressed as demands. Some wants we do nothing about. We may have the necessary information regarding diet and exercise and want the objects to satisfy them, but we may not have the money or time or energy to purchase or engage in them. There may not be facilities within reasonable distance. We may realise that the atmosphere is polluted or that the nature of our jobs exert a toll on our health, but we may think that these states of affairs are inevitable and make no demands for improvement. We may feel the need for health care but we may decide not to visit the doctor for a number of reasons. We may believe that nothing can be done about our condition, we may fear that our condition is serious and wish to remain in blissful ignorance, we may feel that our problem is too minor to bother the doctor with, we may not realise that certain check-up facilities apply to us. Furthermore visiting the doctor has costs which may be perceived to outweigh the expected benefit. Health care visits cost money. We may not have access to cheap transport or be able to afford the earnings lost whilst attending surgeries or clinics. We may not have the time and energy required to wait for appointments or sit in queues. These costs may be perceived to outweigh likely benefits given the quality of medical care itself. The beliefs and values of the medical profession reflect their own class position and consequently inform their attitudes and approaches, which are more likely to be appropriate to their middle class patients.

Townsend and Davidson (1982, p. 68–81) provide clear evidence that the working class place proportionally less demands on the health service than do their middle class counterparts with the same underlying needs. Although the working class make greater use of most GP, hospital and out-patient services than the middle class, this use is disproportionate to the excess mortality and morbidity suffered by that class. For example, Forster (1976 p. 29) shows that in proportion to reported sickness and sickness absence from work semi-skilled and unskilled workers make less use of GP services. Their level of consultation does not match their underlying need.

In the use of preventative and promotional health services it is well documented that manual classes make less use of radiography, cervical cytology, conservative dentistry, ante, postnatal and family planning clinics, as well as immunisation programmes, though it cannot be assumed that they have a lesser underlying need for such services (Cartwright 1970, Bone 1973, Douglas and Rowntree 1949, Gordon 1951, Gray et al, 1970, Bulman et al, 1968).

3 Felt, demanded needs

People may want and demand goods and services to meet their needs without these being acknowledged as need or subsequently satisfied. In the case of medical care this can be because there is no underlying need but can be due to the fact that medical acknowledgement of needs is based on the availability of the supply to meet them. In the US twice as many people per capita are deemed to be in need of surgery than in Great Britain (Cooper 1974). This variation in referrals illustrates how doctors react to supply by realigning their conception of need. The availability of supply is a result both of socio-economic conditions as it is constrained by the State's willingness to pay for services, and of the level of medical progress itself, which is also to some extent dependent on socio-economic conditions.

Acknowledgement of need can be a function of provision, but it may also be a function of the vociferousness of the demand itself. The more stridently the demand is made the more likely it is to be acknowledged. The most articulate can command a better quality of care. Cartwright and O'Brien (1976) show that the middle class have longer consultations, discuss more problems, receive more information and ask more questions than do their working class patients, while doctors know more about their domestic and personal circumstances, thus reinforcing the point made above about the quality of provision available to different classes.

Where the underlying need for medical care is not acknowledged it cannot be satisfied. However, acknowledgement itself does not automatically result in satisfaction. Felt demanded, felt undemanded and unfelt undemanded needs, even if acknowledged, may not be satisfied.

The possibility of satisfaction, like the possibility of acknowledgement of need, relates to the provision of services and access to that provision. Under capitalism the provision of health care must be seen in the context of the limitations on public spending given capitalism's need to reproduce itself and its profit priorities. The particular provision of medical care and resource allocation to various aspects of that care is itself determined by and reflects the socio-economic structure and its concomitant class divisions.

Although the NHS provides a service to all regardless of class distinctions, the private market in medical care reinforces social differences by allowing those with more resources to obtain better and quicker access to services, and results in less satisfaction of need for those without access and who must depend on the NHS.

Private commercial interests operating in the building trade, pharmaceutical industry and medical equipment manufacturing affect both the quality and quantity of provision. Satisfaction is diminished quantitatively, for building programmes, drugs and medical equipment cost the NHS more than they need to. The State is reluctant to intervene and control these industries as its role in supporting them is determined by the objective necessity of facilitating capital accumulation.

Satisfaction is affected qualitatively by the emphasis on curative medical intervention, drug therapy and surgery which continued support of these industries entails, since their products are more conducive to the technological and chemical treatment of the consequences of illness. Thus alternative treatments are limited and prevention of illness and the tackling of causes of ill health are given secondary importance.

The possibility of satisfaction of health needs by medical care also reflects and is diminished by socio-economic arrangements in that distribution of financial resources differs from hospital to hospital and between different geographic areas. Teaching hospitals and acute intervention services benefit from a greater allocation of resources, (Doyall and Pennell 1979 p. 195–6) whereas mental hospitals suffer from under-resourcing, resulting in low standards and demoralisation of staff, reflecting the lack of economic power and productive potential of their patients (Morris 1969). Furthermore there is a marked difference in financial allocation to medical services in the North and South with the poorer regions being uniformly deprived. This increases the negative correlation between the needs of those poorer areas and their satisfaction (Rickard 1976, Coates and Rawstron 1971).

The differential use of those services by different classes exacerbates the inequality of satisfaction.

Summary to Section A

This discussion has shown how the patterns of health, illness and health care itself are determined by the mode of social and economic organisation. The socio-economic causes of ill health are also determinants of whether health needs are felt, demanded, acknowledged or satisfied. Any attempt to undermine the causes of ill health or any intervention to ensure that health needs are experienced, demanded or satisfied would require a radical reorganisation of the process of capital accumulation, the nature of material production, the resulting social relations and the distribution and consumption of goods and services. Present healthcare provision, medical practice and government policy is principally aimed at providing formal equal access to health and social services in order to meet health needs. These alone cannot meet health needs, since many needs are unexpressed, and many demands are unsatisfied due to social, economic, material and non-material disadvantages and inequalities in the availability and use of goods and services. The health service deals with and treats the unhealthy consequences of social and economic conditions and relations. Because of the emphasis on health as an individual condition and the provision only of formal access to health care to meet needs, recognition of the socio-economic dimensions of the real causes of ill health, and the lack of felt need, demand and satisfaction of need is suppressed. The equalisation of the provision of health and social services is not separable from the equalisation of social and economic advantage.

B) Alternative indicators of need

Felt needs and demands are inadequate indicators of need because needs can exist independent of experience and as a result can be unrecognised or unfulfilled. Alternative indicators of need must be developed to provide information for organisation, planning and action if that need is to be met.

If, as I have argued, health itself, health needs, their manifestations and satisfactions are determined by socio-economic conditions which affect the individual's lifestyle, working and living environment and access to goods and services, then indicators of unfelt, undemanded or unsatisfied need will refer to these determining causal conditions.

Indicators of health, ill health and felt need within a population traditionally have been measured without reference to these factors. They have relied on the presence or absence of mortality or morbidity indices. That is they measure the harm done to and felt by the individual only as manifest by discernible symptoms and negative consequences such as impairments, disabilities, handicaps and death (for example, see Table 6.5).

Similarly, negative measures of felt need as manifest in some physical incapacity have been developed in relation to specific disabilities. Guttman

(1944) developed a disability scale where he ranked degrees of patient dependence in respect to activities such as feeding, continence, ambulation, dressing and bathing. Kurtzke (1981) developed a disability scale for people suffering from multiple sclerosis. It lists 12 activities, giving a 0–4 ranking for the patients ability to perform each activity. The patient's overall rating on the scale gives a measure of the extent of their incapacity as a result of the disease.

Traditionally then, health and health needs have been measured negatively, either when those needs are felt or when the harm is observable. Although these measures are useful in that they can indicate the need for treatment or services, they can only do so after the event, when the harm is done, when people actually experience ill health. They do not reflect the multiplicity of socio-economic and environmental factors which influence health or which may ultimately cause ill health. As a result they suggest that the 'cure' for ill health is to be found in medical intervention and treatment, rather than emphasising measures which lead to the prevention of ill health, some of which extend beyond the domain of medical practice into social and economic measures.

There have been a number of papers in medical and social science literature which have tried to develop a set of health status indicators which reflect the many lifestyle, socio-economic and environmental factors influencing health (WHO 1979, Ware et al, 1981, Miller 1973, Levy 1977, Catford 1983).

These indicators show that health could be improved by intervention at these levels, rather than by more provision of treatment services alone.

John Catford (1983) made proposals for measurements of health suitable for field work testing which include measurement of individual factors which increase or decrease the risk of mortality and morbidity. These included information on nutrition, physical activity, drugs, transport, dental health, reproduction, infectious diseases, screening, the activities of health and education authorities and health knowledge and beliefs (see Table 6.6). The data collected would be classified according to age, sex, marital status, ethnic origin, residence, education and income level so taking into account other variables which affect health.

This data would provide direct knowledge of an individual's health to give information for both health service planning and intervention at the level of the individual. It would suggest also that health differences which result from other variables such as age, sex etc. could be subject to social and economic intervention where appropriate.

However assessment of individual health by the measures listed above omits the role of the wider environmental and economic factors which influence health. Therefore Catford suggests examples of positive health measures which relate to these. Health measures which increase or decrease risk to health from the physical environment include data on air, water, noise, sewage, food, workplace, housing, transport and recreation (see Table 6.7).

Catford argues that many of these measures have already been developed and are available at district and national level as well as from Local Authorities through environmental health and transport departments.

Suggested examples of health indicators concerning socio-economic decisions which affect risk reduction and avoidance, include government health, nutrition, transport, recreation and environmental health policies, data on government spending, incentives, subsidies, regulations, legislation and taxation and information on employment, income distribution and education (see Table 6.8).

Data could be collected according to geographical location to accommodate differences in unemployment, income distribution and educational attainment. This information could be obtained from *Social Trends* published by the Central Statistical Office, and from the health policies of ministerial departments.

Catford proposes that the Health Service should be primarily responsible for developing measurements of health along the lines he has suggested and that District Health Authorities could collect information from relevant sources on the physical environment. Regional Health Authorities could provide technical assistance and collate information to provide a regional summary. At Central Government level the Department of Health could ensure the publication of socio-economic indicators and their geographic variations.

Catford also argues that if this information was available and these indicators developed, since they are important determinants on health, collectively they could provide baseline measures for deciding health promotion priorities as well as providing the means for evaluating progress in improving the health of a population. In addition the findings would suggest target areas for social and political action aimed at improving health standards.

Other studies have also attempted to develop health status indicators which reflect the multiple factors influencing health and its expression as felt need, demands and eventual satisfaction. I will discuss some marketing research carried out by the Health Education Council (Farrell 1986) as an example which focuses on resident's own perceptions of the wide ranging influences on health, health needs and satisfactions.

Market research was carried out in a survey of Bath Health District residents. It investigated their definition of 'being healthy', where they considered they stood in relation to that state at present and what change they would like to see in order to improve that state. ACORN (A Classification of Residential Neighbourhoods) was used in addition to socio-economic and demographic classification. This classification was linked to specific residential area. Furthermore ACORN was linked to postal geography – postcodes were ACORN typed to allow for precise targeting. Summary data was presented as an overall distribution of response to each of the 41 health related issues. In addition response data was tabulated by ACORN group, age, sex and social class. It was found that half the differences in response by the ACORN group were attributable to these variables.

For an example of the findings and more importantly for our purposes, the health issues identified, see Table 6.9. It was found that the consumers' perception of 'being healthy' included more than being free from symptoms of illness and disease but also included access to material and non-material resources which influence health: income, hygiene, food, warmth, housing, transport, leisure, living, working and environmental conditions, information.

It was the contention of those who conducted the survey that the results could be used in conjunction with mortality and morbidity data, information on screening and immunisation levels, and information from the General Household Survey to form a picture of the services necessary to improve health or to prevent ill health in that particular area.

From the results obtained a number of specific recommendations were made, for example, the needs for a positive mental health programme and heart disease programme, the need for the provision of information on health services available, and the importance of information on how to keep healthy (diet, exercise etc.), and the need for planning in relation to health services which takes into account their availability, accessibility etc.

The purpose of this report was to provide information which would be fed into the planning and development of health services in the Bath area and the suggestions above are a result of this. However, from the response to the survey it is clear that many of the factors which influence health are outside the domain of the health service and require action targeted at other agencies for the improvement of health.

C) Intervention

I have drawn attention to the above studies in order to show that empirical indicators of determinants on health and therefore measurement of health have been developed and that specific practical recommendations can result from this information. From this I would suggest that it is possible (although beyond my brief in this book) to refine and develop empirical indicators of health and health needs (some of which are independent of experience). These would reveal that, in order for health needs to be satisfied, both the provision of goods and services (including health services) and wider socio-economic measures must be taken. Such indicators would have to take into account the factors in the list below. These have been compiled from other studies discussed. Such a list is not exhaustive, but comprises the major determinants on health, its expression and satisfaction.

N.B. Though these factors influence mental health and specific determinants on mental health affect physical health, I will discuss mental health separately.

Determinants of health and measures of physical health

Lifestyle	1.	Income
	2.	Diet
	3.	Drugs – tobacco, alcohol, other
	4.	Exercise
	5.	Health knowledge
	6.	Education level – communication skills etc.
	7.	Health attitudes and beliefs
	8.	Motivation
	9.	Immunisation
	10.	Screening
	11.	Access to goods, services and facilities
Home environment	12.	Type of house (size)
	13.	Number of people in house
	14.	Area house in
	15.	Heating
	16.	Domestic appliances (safety of)
	17.	Hygiene in the home (shared bathroom, outside WC, fridges)
	18.	Access to communication (phone, car)
	19.	Garden and access to play facilities
	20.	Proximity to shops, facilities, services
Work environment	21.	Lack of work – unemployment, non-wage labour in the home
	22.	Conditions at work – hours, breaks, holidays, overtime, shift work, piece work
	23.	Pay – basic rate, bonus and O.T. rate, sick pay, maternity & paternity pay, pension, allowances and perks
	24.	Amenities at work – canteens, washing and cleaning, safety equipment
	25.	Dangers and risks
	26.	Job satisfaction
	27.	Physical and mental strain
	28.	Stability and security
Wider environment	29.	Pollution – air, water, sewage, nuclear
	30.	Transport – safety of
	31.	Noise levels
	32.	Recreation facilities

These indices can measure individual health and point to unfelt and unmet needs as well as felt needs. The use of such indicators can suggest where intervention is necessary to remedy the situation and can point to practical recommendations as to what is necessary to satisfy needs. The success or failure of intervention policies can be assessed by repeated use of indicators.

The practicalities of intervention have to be assessed. The actual studies mentioned previously have shown how specific health service policies which are feasible now could improve need satisfaction in these areas. They show that information is necessary for people to become aware of their underlying needs and that certain facilities and access to them are necessary for people to convert their felt needs into demands. They also show the importance of extended provision in responding to this demand. To take some examples from the list of determinants on and indicators of physical health:

2 **Diet:** It has been suggested that the Health Education Council (H.E.C.) should provide information on healthy diets. Nutritionists could draw up lists of food low in additives etc. Healthy eating habits could be encouraged in schools and hospitals, for example.

3 **Drugs:** Alcohol and tobacco – Health promotion officers can coordinate action aimed at the dissemination of information and provide counselling, advice and back up services for those at risk from health impairment.

5 **Health knowledge and (7) health attitudes and beliefs:** The provision of general health education, safety education and physical education. Information on what makes you unhealthy, on the side effects of certain drugs, on alternative treatments, first aid, life saving, road safety, accident prevention could be provided by Health Promotion Agencies and the H.E.C. via the media, and through newsletters from GPs.

6 **Communication skills:** The incorporation into doctors' training of sensitivity to the less articulate.

9 **Immunisation and (10) screening plus (1) access to services:** Clearly targeted information could be provided on the services available and their importance. Reappraisal of the accessibility of services. Workplace screening, weekend surgeries, mobile screening units, well-women clinics, child development screening at school, health visitors for all ages, back up nursing services in the home.

But the health service as such is unable to do anything about determinants on health such as income, living, work and environmental issues since improvement in these areas lie outside its realm. Thus various studies make recommendations to government agencies which have the power to provide the resources necessary to improve these. For example in relation to diet, (2) the Government could encourage cereal growing, fishing, wholemeal bread production. In relation to drugs (3) the Government could increase taxation and introduce stricter legislation on advertising and marketing of tobacco products. It could authorise more stringent health warnings and resource counselling services for drug users.

In relation to the home environment the government could provide resources for better public housing, more spacious and built away from polluted areas in pleasant environments with access to gardens, play areas, near to facilities and amenities. It could subsidise heating costs for those most at risk (old and very young).

In relation to the work environment the government could introduce policies which reduce unemployment, job insecurity and provide resources to combat isolation in the home, day centres and nursery facilities. They could employ more safety officers at work and mechanise boring, repetitive work.

In relation to the broader environment the government could employ environmental safety officers, ban the use of leaded petrol and take steps towards a non-nuclear policy. With reference to transport there could be stricter road and traffic legislation, more road safety officers, anti drink and drive campaigns, police spot checks, pelican crossings and cycle lanes.

These policies which the government could implement now, though with difficulty given private interests, are fairly modest. They could improve the prospects for the health of the population to some considerable degree, but, given the material and intellectual resources which are available they only represent the tip of the iceberg of what could be done.

The determinants and indicators of health are all those things which also affect health and whether health needs are felt, demanded or satisfied. Once we can identify them we can see the social, political and economic measures that must be taken if need is to be satisfied. We assess whether it is possible not within the limits of the necessity of perpetuating a particular socio-economic system, but within the limits that are possible given the material and intellectual resources which are available.

Within capitalism, the increase in resources for the health service and the social and economic measures which would be necessary to combat ill health are just not possible. Even the modest improvements relating to food, alcohol and tobacco, and the various health and safety measures relating to work and the environment would be difficult to implement given the private profit interests operating in these respective industries. Additional resources to specific health service programmes such as education and screening would be assessed unfavourably in the light of other economic priorities.

Substantial social, political and economic transformations are required in order to ensure an adequate income for all to enable equal access to certain goods. To ensure the implementation of a public housing programme, the elimination of unemployment, long hours, poor conditions, boring, dangerous and unsatisfying work plus an environment safe from pollution would require such a massive social change that while improving health, would vastly undermine the whole disease ridden edifice of capitalism itself.

Stillbirths

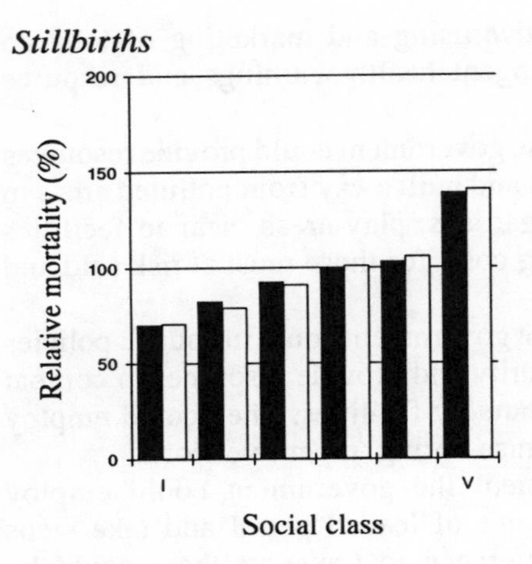

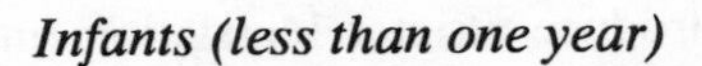

Infants (less than one year)

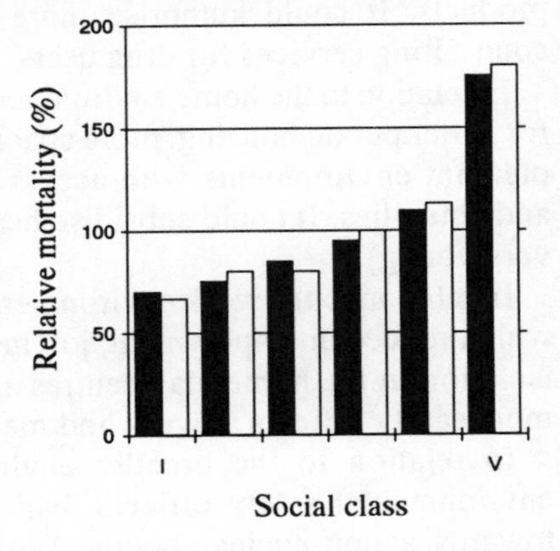

Children (1–4 years)

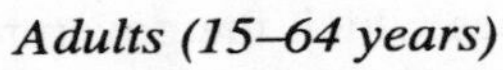

Adults (15–64 years)

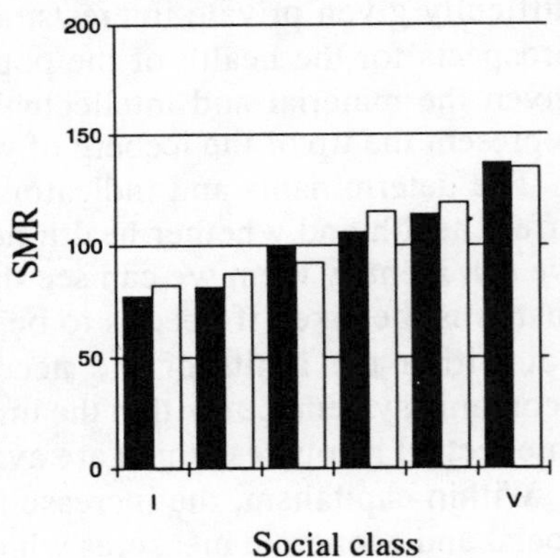

Males

Females

Figure 6.2 Mortality by social class and age

Source: *Occupational Mortality 1970–72,* London, HMSO

Diseases of the respiratory system

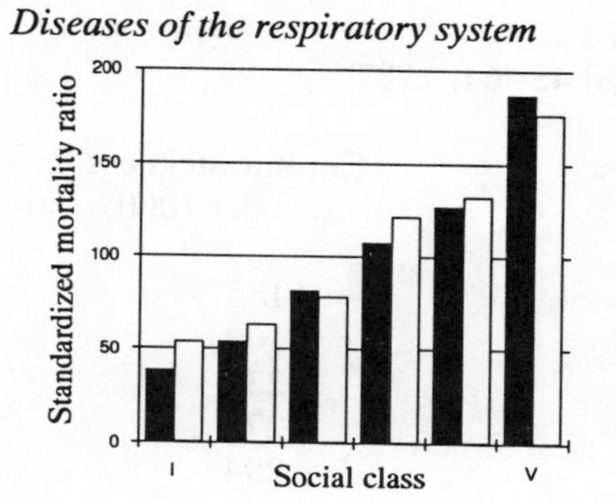

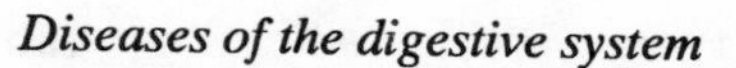

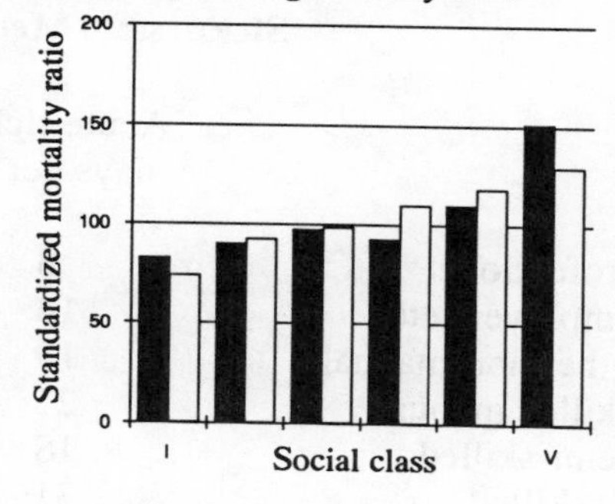

Infective and parasitic diseases

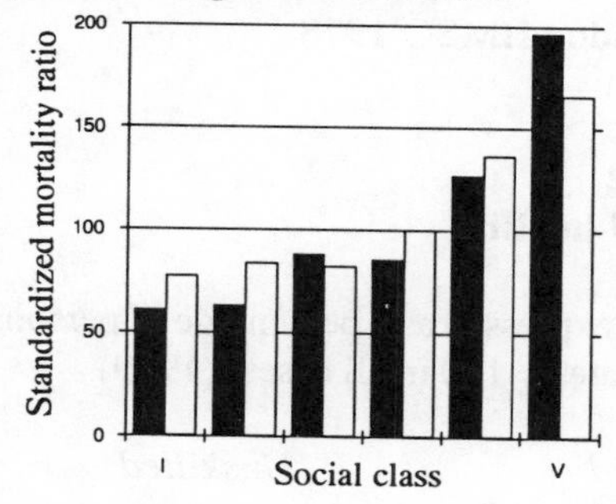

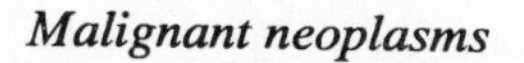

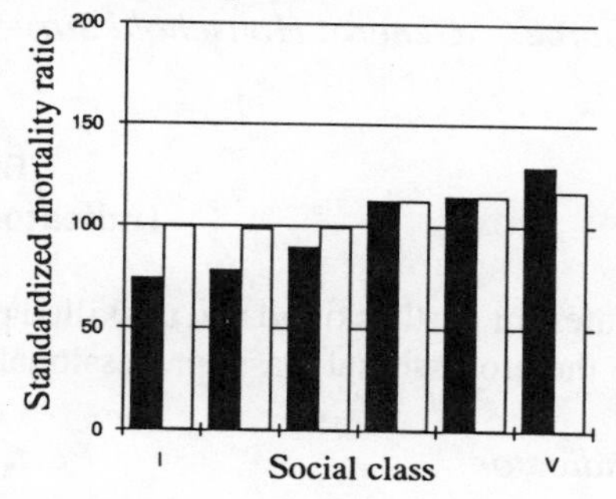

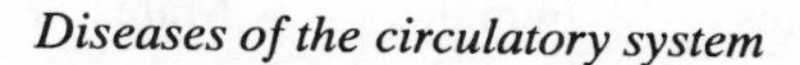

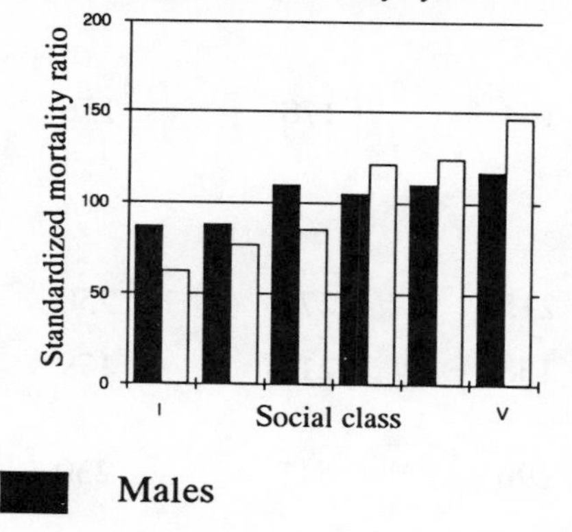

Accidents, poisonings and violence

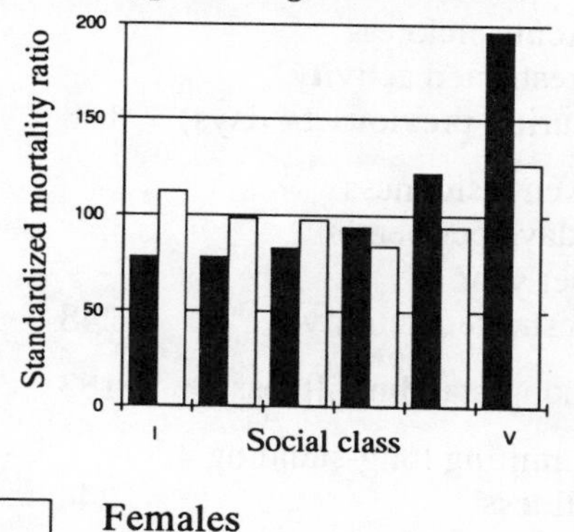

Males Females

Figure 6.3 Mortality by social class and cause of death: Standardised mortality rates for men and married women (by husband's occupation) aged 15–64

Source: *Occupational Mortality 1970–72*, London, HMSO

Table 6.1
Sickness: Men aged 45–64, 1987

	Acute sickness days per year	Chronic sickness rate per 1000
Professional	8	185
Employers etc.	14	160
Other non-manual	19	236
Skilled manual	21	270
Semi-skilled	18	294
Unskilled	31	369

Source: *General Household Survey,* London HMSO 1978

Table 6.2
Indicators of ill health

Rates for partly skilled and unskilled persons expressed as a percentage of persons in the professional class (professional class rates = 100 in all cases) (1979)

Indicator	*Partly Skilled*		*Unskilled*	
	Females	Males	Females	Males
Acute sickness (restricted activity during previous 14 days)	178	144	178	156
Acute sickness (days per person per year of restricted activity)	248	215	273	250
Long-standing illness	183	158	217	179
Limiting long-standing illness	244	190	311	230
GP consultations: persons consulting	167	120	167	130
Number of consultations	167	130	160	120

Source: OPCS, *General Household Survey,* 1979, HMSO, 1981, pp 117–23

Table 6.3
Food consumption by income group in 1977

Ounces per person per week

	Income Group			
	A	B	C	D
White bread	18.0	25.0	28.0	31.0
Brown bread (incl. wholemeal)	4.9	3.4	2.8	3.3
Sugar	9.3	11.0	13.0	15.0
Potatoes	29.0	39.0	49.0	52.0
Fruit	33.0	24.0	20.0	17.0

Source: *Household Food Consumption and Expenditure,* London, HMSO 1978

Table 6.4
Percentage of old persons of different occupational class who were receiving public or private domestic help, or who said help was needed (Great Britain, 1962)

Source of Domestic Help	Occupational Class					
	I	II	IIIN	IIIM	IV	V
	%	%	%	%	%	%
Local Authority	1	2	4	6	4	4
Privately paid	42	27	12	5	3	2
Other (e.g. family) or none, but need felt	10	7	6	6	6	4
Other (e.g. family) or none, no need felt	47	64	78	83	87	90
Total	100	100	100	100	100	100
Number	81	555	396	1,188	1,033	447

Source: Townsend and Wedderburn, 1965

Table 6.5
Negative health measures

	Example
Life expectancy	at birth, age 50
Premature mortality rates*	age 45 – 64
Age, sex, specific mortality rates* by cause	accidents, lung cancer
Age, sex, specific morbidity rates* by cause	arthritis, stroke
Age, sex specific morbidity rates* by degree of handicap	immobility, incontinence
Sickness absence	certification rates
Use of treatment services	consultation rates, hospital admission rates
Self assessment	proportion of public unsatisfied with their own health

* These may also be expressed using the life-table approach, e.g. years of life lost.

Source: Catford (1983) p.127

Table 6.6
Examples of positive health measures concerning the individual

1 Nutrition:	% obese, malnourished % daily intake of fat, fibre, vitamins, salt, sugar % blood total cholesterol <200 mg/dl.
2 Physical activity:	% undergoing vigorous exercise three times per week % who can swim 100 metres, run 400 metres in three minutes
3 Drugs:	% smokers, non-smokers, ex-smokers % consume more than 5 alcoholic drinks per day % abuse medicines, glue sniffing
4 Transport:	% motorcycle users % crash helmet and seat-belt use % drink and drive, exceed speed limits
5 Dental health:	% visiting dentist once a year % own toothbrush, clean teeth daily
6 Reproduction:	% breast feeding at one month % birth weight >2500g % receiving antenatal care by 16 weeks % contraceptive use of sexually active wishing to avoid pregnancy % teenagers pregnant % pregnancies screened for neural tube defects, Down's Syndrome % neonates screened for phenylketonuria, congenital hypothyroidisms, physical abnormalities % births to single parent families
7 Infectious disease:	% immunization uptake % sexually transmitted disease and tuberculosis cases with contact tracing
8 Screening:	% aged over 35 screened for hypertension in last five years % blood pressure >95 mm Hg diastolic % women aged 35–60 with cervical smear in last five years

	% women practising regular breast self examination % aged over 75 who have had 'health visit' in the last year % five year olds screened for sensory, development defects
9 Activities of Health and Education Authorities:	% population at risk offered family planning, cervical smears, antenatal care, childhood screening, blood pressure measurement, general health education, safety education, physical education Preventive services to population ratios: e.g. health visiting, general practitioners, factory inspectors, environmental health officers, road safety officers, health education officers.
10 Health knowledge/beliefs:	% consider health as a valuable asset % understand basic health issues (smoking, diet, exercise, etc) % know basic first aid, life-saving, road safety, accident prevention % consider themselves to be in good health, fit, sleeping well % seeking to change their life-style (smoking, diet, exercise, etc) % satisfied with health promotion, services

Source: Catford (1983) p.129

Table 6.7
Examples of positive health measures concerning the physical environment

Air	-	carbon monoxide, lead, smoking in public places
Water	-	fluoride, nitrates, bacteria
Noise	-	transport flows, tolerable limits
Sewage	-	availability of safe schemes
Food	-	refrigerators, hygiene inspections
Workplace	-	asbestos, mining, North Sea diving
Housing	-	overcrowding, outside W.Cs, no baths
Transport	-	dual carriageways, cycle lanes, roundabouts
Recreation	-	play areas, parking restriction in 'play' streets, sports centres

Source: Catford (1983) p.130

Table 6.8
Examples of positive health measures concerning socio-economic conditions

The presence of a government health policy committee at Cabinet level.

The presence of an explicit National Nutrition, Transport, Recreation, Environmental Health Policy.

Gross National Product per head.

% Gross National Product spent on primary care, health promotion, education, social security.

% involuntary unemployment, income distribution.

Educational attainment, literacy rates.

Disincentive taxes on cigarettes, tobacco, motorcycles.

Absence of incentives for dairy production, tobacco growing, alcohol production, confectionery manufacture.

Licensing laws, advertising restrictions for sales of tobacco, alcohol.

Incentives for cereal growing, fishing, wholemeal bread production.

Subsidies for public transport, speed limit enforcement.

Motor vehicles and driver licensing and regulations.

Drinking and driving legislation including random checks.

Firearm restrictions.

Source: Catford (1983) p.131

Table 6.9
Health issues ranked according to percentage and number of respondents selecting

Being healthy means	% of n*	Number of respondents
Being able to keep clean	91	1455
Having energy	90	1442
Being able to sleep well	89	1423
Not being ill	89	1418
Eating healthy food	88	1409
Being able to relax	88	1410
Being able to keep warm in winter	86	1383
Enjoying my leisure time	84	1339
Not being in pain	83	1327
Having good local health services	83	1321
Being physically independent	82	1312
Having suitable housing	82	1312
Having a good family life	82	1309
Not having too much stress	81	1301
Not using illegal drugs	81	1297
Having an environment free from pollution	80	1288
Taking exercise	80	1281
Feeling good about myself	80	1276
Not drinking too much alcohol	76	1219
Having time to look after myself	75	1197
Being able to do without pills and medicine	74	1191
Not smoking	74	1180
Having friendship	73	1170
Being safe from accidents	71	1132
Having medical check-ups	64	1018
Having enough money to live comfortably on	67	1079
Not being bored	66	1063
Being well informed	66	1059
Enjoying my work	66	1058
Being free from the threat of violence	65	1048
Not being lonely	62	997
Being able to have privacy	61	982
Enjoying becoming a parent	57	918
Having a good sex life	56	899
Having a holiday	55	881
Having a good social life	55	879
Not having too much noise around me	55	875

Having a secure job	50	798
Being free from the threat of nuclear war	46	736
Having good access to transport	45	713
Living in a close community	33	528

*n = 1601

Source: Farrell (1986) Appendix 6

7 Instrumental health: Mental health needs 1

In Chapter 5 it was argued that mental health is analogous to physical health in the sense that it is natural mental functioning. Physical and mental health are objective and essential needs (PHN1, MHN1) as means to achieving other goals. It follows from this that the means to physical and mental health are needs (PHN2, MHN2) any human being has good reason to pursue, desire or value.

Chapter 6 established the empirical content of PHN2, and proposed empirical indicators to identify them and the social means necessary to satisfy them. Chapters 7 and 8 will outline how the same may be established for MHN2.

Chapter 7 will establish what abstract, general psychological needs are. A lengthy argument to establish abstract, general physical needs was unnecessary since we have uncontroversial biological and physiological knowledge for what is necessary for the natural physical functioning of the human organism. But whereas we have sufficiently reliable knowledge of the human body to establish incontestable fundamental physical needs we have far less secure knowledge of the human mind from which to deduce fundamental psychological needs. There are no genetic or neurological techniques to identify the organic basis of psychological need. We do not fully understand the nature of our psychological constitutions and have insufficient scientific knowledge to confirm a theory of natural functioning behaviour. Natural psychological functions are also less specific than physiological functions.

However, in Chapter 5 it was argued that from elementary functional assumptions it is possible to suggest that some conditions currently classed as psychopathologies are unhealthy (schizophrenia, psychosis, neuroses). Furthermore, even without making these assumptions it is possible sometimes to infer internal dysfunction from certain conditions, states or symptoms which interfere with a person's ability to do various things and with their general capacity for action to achieve any other end or aim. These can be thought of as interferences with natural functioning.

These mental conditions, states and symptoms indicate both disturbances in natural mental functioning and the inadequate satisfaction of mental health needs. Instrumental health or MHN2 are whatever is necessary to achieve, maintain or restore natural mental functioning.

The mere presence of these conditions, states or symptoms does not necessarily prove mental dysfunction, nor are all forms of mental dysfunction accounted for by the failure to satisfy needs. But neither of these strong theses is required to sustain the point being made here: that in certain circumstances such symptoms are and can be generally regarded as indicators of disturbances in natural functioning which can be shown to be caused by inadequate satisfaction of need.

Whereas there is an obvious correlation between physical health and need satisfaction it cannot be established with the same degree of precision that all forms of mental dysfunction can be accounted for by failure to satisfy need. The causes of many mental abnormalities are not fully understood or confirmed. Candidates for causal status are physical, biochemical and genetic, cognitive (cultural and behavioural), and emotional (social or individual). It is known that some rare organic psychoses are caused by brain tumour or vitamin deficiency and it is argued by some that there is a potentially bio-chemical basis to mental disorder to all kinds. It is thought that there may be genetic predispositions to certain functional psychoses such as schizophrenia and manic depression and it has been suggested that there is a genetic contribution to alcoholism, anxiety reaction, obsessionality and paranoid reaction (Slater and Roth 1969; Martin 1977). But the extent to which the genetic basis of these disorders is a necessary or sufficient condition for their development is unclear. In cultural behavioural explanations a causal role is given to the characteristics of the individual, their intelligence, skill and dispositions, the way they live their lives, their ideas and behaviour at the onset of illness, even though an individual's characteristics cannot be separated from their social context. Therefore, at the present stage of knowledge it cannot be established that all and every mental pathology or symptom is caused by the social failure to meet need. Nor can it be demonstrated that inadequate satisfaction necessarily leads to pathology, that all particular frustrations have similar effects or that certain effects are caused by particular need frustrations. However, despite the absence of concrete knowledge of the causes of mental illness, it is nevertheless possible to direct attention to the conditions which we have good reason to believe are associated with the presence or absence of illness in various sections of the population and concentrate on those factors which are related to high prevalence rather than idiosyncratic factors which determine individual differences in health. In practice there is sufficiently precise information linking the failure to meet certain needs with the risk of mental breakdown, and showing the necessity to anticipate needs before the effects of their frustration and deprivation are experienced as interferences with natural functioning.

I will argue that in order to achieve, restore or maintain natural functioning (MHN1) human beings must satisfy the abstract psychological emotional needs for security, love and relatedness, esteem and identify and self-realisation. Since the expression and concretisation of these abstract needs and their objects of satisfaction are determined socially, MHN2 also will include the social, material, economic, environmental and cultural factors and conditions known to exert a causal influence on health and the experience and satisfaction of health needs.

It is to the evidence for the first set of these needs, the abstract general psychological ones, that I now turn.

Evidence

The existence of needs for security, love and relatedness, esteem and identify and self-realisation cannot be proved in the same way as that of the physical needs. In the case of psychological needs we have no developed genetic or neurological techniques which enable us to identify or disconfirm the corresponding physiological foundations for these needs, if indeed there are any; for it may be the case that, as Fromm (1956) has argued, the foundation for these needs resides in the total human personality in interaction with the world, so that what I have called 'psychological' needs are 'existential' needs, needs to find answers to the problems of human existence. I shall not debate Fromm's position here or provide an answer to the origin of these needs, but will give what I believe is plausible evidence for their existence and persistence. I shall discuss

1 evidence of common agreement as to what psychological needs are;
2 causal evidence from the effects on natural functioning of need satisfaction and frustration;
3 behavioural evidence of human beings' pursuit of these needs.

1 Common agreements

When we examine any theorist's attempt to specify a list of fundamental human needs, again and again the same needs recur. Strictly speaking, this in itself is not conclusive evidence for the existence of such common needs, but it does give support to the view that there can be common agreement upon what requirements must be included in any conception of the fundamental needs of human beings.

In what follows I shall refer to 10 versions of human needs offered by different theorists (Appendix 1 Lists A–J).

Brentano (1908) suggested a hierarchy of needs, the satisfaction of one need leading to the development of another. Maslow (1943, p. 394) lists five categories of needs in order of their priority. He regards these needs as both instinctive and universal. Fromm (1956, pp. 27–63) discusses 'man's' needs as they stem from 'his' conditions of existence. Nielsen (1977, p. 147) presents a list about which he argues:

> I am not trying to catch all the needs that there would be widespread agreement about, but I think I have caught at least some of the central elements that would be on my thoughtful list of human needs.

Robert Lane (1969, pp. 31–47) suggests ten needs that are important for understanding human motivation in political life. J.C. Davies' (1977, p. 76), view of human needs stems directly from Maslow's with some modifications. Other contemporary need theorists, such as Knutson (1973), Renshon (1974) and Bay (1968) make use of Maslow's hierarchy of needs in relation to politics. Their lists have not been included to avoid repetition. Vance Packard (1960), discussed the eight hidden needs towards which marketing theory is orientated. Galtung (1980, p. 60) argues that when applied to needs:

> the term 'basic', which serves to further qualify the notion of a need as a necessary condition, as something that has to be satisfied in order for the need subject to function as a human being ... when a basic need is not satisfied, some kind of fundamental disintegration will take place.

Of his list of basic human needs as a working hypothesis, Galtung (p. 59) says:

> it does make sense to talk about certain classes of need ... and to postulate that in one way or other human beings everywhere and at all times have tried and will try to come to grips with something of that kind, in very different ways.

Mallman (1980, p. 37) defines a need as:

> ... a generic requirement that all human beings have in order not to be ill, by the mere fact of being members of the human species.

Mallman's list represents his proposal for a system of human needs. Mallman asserts that this system is 'one of the many systems that have been used' and 'that it should be possible to find the relations between the different reference frames' (p. 38). Lederer (1980) argues that the list of human motives given by Krech, Crutchfield and Livson (1969) can be analogously applied to needs.

From a casual comparison it will be apparent that considerable overlap occurs in these lists of need, though some accounts include physical needs and others pre-suppose them and some accounts concentrate on abstract categories and conceptions of needs while others specify their content and satisfiers. In Appendix 2 (categories 1–6) I demonstrate this overlap by re-categorising these lists, reducing them to abstract needs rather than to the concrete ways in which they are satisfied. The six categories are (1) Physiological needs (these have already been discussed under physical health needs) (2) Sexual needs, (3) Safety needs, (4) Love and relatedness needs, (5) Esteem and identity needs and (6) Self-realisation needs. In most cases it will be self evident why I have classified a need from groups A–J as belonging in categories (1) – (6). But, I do not claim that any such classification is absolute. Any division of needs into neat and unique classifications is to some extent open to question. What is not questionable is that there are close connections between the lists, and this suggests that there is common agreement on the content of common human needs.

2 Causal evidence: arguments from the consequence of frustration and satisfaction

In the same way that PHN2 are pre-requisites for physical health, MHN2 are pre-requisites for mental health. If the needs for food, water and sleep are denied the physical organs cannot function effectively. Similarly, if the psychological needs for security, love and relatedness, esteem and identity and self-realisation are denied or frustrated, destructive physical and psychopathogenic effects may occur which themselves hinder or limit the individual's capacity for successful action aimed at other goals. As the obverse of this, satisfaction of psychological needs tends to have positive consequences both for physical and mental health and hence for the capacity to achieve other aims. Furthermore, though this is not essential to this argument, everyday observation and experience show that human beings do not just need security, love, esteem and self-realisation as a means to effective functioning but that their satisfaction is also conducive to a rich and deeply rewarding life. It is contrary to experience to suggest that people could seek health or satisfaction through fear, insecurity, isolation, loneliness, rejection, self-disgust, the squandering of their talents and capacities, the stunting of their development.

I will examine evidence for needs (3) to (6). Needs in category (1) have been discussed in relation to physical health. Needs in category (2) can be subsumed under (1) in their physical aspects or (3), (4), (5) and (6) in their psychological aspects.

Security

Human beings need security in order to pursue other needs and other ends because if our security needs are frustrated destructive effects result. We feel threatened and vulnerable. We become dominated by symptomatic fears and anxieties which reduce our capacity for action. In extreme cases when feelings of insecurity result in clinically pathological conditions such as agoraphobia or compulsive obsessive behaviour, capacity for action is all but paralysed. If however safety needs are satisfied we feel confident, secure and protected, at peace with ourselves. Not only does this enable us to function more effectively but is intrinsically satisfying.

Love and relatedness

Although there is little information about the organic origin of love and relatedness needs it is clear that the fulfilment of these needs is fundamental to effective functioning and even to survival itself. Clinical studies have shown that people have a basic need for human relationships and human contact. Without it children fail to develop normally in any sense of the word and often die. Spitz (1949) made a comparative study of infants raised in nurseries by their own mothers and those raised in a foundling home. 100% of the first group survived and developed into normal healthy adults. In the second group there was a 37% mortality rate by the end of the second year, and those who did survive were apathetic or hyperexcitable. Other studies in this field show how deprivation of early relatedness needs obstructs normal development. Clinical observation of a small boy found in India, reputedly one of the fabled 'wolf children', showed him to be incapable of normal physical functioning – walking and verbal communication – or of behaving normally according to any standards (Goves 1960). Harlow (1958a, 1958b) in his famous study of baby rhesus monkeys separated from their mothers at birth provided two 'substitute' mothers. One was a cold, bare wire structure which held a feeding bottle and the other was a warm, comfortable padded structure which provided no food. The infant monkeys fed from the 'wire' mother but went to the 'padded' mother for comfort and contact when they were tired or afraid. It was found that the monkeys did not develop normally. They exhibited aggressive or apathetic behaviour and they were unable to interact socially, play or breed in adulthood.

Fairbairn (1952), Guntrip (1961), Winnicott (1965) and Balint (1968) have all suggested that the primary motivational drive in human beings is to seek relationships with others. The neo-Freudians of the 1930's, Fromm, Horney and Sullivan all stress that a person's sense of self and value depends on interaction with others and that conflict and breakdown in interpersonal relationships cause distress and even illness.

The assertion that it is contrary to experience to suggest that people could find health or satisfaction through isolation or loneliness is not contradicted by the claim that people can also like doing things on their own, that they can desire privacy and even seek seclusion, as long as examples of these desires and pursuits ultimately cannot be uncoupled from the need for relatedness. For example, evidence of the need for relatedness is not undermined by the fact that there are activities that we enjoy doing as individuals. People often want to occupy their own space and do so not on top of, but among other people. Consider the two young children who do not play 'with' each other but who derive enormous satisfaction from playing alongside each other; and the various members of a household separately engaged in their own different activities. The individual who wants to play, think, sleep, study, read or play the piano on their own is not thereby a social isolate or necessarily lonely. The fact that people may want to withdraw from social participation and protect their private lives is not a counter example to the need for relatedness but rather evidence for it in that many facets of our private lives typically involve close relationships with lovers, family and friends which though personal and intimate are also social in character. Even the hermit who seeks self-reliance and seclusion from society has not renounced all relational ties. The significance of their separation depends on them seeing themselves as playing a useful role in and being part of the community, and on the community in turn respecting that role and function.

People then can be physically isolated without being socially isolated and so have their relatedness needs met, whereas the reverse is not the case. The socially isolated person is still lonely in a crowd. This suggests that it is the experience of social isolation and loneliness which is not conducive to health and satisfaction and there is empirical evidence to support this view. Berkman (1977) showed that people with more social contacts, i.e. marriage, close friends, relationships, church membership, informal and formal group association, had lower mortality rates than those with less. Isolation, and lack of social and community ties increases susceptibility to disease. Kaplan, Casell and Gove (1977) also show the importance of social support in determining vulnerability to physiological disease. And, generally psychotherapists and psychoanalysts believe that many adult neurotic conditions are traceable to the deprivation of loving relationships in early life.

There is overwhelming support for the proposition that human beings cannot live alone, that they need love and that they need to relate to other human beings, that they are social animals, and not just in the sense that people must relate to one another instrumentally in order to meet their needs or to achieve any other end they may have, but that people need to relate to other people to keep alive, sane and human. Aristotle thought that the person who was socially isolated was in some way ahuman, a beast or a god. Aristotle (1962, p. 28) writes in a passage quoted earlier (p. 54):

> ... man is by nature a political animal; it is his nature to live in a state. He who by his nature and not simply by ill-luck has no city, no state, is either too bad or too good, either sub-human or superhuman.

Such a person is a 'non-cooperator like an isolated piece in a game of draughts'. Feelings of love and being loved, of belonging and relating to others, make us confident, strong and secure, able to act effectively and achieve deep personal satisfaction.

Identity and esteem

While it is generally acknowledged that there is empirical support for the universal existence of physiological needs and the needs for security and relatedness, it is often claimed that empirical validation for the so called 'higher' needs for identify, esteem and self-realisation is non-existent (Fitzgerald 1977a, p. 43, Cofer and Appley 1964, Ch. 13, Peters 1958, pp. 17–18, 122–9, 153). One by now familiar attack concerns the unacknowledged and inescapable normative character of such needs. The other line of attack which will be addressed here concerns the denial of the universality of the urge to satisfy the need for self-esteem at all. Fitzgerald (1977a, p. 48) argues:

> It can be denied that the 'need for self-esteem' can be made empirical or universalised. It is also clear in individual cases that a predominance of self-disgust over self-esteem has been highly productive ... Artistic creation is often the product of a critical ambivalence between self-regard and self-disgust.

The need for identify and esteem cannot be shown empirically in the sense that its organic base can be demonstrated. Its origin could be explained via the existential phenomena of realising ourselves to be separate persons, which gives rise to the need to establish a positive sense of self as an individual subject. Hence the connection between this need and the need for relatedness. Individuals develop their sense of an individual self in and through relationships with others. Isolation from other people leads to a disintegration of the self. Relationships with others that deny individual subjectivity, that involve being treated as an object so that the self is defined in deference to another's identify, lead to a lack of self-worth. The sense of self is lost.

Contrary to Fitzgerald's suggestion, there is evidence to suggest that the denial of the need for identity and esteem leads to detrimental rather than productive effects on natural psychological functioning. To illustrate the point perhaps it would be helpful to make distinctions here between a sense of identity and self-esteem which is (1) based on a wholly favourable appreciation or opinion of oneself possibly bordering on egoism and vanity, (2) a self-critical assessment and acceptance of oneself involving acknowledgement of and feelings about negative aspects of oneself, and (3) a strong distaste or repugnance for oneself. Fitzgerald's conclusion that self-disgust can be productive relies on equating self-disgust with the second of these rather than the third.

However (2) falls more properly within the scope of the notion of self-esteem, for critical and negative feelings, such as being annoyed or disappointed with oneself and blaming oneself, are in fact like self-congratulation and self-praise; they all presuppose self-respect. Self-esteem is perfectly compatible with the acknowledgement of one's faults and deficiencies. If it were not then self-esteem would be either a super-human ideal or attainable only by the deluded. That self-esteem understood thus can be productive is then no evidence against the existence of self-esteem. That genuine self-disgust, as characterised in (3) as a strong distaste or repugnance for oneself, could be other than detrimental is an argument difficult to sustain. Aristotle argued that 'undue modesty' was worse than 'conceit' in that the consequence of the former was the lack of confidence to act.

The absence of any self-acceptance can only lead to feelings of inadequacy and inferiority, a reluctance to voice or act upon one's own desires or aims, a denial of one's own right to be or to do anything. This results in despair and impotence rather than productivity. Analogous differences are marked in all religions, where (1) would be analogous to a sense of self-esteem akin to the sin of spiritual pride, (2) to the critical but constructive self-appraisal whose end is atonement and amendment and (3) the antithesis of the cardinal virtues of faith and hope, the sin of despair, which seduces and paralyses the will.

Smail (1984, p. 18) argues that:

> ... in order satisfactorily to function, we depend, throughout our lives on the presence of others who will give us validity, identity and esteem. You cannot be anything if you are not recognised as something.

Without self-esteem and a sense of identity, natural psychological functioning is impaired. Smail claims that behind every symptom of anxiety there is an injury to self-esteem (p. 18). Storr (1979, p. 90) argues that, 'the most striking characteristic of depression is a negative one: an absence of built-in self-esteem'. Ziller's (1973) research with depressed veterans in psychiatric wards showed that in their own estimations, the veterans were suffering from extremely low self-esteem. Bettelheim (1961) illustrates how even survival itself can depend on maintaining a sense of identity. He tells us that the prisoners at Auschwitz who surrendered their autonomy and let the guards determine their existence became like automata and died. Seligman (1975, pp. 175-188), gives examples of 'hex' death and the deaths of American P.O.W.'s in the Philippine campaign in World War 11. In these situations people are traumatically stripped of their social identity and their expectations of stability are destroyed. A non-person, Seligman argues cannot remain alive when the social structure which gives validity to existence predicts his death.

It would seem then that to whatever degree of deprivation of identity and esteem needs occurs the capacity for successful action is also impaired. Even Fitzgerald (1977a) admits that despite his arguments, 'it would be difficult to deny, for most human beings, the desirability of at least sufficient ego-strength to cope with their internal and social environment' (p. 48). And beyond coping, the satisfaction of these needs increase the capacity for action as well as intrinsic satisfaction when confidence and affirmation are felt and acted upon.

Self-realisation

Self-realisation is here defined as the need for human beings to develop their talents and capacities. Critics usually reserve their most hysterical and vitriolic abuse for the concept of self-realisation. But it seems to me that the burden of their complaints is either scepticism regarding the practical implementation of the ideal of self-realisation or criticism of the non-empirical nature of a concept whose champions assume that the self to be realised is the 'good' self thus leading to a justification for tyranny over the 'actual' self. For a discussion regarding the value laden nature of the concept see pp. 164–169.

Criticisms of the practicality of implementing the ideas of self-realisation include the conflict with other values. Elster (1985, p. 523) argues that an extreme emphasis on creative self-realisation comes into conflict with the value of community. However, this supposes that the need to develop one's capacities and talents is selfish and narcissistic and incompatible with living in a community which requires individuals to act selflessly. It assumes that we can either realise our talents and capacities or live in a community, but not both. However, as Mobasser (1987, p. 123) points out the ideals of self-realisation and community are not incompatible. Quoting Marx, she argues that human beings are social creatures, because 'only within the community has each individual the means of cultivating his gifts in all directions' (Marx 1976, p. 78) because 'production by an isolated individual outside society ... is as much of an absurdity as is the development of language without individuals living *together* and talking to each other (Marx 1973, p. 84).

The idea that self-realisation conflicts with community is closely related to other criticisms of the practical implausibility of the idea, that is that self-realisation can only be achieved at other people's expense in various ways. For instance, those people whose self-realisation depended on expensive activities would either be unable to engage in them or prevent other people from achieving their self-realisation by commanding a large share of material resources. Similarly, in order to maintain efficiency in society, some people will have to sacrifice their self-realisation as a result. Given that any society will have finite resources it is not plausible to argue that all self-realisation needs must be met. This, though, does not mean that society could not be organised so that everyone could have equal access to the means of developing their talents and capacities, that the objects for meeting needs could not be communally owned and equal access given. If there is a conflict between efficiency and self-realisation, then it is not necessary for some people to engage in meeting the efficiency needs of society and others to engage in fulfilling activities. All could share both.

None of the standard criticisms amount to a denial of the existence of a need for human beings to develop their talents and capacities per se. And, indeed both liberal and socialist political theory, our actual childrearing and educational practices, and the experiences of everyday life attest to the fact that the need for self-realisation is a presumption of them. Confirmation may be found in the curiosity and exploratory drive of the human infant which Piaget (1953) emphasised. The child that does not want to explore her environment, that never says 'why?', that is content when never stimulated, that is always passive, is thought to be seriously disturbed. Is there a small child who given the opportunity is not a prolific painter, an avaricious lover of stories, a riotous singer, an obsessive builder, an intrepid explorer and a daring adventurer on an indefatigable quest to control and master all that comes within their grasp? And, it is the retention of this capacity for childhood playfulness into adult life (Storr 1976), that is one of the mainsprings of creative activity.

It is odd that the concept of self-realisation has been thought to be such a utopian and metaphysical ideal when observation and experience show that all people have a variety of abilities and talents, and when given the opportunity, receive enjoyment and satisfaction from exercising and developing them. The nature of work and the conditions under which it is performed may facilitate this and/or engaging in activities conducive to self-realisation may be a function of leisure time. Whichever is the case, it is a matter of fact that people when given the choice and the enabling conditions will engage in a whole number and range of activities, mental, manual, artistic, athletic or creative, which are expressive of the many different aspects of their personalities. It is simply not conceivable that there are people who, ceteris paribus, want to do nothing all the time, or who want to spend their lives devoted exclusively to one activity. If there is such a person then their passivity or obsessiveness would be a symptom of some pre-existing illness or herald the advent of one. If a person's capacity for growth is stunted, at the very least they will lead a narrow, restricted, boring life the frustrations of which are non-conducive to their physical or mental health.

Fromm (1977, p. 322) discusses the need for stimulation and excitement in relation to a person's capacity for growth. He distinguishes between 'simple stimuli' and 'activating stimuli':

> Stimuli of the first, simple kind, if repeated beyond a certain threshold, are no longer registered and lose their stimulating effect. Continued stimulation requires that the stimulus should either increase in intensity or change in content; a certain element of novelty is required.

A person reacts to simple stimuli but is not inspired to act. An activating stimulus on the other hand 'stimulates the person to be active' (p. 321) creating a 'productive response'. Contemporary society provides many sources of simple stimuli. 'What is stimulating are such drives as sexual desire, greed, sadism, destructiveness, narcissism' (p. 323) mediated through films, television, newspapers and obtained in the consumption of commodities. These present people with easy, non-demanding ways to satisfy their need. They are quick, require no effort, patience, discipline, concentration, practice or the exercise of critical judgement. However these ways are ultimately unsatisfactory. The need that people initially felt for growth and self-realisation atrophies as they become docile, unspontaneous, passive, reactive rather than proactive. The satisfaction felt is superficial since simple stimuli leave a person's deeper feelings, imagination, reason, all his essential faculties and psychic potentialities untouched. Chronic boredom at the lack of productivity can result; and according to Fromm this 'constitutes one of the major psychopathological phenomena in contemporary technocratic society' (p. 326) manifest in depressive illnesses.

3 Behavioural evidence

So far, I have argued that the objective importance of the psychological needs can be inferred from the negative effects of their frustration and the positive effects of their satisfaction. Certain mental states, symptoms and psychopathologies are effects of need frustrations and indicators of unmet or inadequately satisfied need. Complementary to this, the existence and persistence of these underlying needs can be concluded from the presence of various conscious desires and overt behaviours, the use of and striving for certain satisfiers when these can be shown to represent attempts to satisfy needs. All people are motivated to seek the means to satisfy their mental health needs. However, the conscious desires and the objects of satisfaction of need are dependent on material, social and historical circumstances. Consequently desires and satisfiers differ in time and space, and according to culture and the individual's place within it. Underlying needs that the individual may or may not be aware of are the motivational sources which give rise to different desires. These desires take the form they do because they are structured both by needs and social and environmental forces. For instance, the need for security might be expressed in conscious desires for solidarity, through dependency behaviour or through violence and aggression. It may take the form of demands for certain welfare policies, higher wages, health and safety legislation, law and order enforcement or trade union activity. The need for relatedness is expressed in and through activities and relationships of all kinds, with family and friends, lovers and children, neighbours and workmates as well as with the wider political community. Relationships may be hierarchical and unequal or equal and reciprocal. Behaviour may be dominating, oppressive or submissive, manifest as violence and aggression or sought in supportive and co-operative relationships. The need for identity and esteem is expressed through a desire for recognition, attention and affirmation.

It may take the form of craving for possessions and the consumption of material goods; in a passion for status achieved through dominating or conforming behaviour; in national, racial, religious or class identity; or if all else fails, through delusions of grandeur. The need for self-realisation can be expressed through the desire to engage in various activities, mental, manual, artistic or creative; in and through relationships; in ambition, envy and the desire for glory; in boredom, frustration and destructive behaviour.

The above is not meant to be an exhaustive or even a representative account of how desires are manifestations of needs, but rather an indication that many behaviours and activities can represent strivings to satisfy needs. It is precisely this kind of claim that gives rise to three related criticisms from anti-need theorists:

1 If the diversity of behaviour is evidence of the urge to satisfy underlying needs, almost any behaviour can be cited as evidence for the existence of needs; hence their existence is compatible with everything and cannot be proved or disproved.

2 If needs can be expressed in a diversity of forms, there is no way of distinguishing between desirable and undesirable, appropriate and inappropriate expressions except by introducing a value premise which renders the concept of need non-empirical.

3 In any case governments can in no way promote the satisfaction of needs. For example, the need for love or creativity cannot be satisfied by political means or social activity (Fitzgerald 1977a, p. 49; McInnes 1977, p. 239). The first two criticisms will be dealt with here. The political and social ways of meeting needs will be discussed in Chapter 8.

1 The diversity of behaviour

Springborg (1981) challenges the validity of the claim that diverse behaviours constitute proof for the existence of needs. In her chapter on Fromm's arguments to this effect, which can be applied to the similar arguments formulated here, Springborg (p. 53) says:

> the fact that existential needs can exhibit such heterogeneous manifestations reflect their dubious legitimacy as needs in the first place. Not only do these so called needs lack specificity to such an extent that there is no prescribed form that their satisfaction must take, but it turns out that complete opposites will count as evidence for their existence.

For instance, she argues that if Fromm's 'need for transcendence' (cf. the need for self-realisation proposed here) can be fulfilled from anything from the highest art forms to destructiveness then it cannot be maintained that transcendence is a need. Similarly, if the need for identity is manifested in close mutual relationships or in power relations then identity cannot be a need, and so on. Springborg (p. 152) argues this is because:

> ... the range of acceptable forms of satisfaction that a need permits is strictly limited and does not include complete opposites. It is as absurd to say that the need for food can be met by food or hunger, as to say that the need for relatedness can be met by love or hatred, the need for transcendence by creativeness or destructiveness, the need for rootedness by incest or fraternity and so on.

Springborg (p. 153) complains:

> Fromm is not even logically consistent, because the way he defines the respective existential needs entails that in the positive instances he cites the need is indeed met, but in the negative it is not.

I would submit that Fromm is not saying the equivalent of the absurdity that the need for food can be met by food or hunger. Rather, he is saying the equivalent of 'human beings' need for food can be manifest and met by eating food; and the need for food can be manifested and demonstrated to exist by referring to instances of hunger.' There is no inconsistency here. In the positive instances the need is demonstrable and met. In the negative instance the need is demonstrable and manifest but not met. A more accurate account of Fromm's position would compare the universal need for food which demands satisfaction with the common existential needs which also demand satisfaction. In all cases manifestations or answers (not always satisfactions) to these needs take various forms largely dependent on social conditions. If the need cannot be met in life fulfilling ways (for oneself or others) then attempts at satisfaction will be characterised by life thwarting syndromes. So for example, if there is no nourishing food available, attempts to answer this need will take the form of eating unwholesome food or eating food at others' expense. Similarly, Fromm then is not claiming that the need for relatedness can be met by love or hatred. Rather, he is saying under certain conditions conducive to optimal development human beings meet this need by establishing productive, loving relationships, and when these conditions are absent answers to this need can take the form of seeking power over or submitting to the power of another. Both ways are attempts to answer the problem of pressing needs but both ways do not actually meet needs. Fromm (p. 354) argues:

> ... life-thwarting passions are as much an answer to man's existential needs as life-furthering passions: they are both profoundly human. The former necessarily develop when the realistic conditions for the realisation of the latter are absent ... One might consider him an existential failure, a man who failed to become what he could be according to the possibilities of his existence. In any case, for a man to be stunted in his growth and become vicious is as much a real possibility as to develop fully and to be

productive; the one or the other outcome mainly depends on the presence – or absence – of social conditions conducive to growth.

What Fromm wants to establish is how the existence of a need can be deduced from observations of diverse behaviours and to show that certain behaviours are inappropriate satisfiers precisely because they are not conducive to satisfactions.

However, Springborg emphatically denies that observations of human behaviour can disclose the existence of these needs. She asserts that people ordinarily do not profess to feel needs for abstract metaphysical entities. She says 'it is a characteristic feature of the concept of need that it gives rise to the need claims of the form 'I need x', presumably where x stands for something specific and concrete, for Springborg (p. 153) argues that to say:

> 'I have a need for transcendence' or 'I have a need for relatedness, rootedness etc.', certainly sounds odd, and for good reason. No-one can reasonably claim to have a need for anything as abstract as this.

But this is absurd reasoning. It would rule out the intelligibility of being able to say, 'I need food' or 'I feel hungry' on the grounds that here food and hunger are abstract concepts which do not refer to some specific and concrete satisfiers like sausages or bananas.

Conceptually (though not empirically) there is no greater difficulty in inferring the abstract general need for food from the specific felt need for sausages, than there is inferring the general abstract need for identity from the felt need for a new car. Springborg (p. 154) cannot accept this:

> (It) is both redundant and erroneous to reduce an express need for something specific to an inferred need for something more general. If, in fact, a man says that he feels the need for a car, it is probably the car that he feels the need for and not a sense of identity. It is possible to argue that his express need for a car is motivated by his attempt to create an identity for himself, as long as the motive is clearly distinguished from the need itself. The important thing is that there is no causal necessity such that we can infer in each and every case in which someone desires a new car, a 'need for identity' can be inferred; and this is what these theorists by implication claim.

If indeed this is what need theorists claim, then that claim would be both erroneous and plain silly. The theory does not require that there be a rigid correlation between desires for certain specific satisfiers and particular needs.

We only infer the need for food from the desire for sausages when we know the circumstances under which the desire was expressed. If eating sausages was the craving of a pregnant woman, the obsession of a person with an eating disorder or was believed to be the means to great sexual prowess then the sausage desires and sausage eating behaviour would not be taken to be a manifestation of the need for food. Similarly, every time someone expresses the need for a new car we do not automatically leap to the conclusion that the need for identity informs it. We examine the individual and social circumstances under which this felt need arose and infer the need from within these. Empirically this is no simple task, given the culturally and socially influenced wide range of desires and multiple satisfiers which can correspond to a single need, and the constellation of needs which can crystalise in a single desire. However, given what we do know about human motivation in general and about the individual in question and her place within a society which explicitly invests and inculcates symbolic and psychological meaning into certain commodities, a person's particular desire for a car could possibly be explained in terms of needs relating to self-expression, self-esteem, identity, affirmation and admiration. So the particular desire for a car could be explained by the needs which motivate it plus the social conditions which determine the objects of satisfaction and beliefs about their satisfiability, though a person may be unaware of both the internal motivation of the desire or the socially conditioned nature of its particular focus.

2 *Is the concept of need empirical?*

The kind of criticism usually directed at the concept of self-realisation epitomises the objection which can be applied to all the other proposed needs when behavioural evidence is adduced in their support. Fitzgerald (1977a, p. 49) complains:

> ... it is impossible to make such a metaphysical notion as the 'need for self actualisation' empirical at all. Human selves have many potentialities ... It is clear that to the questions 'What is the self to be realised?' and 'What are the potentialities to be developed or expressed?' the respective answers are 'A good self' and 'good potentialities'.

That is if needs can be expressed in a diversity of forms the only way to distinguish between desirable and undesirable, appropriate and inappropriate expressions is by introducing evaluative standards on which there can be no general agreement since these 'will vary according to different estimates of things that are worth doing and propensities that are worth developing' (p. 50). The 'murderer, sadist, fascist, rapist, incendiarist and machete man' (p. 49) could be seen as developing their potential.

Similarly dependency and aggressive behaviour is expressive of the need for security, dominating and submissive behaviour expressive of the need for relatedness and so on. Fitzgerald supposes that there is no way of condemning certain forms of expressions without resorting to value-laden criteria which, because they are relative, are almost useless.

But if the criteria distinguishing desirable and appropriate expressions of need are so value-laden and therefore according to Fitzgerald too diverse to be of any use, how can it be that he singles out the 'murderer, sadist, fascist, rapist, incendiarist and machete man' as obvious examples, likely to resonate with all his readers, of undesirable and inappropriate ways of self-actualisation? Isn't he implicitly using criteria himself, or at least indicating what those criteria might be, when he argues (pp. 49–50):

> ... even the most inconsequential or destructive forms of human action can be seen as part of the process of self-actualisation unless one specifies only certain forms of activity as properly actualising the self.

While claiming that criteria cannot be found, inadvertently he indicates what those criteria might be, by excluding the inconsequential and the destructive.

Critics who object to the value-laden nature of need theory must at least concede that the definition of a need as means to ends any human being has good reason to pursue, desire or value is an empirical definition and an objective one.

Furthermore, the definition of 'need' advocated here rules out the possibility of there being 'bad', 'destructive' or 'harmful' needs, since needs are the permanent and universal characteristics of human beings at all times and in all places. Given that human beings have and always have had good reason to pursue, desire and value their life and health, the means to the fully successful attainment of these ends cannot cause harm or destruction. On this view, to call fundamental human needs 'bad' is simply a contradiction in terms. There may, however be 'good' and 'bad' ways of expressing these needs and meeting them. Since the ways they are expressed are co-determined by biology and society, and our biological nature could not determine us to need things unconducive to its fulfilment, it is social determinants that are responsible for the 'bad', 'destructive' or 'harmful' expressions of need.

In claiming that a form of expression, a particular desire, behaviour or object of satisfaction is bad, desirable, undesirable, appropriate, inappropriate, can criteria for the distinction be made that avoids if not dictatorship over needs then at least dictatorship over their socialised expressions? I think the answer to this question is that the criteria are both empirical and logical.

Those forms of expression which are not conducive to the satisfaction of one's own need and those of others are those forms which are bad, undesirable and inappropriate. Bad ways of satisfying one's own needs are those ways that do not lead to satisfaction. Bad objects of satisfaction are those that do not satisfy, that are not conducive to health and survival. In relation to other people bad ways of satisfying needs, bad forms of expression are those that impede satisfaction in others. These forms of expression of need are empirically identifiable since it can be ascertained whether or not they are required for one's own health or that of others and whether or not their non-satisfaction causes death, physical or mental illness or prevents people whether oneself or others, from functioning effectively.

Hence, the commonly postulated 'bad' needs, the need to deceive and be deceived, the need to dominate, the need to aggress against others, the need to have power or control over others, the need to oppress or to exploit, the need to degrade or to be degraded, cannot be fundamental human needs on this definition. They can be, though, forms of expression of needs which may be judged 'bad' on logical or empirical grounds.

From an individual point of view dominating, aggressive, oppressive, possessive or degrading behaviour cannot be good ways of satisfying psychological needs for security, love, identity and self-realisation simply because such behaviour is self-defeating. It does not satisfy the needs of individuals who depend on the these relationships for satisfactions. Hegel's description of the Master-Slave relationship in the 'Phenomenology of Mind' (1931; Section IVA) might help explain why. According to Hegel, the master requires recognition and acknowledgement from his slaves. He needs them to confirm his own power and dignity as a person, that is, as an independent and autonomous agent.

But, he cannot achieve what he is trying to guarantee. The slave is not an independent agent: he is merely obeying orders. Any recognition he gives the master is not freely given: therefore it cannot confirm the master's identity. Genuine recognition as a free man can only be given by another free man. Given this, wherever prevailing social relations are of hierarchy and submission, neither the master nor the slave can fully satisfy their needs. However, these behaviours do represent attempts to satisfy needs and are ways of satisfying needs which may be superficially functional and rational. They may be functional in the sense that they achieve an immediate effect. Aggressive behaviour or defensive behaviour may achieve the effect that the world is safe. They may be rational in the sense that they are defensive attempts to satisfy needs. Aggressive or degrading behaviour may both be defences against insecurity. So that, at this level the person who can say, 'Unless I dominate you I will not feel secure' or, 'Unless I degrade you I cannot preserve my sense of identity' seems to refute my claim that these behaviours are excluded as 'good' ways of satisfying needs on logical and empirical grounds.

However, though superficially these behaviours represent attempts to satisfy need and though there is a sense in which they might be said to do so, at a more fundamental and important level they are both dysfunctional and irrational. They merely relieve symptoms of need frustration, so that the individual feels that these objects are necessary if need is to be satisfied, if they are to function effectively. But this is symptomatic relief, inappropriate because not directed towards the causes of that need frustration and the objects that will satisfy it; dysfunctional because ultimately the underlying need is not content with palliatives. These ways of behaving are attempts to solve the problems of feeling insecure, lonely, unimportant, unacknowledged that mask the causes of these feelings and which therefore provide no path to security, love or esteem. The behaviours referred to here then ultimately frustrate the satisfaction of needs. And is it not also the case that there is something manifestly absurd about the claim that people need to be aggressive, degraded, oppressive or oppressed, tyrannical or cruel in order to be secure and loved, to have a sense of self-esteem or to function and fulfil themselves as human beings? Are not these the very behaviours (quite apart from their effect on other people) we tend to think of as not fully human, as indicators of crippled, dwarfed, stunted, debased, diminished human beings? And is this not because we have good reason to believe that such behaviours are either (a) symptoms of some prior or occurrent mental distress or mental dysfunctioning and/or (b) themselves the cause of subsequent mental distress or dysfunctioning?

It might be thought that Fitzgerald's 'murderer', 'sadist', 'fascist', 'rapist', 'incendiarist' or 'machete man' really do satisfy their needs for self-realisation in and through their overt behaviour, and this is shown by the fact that the behaviour was motivated by their need; this is what Fitzgerald's position suggests (p. 149). But simply because my needs motivated my behaviour it does not follow that what I do satisfies my need, or that satisfaction is conducive to natural mental functioning. According to Fitzgerald people who kill, torture, rape, or burn other human beings, cause pain to them or hack them to pieces can never be described as engaging in 'bad' ways of fulfilling their needs; they can only be 'disapproved of' if one happens to disapprove of these activities. If one disapproves of these activities could it not be the case that one of the reasons for the disapproval was precisely the empirical one that these ways of attempting to satisfy need do not in fact do so, so that these behaviours are both symptomatic of mental ill health and hazardous to future natural mental functioning?

Such a claim is clearly empirically refutable. If it turned out to be the case that behaviours I have termed 'bad' ways of satisfying needs turned out to be 'good' – that aggressive or submissive behaviour was conducive to the deep intrinsic satisfaction of psychological needs and psychological health, something I believe not to be the case and to have never been demonstrated, and for which there is much counter-evidence – then clearly the distinction between 'good' and 'bad' ways of satisfying needs would have to be abandoned.

But even in this unlikely eventuality all would not be lost. The same criterion for distinguishing between 'good' and 'bad' expressions could be transferred to those individual expressions of need which impede the satisfaction of other people's needs. Galtung (1980, p. 85) suggests this logical criterion as a way of distinguishing between what counts as a 'need' and what does not:

> ... one possible approach would be to stipulate that what cannot even for logical reasons be met for everybody should not be referred to as a 'need' – or at most a 'false' need – for if I shall have or be more than anybody else, others cannot be in the same position; that would constitute a logical contradiction.

For my purposes, this criterion would designate as 'bad' (but not false) those forms of expression of need which for logical reasons cannot be met by all.

This criterion does not exclude interpersonal and intrapersonal conflict and dilemmas which arise between different ways of expressing need and which are the result of empirical causes such as scarce material or non-material resources. The forms of expression that are excluded always can be ascertained empirically from a content point of view. The forms of expression of need that were described above as 'bad' clearly fall into this category. So, even if it is possible to make sense of the idea of needing to harm oneself if that is what one is motivated to do, the things that harm oneself can be classified as 'bad' on different grounds, their direct or indirect effect on others.

From a moral point of view the interpersonal complications involved in meeting 'bad' needs are stressed by Braybrooke (1987). He focuses on the supposed need to be deceived, and the need for aggression and self-abasement. He argues that if such needs were the central and pervasive pre-occupations of most people the establishment of a moral community would be difficult. Braybrooke (p. 272) writes:

> The need to be deceived, if it is to be met, raises the complication that someone may have to do the deceiving.

To deceive someone or even to allow people to deceive themselves, he argues, is tantamount to 'failing to treat people as fully capable moral equals' (p. 273) and will

> involve some people not only in specific moral delinquencies but also in general defection from the principles of mutual respect implied by a moral community.

The interpersonal complications with meeting the needs for aggression and self-abasement are even more telling from this point of view.

Heller (1980, p. 217) also uses an ethical argument to back up her logical point that:

> ... those needs must be excluded from acknowledgement that prevent all needs from being acknowledged and satisfied.

The ethical norm on the basis of which such exclusion is made, providing criteria for the distinction between 'good' and 'bad' needs is one of Kant's (1956, p. 96) formulae of the Categorical Imperative: man ought not to be mere means for another man.

> Act in such a way, that you always treat humanity, whether in your own person or in the person of any other, never simply as a means, but always at the same time as an end.

On the basis of this Heller (p. 218) formulates the thesis that:

> All needs should be acknowledged and satisfied with the exception of those whose satisfaction would make man into mere means for the other. The

categorical imperative has, therefore, a restrictive function in the assessment of needs.

But the 'bad needs' that belong to the category whose satisfaction requires one man to become the means of another, because they are the same needs which create a dilemma with respect to overall need satisfaction, can be condemned on these logical grounds alone with or without the introduction of moral imperatives. This can be seen from the last sentence of Heller's (p. 222) assertion that:

> ... the above formula of the categorical imperative excluded the need for degrading the other man into a mere means. Wherever social relations are based on subordination and hierarchy, wherever possession of property (the right of disposition) is granted to some but not to others, there exists the need of using another individual as a mere means. In these societies it is practically impossible to acknowledge all needs, let alone satisfy them.

Treating people with respect, as ends in themselves, involves respect for their liberty and autonomy as agents who have purposes and ends of their own. The principle of respect for persons as free beings with their own ends can also provide an argument for need satisfaction compatible with others' satisfaction. As Plant et al (1980) suggest, 'I can only be serious about my respect for other people's ends insofar as I am equally serious about their means, in this case their needs' (p. 92).

Criteria for distinguishing 'good' and 'bad' expressions of need can be logical and empirical. Bad expressions of needs are those that for logical or empirical reasons impede satisfactions of others' needs. What these expressions are is empirically discoverable. If fundamental human needs are what is required for survival and health then the forms of expression that have been disqualified because non-conducive to the survival and health of others also empirically can be shown to be non-conducive to the survival and health of oneself. Their denial neither causes illness nor prevents people from functioning as human beings, but rather their presence is a sign of dysfunctioning or will lead to it.

Conclusion

In this chapter I have established that there are abstract, general, universal psychological needs and that it is possible to list them. Empirical evidence for these was provided by arguments from common agreement, and deduced from the negative effects of their frustration and positive effects of their satisfaction and from behavioural evidence of the use of and striving for certain satisfiers.

In addition, it was argued that though these needs are neither 'good' nor 'bad' it makes sense to say that there are good or bad, appropriate or inappropriate ways of expressing needs and satisfying them. The criteria for distinguishing good or bad ways of expressing and satisfying needs are empirical and logical.

Appendix 1: Lists A – J
Lists of human needs offered by different theorists

List A *Brentano (1908)*

1 Maintenance of life – food, clothes, rest or recreation
2 Sexual needs
3 Recognition by others
4 Provision for well being after death
5 Amusement
6 Provision for future
7 Healing
8 Cleanliness
9 Education in Science and Art
10 Need to create

List B *Maslow (1943)*

1 Physiological needs
2 Safety needs
3 Belongingness and love needs
4 Esteem needs
5 Self-actualisation needs

List C *Fromm (1956)*

1 Relatedness
2 Transcendence – creativity
3 Rootedness
4 Sense of identity and individuality
5 The need for a frame of orientation and devotion

List D *Nielsen (1977)*

1 Love
2 Companionship
3 Security
4 Protection
5 Sense of community
6 Meaningful work
7 Sense of involvement
8 Adequate sustenance and shelter
9 Sexual gratification

10 Amusement
11 Rest
12 Recreation
13 Recognition
14 Respect of person

List E Robert E. Lane (1969)

1 Cognitive needs (curiosity, learning, understanding)
2 Consistency needs (emotional, logical, veridical)
3 Social needs (affiliation, being linked)
4 Moral needs
5 Esteem needs
6 Personality, integration and identity needs
7 Aggression expression needs
8 Autonomy needs
9 Self-actualisation needs
10 Need for instrumental guide to reality, object appraisal and attainment

List F J.C. Davies (1977)

1 Physical needs – food, shelter, health, safety from bodily harm
2 Social affectional needs
3 Self-esteem and dignity needs
4 Self-actualisation needs

List G Vance Packard (1960)

1 Emotional security
2 Self-esteem
3 Ego-gratification
4 Recognition and status
5 Creativity
6 Love
7 Sense of belonging
8 Power and a sense of immortality

List H Galtung (1980)

1 Security needs (survival needs) – to avoid violence
  a) against individual violence (assault, torture)
  b) against collective violence (wars, internal, external)

2 *Welfare needs* (sufficiency needs) – to avoid misery
- a) for nutrition, water, air, sleep
- b) for movement, excretion
- c) for protection against climate, environment
- d) for protection against diseases
- e) for protection against excessive strain
- f) for self-expression, dialogue, education

3 *Identity needs* (needs for closeness) – to avoid alienation
- a) for self-expression, creativity, praxis, work
- b) for self-actualisation, for realising potentials
- c) for well-being, happiness, joy
- d) for being active and subject; not being passive, client, object
- e) for challenge and new experiences
- f) for affection, love, sex; friends, spouse, offspring
- g) for roots, belongingness, support, esteem: association with similar humans
- h) for understanding social forces; for social transparence
- i) for partnership with nature
- j) for a sense of purpose, of meaning with life; closeness to the transcendental, transpersonal

4 *Freedom needs* (freedom to: choice, option) – to avoid repression
- a) choice in receiving and expressing information and opinion
- b) choice of people and places to visit and be visited
- c) choice in consciousness formation
- d) choice in mobilization
- e) choice in confrontations
- f) choice of occupation
- g) choice of place to live
- h) choice of spouse
- i) choice of goods and services
- j) choice of way of life

List I Mallman (1980)

Mallman makes the following 4-term distinctions:

1 existence/living
2 coexistence/co-living
3 growth
4 perfection

which group the following 8 term distinctions:

1' subsistence
2' security
3' belongingness
4' esteem
5' development
6' renewal
7' transcendence
8' maturity

He also redefines the same need field in terms of 9 distinctions:

1" maintenance
2" protection
3" love
4" understanding
5" self reliance
6" recreation
7" creation
8" meaning
9" synergy

List J Krech, Crutchfield and Livson (1969)

Survival & security (deficiency motives)	Satisfaction & stimulation (abundancy motives)
1 Pertaining to the body	
a) avoiding of hunger, thirst, oxygen lack, excess heat or cold, pain, overfull bladder and colon, fatigue, overtense muscles, illness and other disagreeable bodily states, etc.	a') attaining pleasurable sensory experiences of tastes, smells, sounds, etc.; sexual pleasure, bodily comfort, exercise of muscles, rhythmical body movements, etc.
2 Pertaining to relations with the environment	
a) avoiding of dangerous objects and horrible, ugly and disgusting objects	a') attaining enjoyable possessions
b) seeking objects necessary to future survival and security	b') constructing and inventing objects
c) maintaining a stable, clear, certain environment	c') understanding the environment
	d') solving problems, playing games
	e') seeking environmental novelty and change, etc.
3 Pertaining to relations with other people	
a) avoiding interpersonal conflict and hostility	a') attaining love and positive identifications with people and groups
b) maintaining group membership, prestige and status	b') enjoying other people's company
c) being taken care of by others	c') helping and understanding other people
d) conforming to group standards and values	d') being independent, etc.
e) gaining power and dominance over others, etc.	

4 Pertaining to the self

a) avoiding feelings of inferiority and failure in comparing the self with others or with the ideal self
b) avoiding loss of identity
c) avoiding feelings of shame, guilt, fear, anxiety, sadness, etc.

a') attaining feelings of self-respect and self confidence
b') expressing oneself
c') feeling sense of achievement
d') feeling challenged
e') establishing moral and other values
f') discovering meaningful place of self in the universe.

Appendix 2: Categories 1 – 6
Recategorisation of lists A – J

Beneath each category 1–6 will figure needs from each theorist's list A–J, the needs themselves numbered as before.

Some needs in the category of sexual needs (2) are either part of (1) for example A(2) and B(1) or can be subsumed under (3) and (4)

Category 1 Physical survival needs

A) 1 Maintenance of life – food, clothes, rest or recreation
7 Healing
8 Cleanliness
B) 1 Physiological needs
C) pre-supposed
D) 8 Adequate sustenance and shelter
11 Rest
12 Recreation
E) pre-supposed
F) 1 Physical – food, shelter, health, safety from bodily harm
G) pre-supposed
H) 2 Welfare needs
I) 1 Existence, living
1' Subsistence
1" Maintenance
J) 1 Pertaining to the body

Category 2 Sexual needs

A) 2 Sexual needs
B) 1 Physiological needs
3 Belongingness and love
C) 1 Relatedness
D) 1 Love
9 Sexual gratification
E) 2 Consistency – emotional
3 Social – affiliation, being loved
F) 1 Social affectional needs
G) 1 Emotional security
6 Love
7 Sense of belonging
H) 3 f) Affection, love, sex, friends, spouse, offspring
I) 2 Co-existence, co-living
J) 1 a') sexual pleasure

Category 3 Security needs

A) 4 Provision for well being after death
   6 Provision for future
B) 2 Safety
C) 3 Rootedness
D) 3 Security
   4 Protection
E) 2 Consistency – emotional, logical, veridical
F) 1 Safety from bodily harm
G) 1 Emotional security
H) 1 Security needs – to avoid violence
I) 2' Security
   2" Protection
J) 2 Pertaining to the environment:
   - a) avoiding dangerous objects ...
   - b) seeking objects necessary for future survival and security
   - c) maintaining a stable, clear and certain environment

   3 Pertaining to relations with other people:
   - a) avoiding interpersonal conflict and hostility
   - c) being taken care of by other people
   - d) conforming to group standards and values
   - e) gaining power and dominance over others

Category 4 Love and relatedness needs

A) 2 Sexual needs
   3 Recognition by others
B) 3 Belongingness and love
C) 1 Relatedness
D) 1 Love
   2 Companionship
   5 Sense of community
E) 3 Social needs
F) 2 Social affectional needs
G) 6 Love
   7 Sense of belonging
H) 3 f) for affection, love, sex; friends, spouse, offspring
   h) for roots, belongingness, support, esteem, association with other human beings
I) 2 Co-existence, co-living
   3' Belongingness
   3" Love

J) 3 Pertaining to relations with other people:
a, b, c, d, a', b', c', d'

Category 5 Esteem and identity needs

A) 3 Recognition by others
B) 4 Esteem
C) 4 Sense of identity and individuality
D) 13 Recognition
14 Respect of person
E) 4 Moral needs
5 Esteem
7 Aggression expression needs
F) 3 Self-esteem and dignity needs
G) 2 Self-esteem
3 Ego gratification
4 Recognition and status
8 Power and a sense of immortality
H) 3 Identity needs, a–j
I) 4' Esteem
J) 4 Pertaining to the self, a–c, a'–f'

Category 6 Self-realisation needs

A) 5 Amusement
9 Education in science and art
10 Need to create
B) 5 Self-actualisation
C) 2 Transcendence and creativity
D) 6 Meaningful work
7 Sense of involvement
10 Amusement
E) 9 Self actualisation needs
G) 5 Creativity
8 Power and a sense of immortality
H) 2 f) for self-expression, dialogue, education
3 a) for self-expression, creativity, praxis, work
3 b) for self-actualisation, for realising potentials
3 c) for well being, happiness and joy
3 d) to be active and subject, not being passive and object
4 Freedom needs
I) 3 Growth
4 Perfection
5' Development

6' Renewal
7' Transcendence
7" Creation
8" Meaning
9" Synergy

J) 2 a') Attaining enjoyable possessions
b') Constructing and inventing objects
d') Solving problems
e') Seeking environmental novelty and change
4 b') Expressing oneself
c') Feeling a sense of achievement
d') Feeling challenged

8 Instrumental health: Mental health needs 2

A) Identifying mental health needs

Felt needs and demands are inadequate indicators of need

It has been argued that human beings have general psychological needs for security, relatedness, esteem, identity and self-realisation in order to be mentally healthy. The forms of expression of these needs can be deemed 'bad' if they do not satisfy the individual's needs or if they lead to non-satisfaction for others. These abstract psychological needs as conditions for mental health are determined by the psychological nature of human beings. Their manifestations, forms of expression and the choice of objects to meet them are determined socially and economically. Hence, whether or not they are manifest and satisfied, the ways (good and bad) in which they are satisfied are dependent on the structure of society, the mode of production in that society, its particular social and political organisation. Mental health needs will include the social and political means necessary to achieve, restore or maintain mental health. For these reasons mental health needs, like physical needs, cannot be identified by relying on felt needs or demands alone (see Ch. 6).

Health and illness are socially produced

The social and economic factors which produce or create risks to mental health also determine whether mental health needs are felt, demanded, acknowledged or satisfied. Parallel to the case of physical health, I will examine first how mental health and illness are socially produced.

By investigating mental health in its social context, and demonstrating how mental illness is socially produced when mental health needs are unmet, and how needs take forms unconducive to fulfilment, I hope to answer Fitzgerald's claim that he cannot fathom how needs are related to government. He asks. 'How can ... governments promote attachment behaviour?' (1977a p. 48) and claims that, 'certainly there is no way one can secure artistic creation by political or psychological means' (p. 48).

Specific health needs, demands and satisfactions are produced by, and can only be explained within, the mode of production within which they occur.

Whatever the genetic or biochemical basis of susceptibility to mental illness or mental distress that might be found, differences in the instances of mental health found between different social classes, the employed and unemployed, and between men and women testify to the significance of socio-economic determinants in the explanations of the distribution and occurrence of mental illness within a given population (Plog and Edgerton 1969, Coulter 1973).

Studies of the social distribution of mental illness use mental hospital admission rates and community surveys to provide evidence for their hypotheses. Studies which use mental hospital admission rates attempt to show the social distribution of psychiatric disorder where the latter is understood according to the major categories used by psychiatrists and classed here as those pathological conditions which interfere with natural functioning. Data from mental hospital admissions obviously provides a limited picture of the incidence of mental illness. Not all mentally ill people are treated in hospitals, some are treated in out-patient departments or day care centres and some are not treated at all. The number of hospital admissions could reflect other factors such as the availability of beds and other resources, the patients' access to these and their general response to their own psychological state.

Studies based on community surveys are designed to discover the actual prevalence of psychological disorders in a population. They take a scientifically drawn sample of the population, collect social and personal data about each individual and test them to see if they could be classified as suffering from psychological symptoms characteristic of the mentally ill. On the basis of this information they form a picture of the factors important in the eteliology of mental illness. Such surveys do not show the people they measure to be mentally ill; rather they show the degree to which they suffer from psychological problems. They measure the extent to which an individual has the psychological traits or symptoms judged by psychiatrists to be characteristic of mental hospital patients and most significant in the clinical diagnosis of mental illness. They commonly use Langer's 22 Item Index (Langer 1962).

Class differences

There is a mass of evidence relating social class to susceptibility to psychological disorder and mental illness. Cochrane (1983) discusses evidence gleaned from mental hospital admissions and community surveys. In the USA

Hollingshead and Redlich's study (1958) of individual patients admitted to mental hospital showed a strong relationship between social class and patient status. Myers and Bean's (1968) updated study reinforced these findings. In Britain, Birtchnell (1971) found mental hospital patients over-represented in Class IV (semi-skilled manual workers) and Class V (unskilled manual workers).

Community survey studies corroborate these findings. The Midtown Manhattan survey (Strole et al 1961; Langer and Michael 1962) developed and used Langer's 22 Item Index in one of the first large scale surveys of psychological impairment in a community. Cochrane (1983) reports that their findings show a marked social class influence in the proportion of people with and without symptoms. In the highest social class group there were four times as many people considered to be well as were considered to be psychiatrically impaired while in the lower social class group there where almost twice as many ill people as there were people diagnosed as well (p. 25). More recent British studies by Cochrane and Stopes-Roe (1980a) using the Langer Index found a very similar pattern.

Sex differences

Higher incidences of mental distress and mental disturbance occurring in women rather than in men have been indicated by differential rates of mental hospital admissions and in the results of community surveys. Cochrane (1983) reports that about 40% more women than men are admitted for treatment in mental hospitals in England every year (p. 40). Depression is the largest diagnostic category exhibiting the major differences between the sexes (p. 41). He records that several reviews of a large number of community surveys show the consistency of the different rate of psychological disturbance between men and women noted on other indices. (Dohrenwend and Dohrenwend 1969; Goldman and Ravid 1980: Schwab et al., 1978 in the USA; Cochrane and Stopes-Roe 1981b in Britain).

Differences between employment and unemployment

There is a considerable body of empirical work linking unemployment to mental illness and indeed to illness of all kinds. Brenner (1976) showed that unemployment in the USA is associated with increasing rates of total mortality, alcoholism, suicide, prison and psychiatric hospital admissions. Stokes (1981) found a positive correlation between unemployment and hospital admission levels in England and Wales.

Community surveys of symptom levels by Cochrane and Stopes-Roe (1980a) found that unemployment was one of the main determinants of poor mental health of both unemployed men and their wives. A recent report for the BMA (BMA 1987) showed that the wives of unemployed men have higher death rates than those that are married, their babies suffer higher death rates, their children are shorter and that young unemployed men are more likely to use drugs. Kirsch (1983) listed a large number of health problems resulting from unemployment including heart disease, psychiatric and emotional problems and violent death. Smith (1987) using figures based on reports of death and disease among unemployed men published by the government statistics service, the Office of Population Censuses and Surveys shows a similar story. Unemployed men are more likely to commit suicide than the rest of the population. They are 40% more likely to die of cancer and 75% more likely to die of lung cancer. Surveys had shown that unemployed men were more likely to need medical help and to be referred to hospitals for treatment. Middle-aged men on the dole report higher rates of psychiatric symptoms – depression, anxiety, and suicidal wishes, according to the biggest non-government health survey so far by the tobacco industry financed Health Promotion Research Trust.

Class, sex and work influences on health: explanations of social class/sex/work differences in mental health

Various research studies show that the lower social classes, women and the unemployed are more vulnerable to mental illness or psychological distress than their higher social class, male and employed counterparts.

Explanations for these phenomena that will be considered below are that it is prior psychological states that cause social and work status (low social class and unemployment) and that it is the biological basis of sex differences which causes more women than men to suffer from mental disorder. It will be argued that these are inadequate explanations for the differences in mental health and that as with physical health aspects of capitalist social and economic relations are the major determinants of health, though this explanation does not preclude the contribution of other factors to ill health .

Myerson (1941) first suggested that the preponderance of people in lower social classes suffering from mental ill health was the result of the inability of psychologically disturbed people to maintain the socio-economic position of their family of origin. Other varieties of the social selection hypothesis concur with the view that it is psychological impairment which effects the social structure rather than the other way around. Birtchnell (1971) argues that schizophrenia so disables people that they are unable to maintain their class position. Gerrard and Houston (1953) argue a similar case for other mental disorders (except for neurotic conditions). However, Cochrane (1983) argues that most of these studies do not rule out other explanations for the higher rates of mental disturbance in the lower social classes. Studies explicitly designed to compare the competing explanations of social causation and the 'drift' hypotheses have found evidence for both but concluded that social causation is the more plausible explanation (Lee 1976). Whitehead (1988) after assessing the available evidence for physical and mental health concludes that whereas unhealthy people are likely to move down the social scale, the evidence suggests that this effect would only make a small difference to the overall figures (p. 288). Therefore other explanations, notably material or structural ones, are needed to account more adequately for the gap between the classes in health status.

For the greater susceptibility of women than men to mental illness to be explained as the result of their intrinsic nature the following would have to be shown: that these differences persist over time and place; that they are consistent over a range of social groups; and that they are caused by some sex-linked mechanism. This cannot be done. Sex differences in mental health do not persist over time and place. Lowe and Garrett (1959) argue that the greater proportion of women admitted to mental hospital is a relatively recent phenomena. Cochrane (1983, p. 45) states that there are societies and ethnic groups within our society where the pattern is reversed, notably in the Republic of Ireland and Scotland. In a Scandinavian study it was found that sex differences in symptoms of anxiety were much smaller in Finland and Sweden than in Denmark and Norway. When psychiatric admission rates were considered they were higher for women than for men in Norway, whereas in Finland and Sweden men had higher rates (Haavio-Mannila 1986).

Sex differences in mental health are not consistent over social groups. Haavio-Mannila's 1986 study showed that the excess of female morbidity was due to higher rates for female manual workers and full time housewives, suggesting that types of employment and unemployment are relevant to rates of illness and hospitalisation. Further it seems that paid employment is associated with less illness among middle class women with children and more illness among their working class counterparts. The results of the Health and Life-Style survey on differences in rates of mainly physical illnesses between working and non-working married women (Cox et al., 1987) confirms this. Working class women living in urban areas have also been found to run a higher risk of depression, with a threshold difference between the rates for working class and professional women (Brown and Harris, 1982). In addition to this it is a common observation that married women are more vulnerable to mental illness. Haavio-Mannila (1986) found that mental health tends to be best among married men, followed by single men and women, with the greatest number of most psychiatric problems found in married women. Given this, any explanation in terms of sex mechanisms connected with female reproductive functions as causes of sexual differences in mental health would seem an inadequate account of them. For women, marriage would on this analysis, be conducive to mental health as a means of fulfilling their reproductive functions. If biological differences were a major factor they would not have appeared only recently, in certain societies and ethnic groups, particularly amongst working class women in paid work, housewives and married women.

There is strong evidence to support the view that unemployment causes a deterioration in mental health rather than vice versa. Several studies of people before and after losing their jobs show a marked deterioration in their mental health after becoming unemployed. Pearlin et al (1981) in the USA analysed data from a longitudinal study of 2,300 people based on two interviews at four-yearly intervals. Those people who became unemployed during the intervening period became significantly depressed. In Canberra, Australia, Finlay-Jones and Eckhardt (1981) studied 400 young unemployed people. They were interviewed and given a short version of Goldberg's General Health Questionnaire (GHQ) (Goldberg 1972). The results indicated that 56% of the sample were suffering from serious psychological disturbance. During interviews with psychiatrists which corroborated this, it was established that 70% of those affected had become disturbed only after their experience of unemployment. In Britain, Stafford et al (1980) used the GHQ and interviewed 650 young people just after leaving school. Several months after it was found that those who were unemployed obtained the highest score on the symptom scale. Eight months later for those who became employed there was a large drop in the symptom level and for those who had lost their jobs the reverse was the case (Jackson and Stafford 1980).

It will be argued that sex and unemployment are important factors in susceptibility to mental illness because they are associated with many other factors which can affect mental health, the impact of which can be subsumed under the variable 'stress'. Lower social classes, women and the unemployed experience more stress as a result of their material and social circumstances. They are more likely to suffer material and emotional deprivation and therefore less likely than their counterparts to have their physical or their psychological needs met.

Antonovsky (1970, p. 72)) defines a stressor as:

> a demand made by the internal or external environment of an organism that upsets its homoeostasis, restoration of which depends on a non-automatic and not readily available energy expending action.

These stressors can be either physical or psychological, causing psychological changes, an increase in heart rate and blood pressure, changes in the distribution of blood, release of glucose, fatty acids and adrenalin into the bloodstream. There is much empirical evidence showing that frequent experience of stress plays a causal role in both physical and psychological illness. Cochrane (1983, pp. 113–116) quotes many studies showing that people with psychological problems ranging from mild neurotic symptoms, to depression, anxiety, schizophrenia and attempted suicide had been exposed to stressors in the immediate past.

To some extent 'stressors' are an inescapable feature of the human condition regardless of class, sex or any other variable. Certain exigencies of human social life are broadly agreed to be stressors because they are statistically significant risk factors and are no respecters of persons or status. For instance, physical trauma, poor physical health and death in the family, natural disasters, wars, life changes, re-location, moving house and retirement do not hit the lower classes, women and the unemployed exclusively, though these events do hit these groups disproportionately and effect them more dramatically because of their reduced ability to cope with them. However, other generally agreed stressors do directly correlate with these categories, for example, low income, debt, poverty, homelessness, poor housing, unemployment, alienating working conditions and social relationships.

In what ways, then, do the groups in question experience stress?

The working class, women and the unemployed's exposure to stress: access to resources, production and consumption

Explanations of differences in mental health, like explanations of differences in physical health, relate to differences in access to material and non-material resources, the physical process of commodity production and patterns of consumption. The working class are more likely to have their non-material, as well as material needs poorly satisfied.

i) Access to resources Lack of income limits access to the basic goods, amenities and services and to the physical environment conducive to the satisfaction of physical health needs (see previous chapter). The inadequate satisfaction of these needs plus limited access to the non-material goods of education, information, skills and personal resources also affects the possibility of working class people adequately satisfying their psychological needs for security, relatedness, identity, esteem and self-realisation. Poor physical health, living and working conditions, economic and environmental insecurity adversely affect the satisfaction of security needs. Hierarchical, divisive, competitive, oppressive relationships in society at large and particularly at work threaten relatedness needs in all aspects of life. Identity and esteem needs are difficult to satisfy when the ability to buy commodities and engage in work and leisure activities that confer status and to affect a sense of achievement and satisfaction is limited as a result of the material and non-material deficiencies arising from class positions. Self-realisation needs are thwarted through lack of time, money, energy, education and meaningful work. As a result there are limited opportunities for leisure, political, cultural and educational activities and creative self-expression or intellectual stimulation at work.

ii) Commodity production: class and patterns of work It is the organisation of work in industrial society that is particularly detrimental to the satisfaction of psychological needs. Characteristics of work under capitalism are hierarchical structures of command and the loss of control over work and the labour process, and the fragmentation of tasks with reduction in skills, which compels people to engage in narrow, boring, repetitive work with little job satisfaction or intrinsic interest. The demands of capitalist production and the use of new technology together with low wages necessitate work at increased pace and pressure for long, unsocial and irregular hours.

The nature of work and the conditions under which it is performed fail to meet psychological needs and have negative health consequences.

Many empirical studies (Gardell 1972; Friedlander 1967) show that workers consider work to be the major determinant of life satisfactions and self-esteem, far more important than non-work activities such as education and leisure, Gardell (p. 26) writes:

> Unless these needs are satisfied at the workplace, the individual experiences a basic frustration that manifests itself in different efforts to achieve adjustment.

Gardell and Gustavsen (1980) show that the most important conditions that have a negative health effect on workers are machine pacing of work rhythms and machine control of work methods; monotonous, repetitive work, activating only a limited part of total human capabilities; lack of possibilities for contact with other people as part of the ongoing work; piece rates and related payment systems, which in addition to contributing to employee wear and tear, are often detrimental to the observance of safety requirements; and authoritarian detailed control of the individual, be it through foremen or impersonal systems (e.g. computer based planning).

Gardell (1982) corroborates the above and reports evidence from many empirical studies to suggest that the following properties of job content are critical from a health point of view: quantitative overload – too much to do, time-pressure, repetition and one-sided demands; qualitative overload – too narrow and one-sided job content, lack of stimulus variation and no demands on creativity, problem solving or social interaction; lack of control, especially in relation to planning, pace and work methods; lack of social support from 'people who count'. All these are detrimental to the fulfilment of psychological needs, cause stress and can produce different adverse effects on health.

Frankenhaeuser and Gardell's 1976 study concluded that lack of control over work conditions was probably a key factor in the explanation of general mental strain and exhaustion, greater morbidity, incidents of psychosomatic illness, stress and cardiovascular disease in Swedish sawmill workers. Caplan's study (1975) showed that for certain types of conditions morbidity and mortality is higher among individuals doing routine types of work than work that demands a large number of skills and which allows for some control over what one does. Lack of control over workplace and over physical movement was reputed in some studies to be the most critical variable for stress and ill health, (Johansson et al 1978; Katz and Kahn 1978). Johnson (1980) found that machine paced workers whose workload allowed no opportunities for creative experiment and individual expression reported higher levels of anxiety, depression and irritation as well as difficulties in sleeping, loss of appetite, accelerated heart rate and other symptoms of psychological strain.

iii) Class and consumption patterns The non-satisfaction of psychological needs at work also limits the possibilities of their satisfaction outside work. Johanssen (1975) and Lundhal (1971) report that a greater proportion of those involved in monotonous and strenuous work than those in less stressful jobs need to rest after work and therefore have less time for leisure and for other activities. Gardell (1976a) reports that such workers are less likely to engage in leisure activities that require participation and effort rather than those that are passive and unrewarding. Gardell (1976b), Meissner (1971) and Weslander (1976) report that workers whose jobs entail serious constraints with respect to autonomy and social interaction at work take far less part in organised and goal orientated activities outside work that require planning and cooperation with others.

iv) Unemployment and access to resources Not all unemployment has negative psychological consequences for the individual affected. The extent to which unemployment causes stress and ill health varies according to contingent factors relating to the particular individual and their social circumstances. Obviously the material deprivation of the unemployed is a factor in their susceptibility to stress and ill health. In addition to this the satisfaction of psychological needs is likely to be further undermined by their reduced status. Financial insecurity and social isolation affect security and relatedness needs increasing family tensions. Stokes (1981), in a comparative study between employed and unemployed taken from a matched sample, reported that those who became unemployed had significantly higher levels of psychological distress, felt more hostile and guilty, less satisfied with themselves and reported more family and marital tensions. Pearlin et al's study (1981), referred to earlier showed that unemployment not only causes depression but also adversely influenced marital satisfactions and the success of parent/child relationships and brought about economic difficulties. Other studies have documented the effect of unemployment on family life, showing that the wives and children of the unemployed can also suffer psychologically (Fagin and Little 1984).

v) Production: patterns of work – unemployment Given that work can be a major source of esteem and identity in our society, its loss can precipitate negative self-attitudes and feelings of degradation and purposelessness. However, since not all kinds of work provide satisfactions for relatedness, identity and esteem needs (in fact quite the reverse) the extent to which individuals are affected by unemployment will differ according to the nature of the job lost. Moreover the loss of a job and the potential loss of identity and esteem can be mitigated or accelerated by the social and economic context in which the unemployment takes place, the reason why the unemployment occurred and society's attitude to it. An individual is likely to respond differently depending on the cause of their unemployment, i.e. whether it was a result of mass sackings after trade union activity, mass redundancies following the introduction of new technology, victimisation, unfair dismissal, individual dismissal, voluntary redundancy, early retirement or whether the individual concerned is a school leaver who has never had a job. Their response will be further affected depending on how other people view them; whether they are seen as mindless militants who get their just deserts, Luddites or heroes, victims or lazy work-shy scroungers. The effects of job loss on particular individuals will also depend on whether their job was a source of self-realisation and whether alternative sources for fulfilling this need can be found. If there were opportunities at work for self-expression, creativity and intellectual stimulation their removal could lead to inertia and boredom. Exploring new possibilities for replacement activities can be problematic given this general mental state together with reduced resources for pursuing them.

i) Women and access to resources, (ii) work and (iii) consumption Given the inadequacy of biological explanations of women's susceptibility to mental illness and the categories of women most at risk, the stress and consequent ill health experienced by women can best be attributed to the non-satisfaction of their psychological needs explicable with reference to their sex roles which form part of structural power relationships and social inequalities. Women as a group are notoriously economically insecure. Working class women in particular are disadvantaged in employment, and commonly either in low paid jobs with poor conditions and prospects; or labouring at unpaid work in the home and dependent on their husbands or the state. They are disadvantaged in their personal relationships and socially isolated in the home, lonely, frustrated and bored. The power relationships operating in society in general allot them to passive, submissive, helpless sex roles, the objects of male domination, degradation and violence. Seligman (1975) suggests that low capacity to influence the environment and lack of control over one's own life make people vulnerable to depression. Their identity and esteem needs are hard to meet given the fact that economic and male oppression determines and delimits the range of identities possible: housewife/mother/whore – and affords none of them admirable status. Women's paid work outside the home is most likely to be an extension of one of these undervalued roles and/or poorly paid, e.g. cleaning, cooking, nursing, teaching, prostitution. Women's main sense of identity comes vicariously through their husbands' and children's. Women spend their time nurturing other people, massaging male egos and ignoring their own need. Self-realisation for women is an almost unintelligible ideal. With no financial security, no productivity, no job satisfaction, no independent identity and little leisure time it is not difficult to see why women are under stress and liable to ill health.

These comments relating the non-satisfaction of women's psychological needs to their social roles are confirmed by research findings which highlight that the women most at risk are those who for whatever reasons are particularly entrenched in those social roles. Studies quoted earlier show that married women in general are more vulnerable to mental illness, but particularly working class women who are full time housewives or who are at work and have young children. And, it is suggested that this may be because if they are working class housewives they are likely to be financially insecure, doing low status, unrewarding work; they may be socially isolated and have only their role in the home as a vehicle for the fulfilment of their psychological needs (Gove 1972; Gove 1973; Gove and Tudor 1973; Gove and Herb 1974). Brown (1982) and others show that psychiatric symptoms in women are related to isolation in the home, the stress produced by poverty and lack of employment. Married women in paid work outside the home are more protected depending on their social circumstances and family responsibilities (Cox et al., 1987). Working class women with children are the worst off. This supports the view that women in low paid jobs are unlikely to have their psychological needs met at work and have the double burden of returning home to other psychologically unrewarding labour. Arber et al (1985) reviewing evidence on work and health concluded:

> ... full time work for young mothers may be detrimental for their health unless there is adequate financial resources for maintaining the multiple roles of housewife, mother and employee, or until the sexual division of labour in the home changes.

Different responses to stress

It has been argued that lower occupational classes, women and the unemployed experience more stress as a result of material and psychological deprivations caused by their social circumstances (their access to resources, place in production and consumption) and that this results in their comparatively high rates of mental ill health. However it is widely acknowledged that different people experience the effects of stressors in different ways, and this too is largely determined by their social circumstances.

It is known that stressors play a causal role in psychological disturbance, but the experience of stressors does not always lead to breakdown. Stressors have different effects on different people because of their different levels of vulnerability and different coping resources. These latter are called 'Generalised Resistance Resources' (G.R.R.'s) by Antonovsky (1970, p. 99) who defines them as 'any characteristic of the person, the group or the environment that can facilitate effective tension management'. He claims that the extent to which these G.R.R's are available plays a decisive role in health status. He identifies three kinds of G.R.R's: the physical and biochemical; the artificial-material, wealth and material resources and interpersonal relationships; and the cognitive and emotional-knowledge, intelligence and information and skill at getting it. He singles out ego-identity and social support as vital G.R.R's and quotes from the vast literature on the importance of ego-identity in facilitating effective tension management.

Schachtel (1962), Erikson (1960), Seligman (1975) and Kaplan (1972) stress the significance of self-esteem in explaining why some people under stress resort to a range of deviant behaviour (drink, drugs, violence) and mental illness while others do not. Other studies show the importance of personal relationships and social support as defences against stressors' potentially pathogenic effects. Gove (1973) analysed cause specific mortality data which showed the protective function being married played in relation to cause of death (especially for men). Berkman (1977) found that people with more social contacts (spouses, friends, relations, church members, formal and informal group association) had the lowest mortality rates. Cochrane (1983, pp. 122–123) quotes several studies which show the importance of social support in determining the susceptibility to disease. Myers et al (1975) found that the unmarried, the unemployed and the generally dissatisfied were more susceptible to the damaging effects of stress than the married, employed and well integrated socially. Brown (1978), in a study of depressed women, found that close, confiding, supportive relationships with another person was a protective factor in proneness to depression in the face of stress. Williams et al (1981) suggests that social support is a positive predictor of good mental health and its absence a predictor of poor mental health, whether or not stress is present. Gardell (1982, p. 35) quotes several studies of the 'buffering' effects of social support in working life which shows that such support may effectively help people to cope with stress: Gardell (1979); House (1981) Cassel (1976); and Cobb (1976).

It had been argued that everyone experiences stress, but that in addition to sources of stress which are independent of class or gender the working class, the unemployed and women experience more stress because of the socially caused failure to meet their material and psychological needs. Consequently these social groups are more susceptible to mental illness on this account. It was then argued that not all people exposed to stress become mentally ill and that the availability of G.R.R's was an important factor in people's ability effectively to cope with stress. It can be seen that the distribution of these material and psychological resources is again determined by the social categories to which people belong, thus making people belonging to these categories doubly vulnerable to ill health. Some people are at risk because they experience a high level of stress as a result of their role in the productive process and their patterns of consumption. Their social circumstances limit access to the material and psychological resources required to meet their health needs thus causing stress. Their inability to cope with stress derives from the same social circumstances. That is if types of work, unemployment and material resources (wealth, income, food, shelter, clothing, availability of services) are G.R.R's, then it is clear that the working class and the unemployed are most likely to suffer from their inadequate supply. Consequently the whole range of physical and psychological health needs and the ability to cope with stress caused as a result of inadequate provision will be inadequately satisfied.

If high self-esteem is a G.R.R. then it is probable that certain groups, e.g. men and the employed, are better able to maintain self-esteem and thus deal with stress more positively. Men are more privileged in this respect as a result of socially caused differential status being conferred on men rather than women; they are more likely to be employed and in jobs with high status in which they can achieve success, intrinsic satisfaction and social recognition. If intimate social relations are G.R.R's then this resource can be seen to fulfil the need for relatedness, security and a sense of identity and personal worth. This resource is more likely to be available to middle class men and the employed. Men of all classes are supported and nurtured in the home by their wives; working class men are subject to oppressive relationships at work but women are subject to them both at home and at work. Women in unpaid labour in the home and the unemployed are also likely to be deprived of social contacts. Meeting mental health needs thus depends on access to resources, the nature of the production process and patterns of consumption.

Dealing with problems: felt needs, demands and satisfactions are socially produced

Social and economic conditions, then, are important determinants on an individual's exposure to stress and ability to cope with its effects. They also play an important role in determining the way in which individuals respond to psychological problems, i.e. whether people recognise the psychological cause of their symptoms, demand and receive treatment. Cochrane (1983, p. 12) (Figure 8.1) shows the stages through which an individual must progress from the occurrence of a psychological or psychosomatic symptoms such as early wakening, loss of appetite, and lethargy to admission to mental hospital. Cochrane argues that the many steps taken before the person themselves recognise the psychological nature of their problem and the further steps that must be taken to ensure treatment are made at different rates in different social groups.

Gurin et al's study (1960) of mental health in America supports the view that the social and economic situation of the person experiencing emotional distress is an important factor in whether or not they recognise their need and whether they seek help. The 9% of Gurin's sample who did not go for professional help were men, the old, the lower educated and those living in rural areas. Gurin (p. 352) found that:

> In most cases the methods people did use to handle their problems indicated a lack of strong internal or external resources to fall back on; the act of going for help was either doing nothing, or tentative attempts at resolution that were not completely effective.

The people who did not seek professional help did not make any substitute use of their own internal coping resources or of informal group ties. Gurin (p. 380) writes:

> ... lack of help seeking behaviour reflects lack of facilitating conditions as well as lack of motivation or experienced need. Thus it would appear that the lower use of professional help resources by the lower educated and older ages is a sign neither of their greater mental health nor a more successful handling of their problem by other means but rather reflects mental health needs that have been less adequately met.

Those who define their problem in psychological terms – women, the young, the more educated and those living in urban areas are those who seek psychiatric help: the high income groups, the better educated and again those living in urban areas do so also as a function of internal and external facilitating factors. The differential demand for help in urban area reflects the availability of those facilities and services in these areas. Those in contact with resources more often go for professional help. Supply of resources interacts with high income, which reflects ability to pay as a facilitating factor; and with high education. Education reflects psychological insight in specifying the nature of the problem, non-shameful attitudes towards emotional distress, knowledge and information about resources and ability to make use of them that are the benefits of higher education. Gurin (p. 404) concludes that there exists a large unfulfilled subjective need:

> the differences between income groups lie more in the extent to which felt needs get translated into an actual use of help, particularly psychiatric resources, than in the degrees of deferential insight, introspection, and subjective need for help.

The foregoing section has shown how social and economic conditions affect individuals' vulnerability to mental illness, their ability to cope with it and even their recognition of their distress and demands for professional help.

1 Unfelt, undemanded needs

Underlying need can be unfelt, undemanded, unsatisfied and people can be mistaken about their needs. A person may have psychological or psychosomatic symptoms. People may feel isolated and lonely, tired and irritable, suffer from headaches, shortness of breath, poor appetite, sleeping difficulties, cold sweats or stomach troubles. The effects of the unmet psychological need are felt but the need itself or the objects that will satisfy it are not. Therefore people can be ignorant of or mistaken about the causes of their symptoms. They may attribute them to other causes such as a physical condition. Thus people will be ignorant about what they do need to remain healthy, the psychological states and the objects to achieve health.

2 Felt, undemanded needs

People may recognise the psychological nature of their symptoms but do nothing about them. They may believe the problem to be intractable or inevitable, they may think it will simply go away if it is ignored. They may not know what to do about it. They may 'treat' themselves with medicines, drugs, alcohol or prayer. They may be ignorant of the objects of satisfaction, they may have no access to them or they may mistake them.

3 Felt, demanded needs

People may recognise their need and demand help from family, friends, neighbours, clergy or other professionals. They may seek help from a doctor who refers them to a psychiatrist. Any of these may be mistaken ways of satisfying underlying need because none of these means will lead to the fundamental changes in socio-economic conditions that largely produce ill health.

Summary to Section A

Socio-economic factors have been judged to be the major contributors to ill health and health differences between various groups. The same factors contribute to whether health needs are felt, demanded and satisfied. This judgement does not deny the possibility of there being individual, biochemical or genetic differences between people which also play a part in susceptibility to mental ill health. I have though focussed on identifying the socio-economic factors associated with the high prevalence or absence of illness to draw attention to the vital importance of factors which we have good reason to believe are harmful. This illustrates as in the case of physical health, that indicators of health cannot be just people's felt needs and demands, and that improvement in health cannot come about simply by providing formal access to health care.

B) Alternative indicators of mental health needs

Indicators of need which reflect the causes of achieving, restoring, maintaining or avoiding risks to mental health must be found if mental health needs are to be met. Traditional measures of mental health have reflected negative definitions of mental health as the absence of mental illness plus (sometimes) the absence of presenting symptoms associated with mild psychopathologies. Where mental illness is defined and classified with respect to psychosis, psychosomatic disorder, mental retardation and deviant behaviour, measures used as indicators have been biochemical assessments, genetic characteristics, behavioural syndromes, psychophysiological items, the use of mental illness facilities and role function incapacities (Braren 1973). Other negative measures of specific psychological traits, physiological or psychosomatic symptoms have been used as clinical diagnostic indices of the emotional distress and disturbance characteristic of undifferentiated psychopathologies (Gurin 1960, pp. 176–177 for a list of 20 symptom items; and Langer's 22 Item Index).

Dissatisfaction with the limited clinical psychiatric notion of mental health as the absence of mental illness implicit in the use of negative indicators led Jahoda (1958) to call for research into the concept of positive mental health and the development and application of empirical measures of it to the general population. Through reviewing the literature in the field she proposed a list of indicators and criteria for positive mental health. They overlapped in meaning and intention and were both theoretically and empirically related. They included attitudes towards the self, growth, development, self-independence and self-realisation, the integration of personality, a correct perception of reality and environmental mastery. While recognising that the present state of knowledge is inadequate to resolve the problem of clarifying the psychological meaning of mental health, she advocated this multi-criteria approach to its empirical study in order 'to do justice to the complexity of human functioning' (p. 73).

Empirical attempts to study mental health in given populations explicitly acknowledged and reflected in their choice of measures Jahoda's multi-criterion approach: (Gurin et al 1960, Bradburn and Capolitz 1965). Subsequent social indicator research which attempted to measure weighted components of the quality of life, and the multi-variate structure of well-being, is based on the implicit assumption that mental health, happiness, satisfaction and psychological well-being are roughly synonymous concepts. In these studies criteria for and indicators of the quality of life are directly or indirectly informed by items from Jahoda's list on the grounds that they are part of common conceptions and generally held ideas about what it means to be mentally healthy beyond the absence of disease.

Much of this QOL social indicator research measures aspects of well being subjectively in terms of the actual happiness or perceived satisfactions of the people under study. People are asked how satisfied or dissatisfied they are with the various factors that are thought to be significant in determining health or happiness. Dalkey (1972) epitomised this strategy. The dimensions of the quality of life he chose to measure were influenced by Maslovian items on Jahoda's list and the quality of life was measured in relation to people's satisfactions and dissatisfactions in these dimensions. The most definitive work on subjective quality of life by Andrews and Withy (1973) used a two dimensional model; the sum of the interaction between values or criteria such as achieving success, self-development and safety (again influenced by Maslow) and domains or role situations such as job, family life, friends. The individuals evaluative response to these is their perceived quality of life.

Similarly, studies by Rodgers and Converse (1975) and Campbell et al (1976) further demonstrate the subjective measurement of the QOL. Like Gurin et al (1960) before them they assess feelings of happiness/unhappiness, satisfaction and dissatisfaction in attitudes towards the self, feelings of competence and identity, self-esteem, security and status in relation to central life roles, e.g. marriage, parenthood, family, friendship, job.

It is my contention that it is not necessary to use a concept of positive mental health in order to develop indicators which measure more than what is classed as actual illness or emotional distress; and that in addition to subjective indicators which only measure felt satisfactions, objective indicators of mental health needs must be used to see the true picture of unmet needs in any given society.

If health is understood, as has been argued for here, as natural functioning, and what is regarded as mental illness and psychological distress are taken to be interferences with functions, then the category of instrumental health, (MHN2), that is whatever is necessary to achieve, maintain or restore natural functioning, replaces that of emotional and cognitive states thought to be synonymous with the concept of positive mental health and advocated as such by its proponents (see Ch. 6).

Security, relatedness, identity, esteem and self-realisation are part of the concept of instrumental health. They are what is necessary for natural functioning. They could be part of the concept of positive mental health if maintaining these states was healthy in itself and not just in virtue of its contribution to the avoidance of impairments in functioning (see Boorse 1977, pp. 542–573). Being healthy is not the same as being secure, being loved or having high self-esteem, much less feeling happy or satisfied. Similarly being insecure, unloved, self-disgusted or failing to develop capacities, feeling unhappy or dissatisfied are not in themselves pathological states. Rather the presence of these positive states is conducive to health and of the negative ones to ill health. As positive states contribute to health, so they contribute to happiness and satisfaction. And, though health is not happiness, nor happiness health, for it is possible to be healthy and unhappy, happy and unhealthy; just as there is a causal connection between certain mental states and health, so there is between health and happiness.

The category of instrumental health (MHN2) can also accommodate the social, economic and environmental factors (see chapter 6,) known to be important in influencing health that are excluded by reliance on negative indicators alone and implicitly acknowledged by the social indicator approach that measures subjective satisfactions and dissatisfactions in relation to the various role situations and life domains which incorporate these factors. However, subjective indicators alone only measure how satisfied people actually feel in relation to the socio-economic factors known to be important in determining health status. That is, they measure the perceived health status of the individual in question and point to the gap between felt need and actual satisfactions obtained. Even advocates of this research approach acknowledge the limitations of this method. Rodgers and Converse (1975, p. 128) write:

> ... people have demonstrated a remarkable ability to adapt to situations that others would consider unsatisfactory or even intolerable, so that subjective data taken by themselves could conceal the extent of real requisites within a population.

An alternative approach is to develop objective indicators of what is needed for health, which can then measure the extent of real requisites within a population; the unfelt and unmet needs which in themselves indicate action necessary to convert unfelt need into satisfactions. Criteria for inclusion in a list of objective indicators would be causal connections between the proposed indicator and the achievement, maintenance or restoration of mental states conducive to mental health. This approach is similar to that exemplified by Storrs McColl (1975, p. 229) who defines the quality of life as:

> ...the obtaining of the necessary conditions for happiness throughout a society. These conditions being necessary not sufficient, high quality of life is compatible with actual unhappiness. The necessary conditions in question are identified with the availability of means for the satisfaction of human needs rather than human desires, and a Maslovian analysis of the former is proposed in defiance of any more satisfactory analysis.

Any list of indicators would have to take into account the lifestyle, work and home and environmental factors known to influence physical health listed in Chapter 6, and in addition would measure whether means necessary for the achievement of security, belonging, identity, esteem and self-realisation were available in relation to these factors and any other life domains not included in them which are known to be relevant. That list would then relate to and include aspects of lifestyle, housing, home and family life, work and working life, free time and leisure, cultural and social activities, education and the wider physical and political environment.

An example of how psychological needs might be measured in relation to work would be by examining conditions at work rather than how satisfied the individual feels with those conditions alone, viz:

Table 8.1
Work

Security	(1)	Income
	(2)	Insurance
	(3)	Pension plans
	(4)	Type of contract, venue etc.
	(5)	Health and safety at work
Relatedness	(1)	Social contact with workers and superiors
	(2)	Social relationships at work – competitive, authoritarian, cooperative, participatory
Identity/esteem	(1)	Job status/prestige
	(2)	Control over work
	(3)	Job involvement
Self realisation	(1)	Opportunities for promotion and training
	(2)	Opportunities for variety, self expression and creativity

The insistence on the importance of objective indicators of health needs does not mean that subjective indicators are redundant, for these do show the extent of unsatisfied felt need. Unlike physical ill health, which may be asymptomatic, in mental ill health, felt dissatisfaction and symptoms are indicators of unsatisfied felt need. But, because people may misidentify the causes of these dissatisfactions, objective indicators must be used in conjunction with them. Research is necessary to develop an integrated set of empirical tools to bring together objective and subjective indicators and to form a picture of needs and their manifestation as wants which could verify, modify, stimulate, complement and correct each other. Objective indicators cannot provide an exact quantification of the degree to which individuals are mentally unhealthy, nor do they mean that people in certain situations or social circumstances need treatment. They merely show that for mental health needs to be satisfied a wide range of social and economic factors, ranging from individuals' and groups' access to material and non-material resources to the production process and consumption patterns in society, need to be taken into account and improved.

C) What can be done

To be mentally healthy people need security, relatedness, self-esteem, a sense of identity and the ability to realise their potentials, and the objects which are necessary for the satisfaction of these needs (MHN2). Whether people express these needs in 'good' ways, that is, in ways conducive to their satisfaction and that of others, and whether individuals' needs are expressed and satisfied at all, is largely dependent on the structure of society. Human beings' health is directly related to their social, economic and material conditions. Therefore, attempts to remove the causes of ill health and intervention to ensure that needs are expressed in 'good' ways and satisfied lie largely outside the health sector and outside the domain of capitalism.

The improvements in health that can take place are those compatible with the maintenance of the system, that is, those that compensate for or reduce the effects of that system. Capitalism can and must within limits cater for the satisfaction of health needs. It provides medical goods and services and can improve these by increasing state expenditure on health, ensuring a more equal distribution of medical resources and by re-evaluating quantitative aspects of the current organisation of medicine. The state must provide nationalised medicine in response to the organised demands of the public. For most people the state provision of medical care is necessary to solve the problems it creates. Further, the state must meet health care needs in order to reproduce the labour force. Nationalised medicine is both a cost and a necessity. In addition to this, the state can improve health care to the extent that nationalised medicine is responsive to the economic requirements of the health industry, which is itself an arena for capital accumulation. Therefore capitalism can provide more complex technology, physicians, lab tests, pills, and surgery, which all profit the system with its emphasis on curative medical intervention. The State can also facilitate improvements in health by emphasising the role of the individual in preserving their own health through preventative medicine programmes and health education.

None of these measures threaten capital accumulation or the organisation, control and management of the economy. They legitimate individual and therapeutic cures rather than tackle social and economic causes. Hence, they do not lead to significant improvement in the health of the population because health and illness, health needs and satisfactions are determined socially and economically. Capitalism cannot reorganise the productive process and the set of relations it determines so that less illness is produced, because to do so would involve undermining the necessary conditions of its own existence. The survival of capitalism depends on the continuing existence of capital accumulation, differential power relations and economic inequalities.

The demands of capital accumulation mean that unemployment is a permanent feature of advanced capitalist economies. The nature of work and the conditions under which it is performed fail to meet people's psychological needs, and capitalism is unable to radically alter those conditions without threatening capital accumulation. Thus the economic insecurity, the hierarchical structures, the loss of the control, the fragmentation of tasks so injurious to the health of the worker remain intact. No measures that could be taken could alter the fact that workers are commodities used for output, efficiency and profit, that any consideration as to their health status will always be ultimately subordinate to the requirements of the self expansion of capital. The sex roles that are allocated to women in society, which limit their ability to satisfy their needs, are the result of power relations and social inequalities. Even if it were the case that capitalism could survive the economic equality of women (Meiksins-Wood 1988), it remains likely that in practice and for the foreseeable future capitalism will decline the 'cost' of such an exercise and make use of gender oppression to provide cheap reproduction of labour power and care for otherwise social dependents.

It is the case that the 'good' ways to satisfy needs and the satisfaction of all needs are incompatible with competitive, hierarchical social relations and economic inequality. The means necessary for the achievement of security, relatedness, identity and self-realisation needs, for economic and psychological security, for supportive personal and social relationships, for varied, meaningful and interesting work with participation and control, for the time, energy and education for leisure and other activities, require equal distribution patterns, the absence of exploitative and oppressive relationships, and the re-organisation of the process of production and consumption.

The achievement of the social and economic conditions necessary for the provision of MHN2 obviously would not prevent any specific person from becoming ill. An individual's health may depend on factors peculiar to that individual rather than the socio-economic factors associated with illness. The obtaining of the means to satisfy health needs is a necessary but not sufficient condition for health itself. A society where MHN2 are met is compatible with actual instances of ill health but provides the opportunity to satisfy the needs of all in ways conducive to the satisfaction of all.

Decisions leading to hospital	*Decisions not leading to hospital*

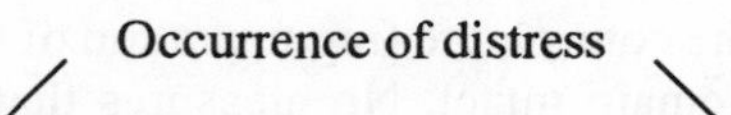

Decisions leading to hospital	*Decisions not leading to hospital*
Acknowledgement that something is wrong	Failure to recognise as a problem or problem masked
Conscious recognition as an emotional problem	Defined as physical problem (menopause, etc.)
Belief that problem can be overcome	Belief that problem is intractable or inevitable
Decision to seek help	Self-medication, antidepressive behaviour, drinking, etc.
Going to a doctor	Seeking help from friends, family, other professionals
Recognition as psychological problem by doctor	Defined by doctor as physical disorder, minor upset, overwork, etc.
Referral to a psychiatrist	Doctor prescribes psychotropic drugs or other treatment
Diagnosis of depression made	
Admitted to hospital	Outpatient treatment or other care offered

Figure 8.1 Stages in becoming admitted to a mental hospital

Source: Cochrane 1983, p. 12

9 Summary and conclusion

It has been argued that needs can be defined objectively and empirically as means to ends any human being has good reason to pursue, desire or value if they are to act successfully and purposively to achieve any ends or realise any values, whatever they may be. In order to act to achieve any ends human beings must have the necessary means to and conditions of action. The necessary conditions of action are what constitute the fundamental human needs of every actual or prospective agent (FHN1). Following from this it was claimed that survival and physical and mental health are fundamental human needs as necessary conditions for any action and for successful and purposive action.

Furthermore, since survival and health can be valued intrinsically as well as instrumentally, fundamental human needs also include whatever is necessary to achieve survival and health (FHN2).

Fundamental human needs are the objective requirements for survival and health. Insofar as they are effects of our biological and psychological constitutions they are general, abstract and relatively unchanging. What changes over time and place are the specific socio-historical forms they take, their content and ways of satisfying them. The requirements for survival and health are determined both biologically and socially.

Fundamental human needs were distinguished from felt needs and wants. Felt needs are what we feel our needs to be. They are subjectively experienced and belief-dependent. Wants are demonstrable dispositions to desire or prefer something and are the result of deliberation, belief, choice and judgement.

Both needs and wants are instrumental. However, wants can relate to any end whereas needs relate to the objective, universal goals of survival and health. Hence wants are subjectively valuable and needs are objectively valuable. Because needs are objective requirements they are not mind-dependent. They are not necessarily known to us or experienced by us in the direct way felt needs, wants and preferences are. Evidence for the existence of needs cannot be conclusively inferred from subjective avowals about what people say they need. However, empirical evidence about means to ends, behavioural and causal evidence of the effects of unmet needs can verify their existence. Felt needs and wants involve beliefs about what we think we need and want, and therefore we can be mistaken about our needs. If we need something it is because it is essential to survival and health and this is independent of beliefs and feelings concerning necessity. For this reason we cannot be said to choose our needs. In contrast to this, choice and preference are involved in the formation, pursuit and satisfaction of wants. Desires and preferences are motivational forces and so part of an agent's own reasons for action. Needs are not motivational forces in this way. We may not know what we need or want it. However needs are reasons for action even if the agent does not desire to act. The desirability of action is independent of the desire itself.

Having established that needs can be defined objectively, intuitively it would seem that facts about needs must have bearing on what we ought to do. This was justified by examining the general connection between facts and values and between the factual statement 'x needs y' and the moral conclusion 'x ought to have y'.

It was conceded that value judgements cannot be logically derived from facts but argued that they can be rationally supported by them. It was argued that the inability to justify a conclusion unless entailed by the premises is not a state of affairs peculiar to moral discourse but occurs in non-moral 'ought' statements and ordinary factual 'is' statements which all require for their intelligibility and justification references to facts, reasons and evidence. It was further argued that:

1 Moral judgements cannot simply be descriptions or expressions of emotional commitment.
2 Facts, reasons and evidence are relevant both to moral judgements and to ultimate moral values.
3 Some of the facts that are relevant to moral judgements are facts about needs.

If survival and health are indispensably necessary then at least they provide the agent with prudential reasons for acting to achieve survival and health needs, (a) by virtue of the agent having any ends they want to achieve and these needs being a means to them, and (b) by virtue of fundamental human needs being ends in themselves any agent has good reason to pursue, desire or value.

If an agent has survival and health needs that are practically necessary in order to achieve any end it follows that all agents have equally strong prudential reasons for meeting their needs. In accepting that my own needs ought to be met, I must accept that all other agents' needs ought to be met. If I interfere with the satisfaction of their needs or do not help meet them, then I deny what I have previously accepted, that fundamental human needs are necessary conditions of any action and therefore necessary goods to all agents. Insofar as other agents are potential recipients of my action, I ought to act in accordance with meeting other people's needs.

This argument was supplemented with Gewirth's claim that needs as the necessary conditions of human action are the subject of human rights, adapted to provide support for the contention that facts about needs rationally support and are relevant to moral judgements regarding their satisfactions.

Since needs are objectively necessary, and meeting them is prudentially and morally obligatory, it would appear that fundamental human needs are the proper criterion for deciding and evaluating social policy. Traditional liberal-democratic theorists disagree and argue instead for policies informed by felt needs and wants. Needs are thought to be an unsuitable criterion because they presuppose a metaphysic, therefore their existence cannot be proved. Needs are hypothetical constructs and cannot be known. They involve normative assumptions and cannot be made empirical. Need theory and practice threatens individual freedom and leads to tyranny over wants. In response to this it was established that needs can be made empirical, their existence can be verified, they are objectively valuable and important for freedom. Explanation and information regarding needs and the provision of the ability, opportunities and resources to meet them enhance the possibility of acting to achieve any end and in particular our most significant ends and purposes. Though wants and preferences could be justifiably overridden in order to promote other people's freedom or my future freedom, caution in such imposition has been advocated. The aim of putting forward a theory of needs is rather that people would come to feel those needs and be motivated to satisfy them.

Need theory was then defended against objections; and the advantages of the concept of wants were shown to be false or overridden by other considerations. Liberal theory claimed that the concept of felt needs or of wants requires no metaphysical assumptions and raises no ontological issues. They are the only needs that can be said to exist. Wants are facts; they can be identified from subjective avowals, or from reading them off from what people actually consume or use. Emphasising wants avoids coercion because political policies based on them seek to satisfy the given wants people have. In the free market existing needs dictate to political institutions and economic processes and as actual needs are revealed through effective demand this form of political and economic organisation is conducive to the maximum and equitable satisfaction of need. Against this it was argued that liberal theory conflates ontology with epistemology and falsely assumes that the real needs are those felt, demanded or satisfied in actual consumption. Even if it were the case that wants are easily identifiable, wants are not simply given facts about people's preferences. They are effects of perceptions and beliefs and the effects of the system of production, consumption and distribution. Emphasis on felt needs and wants ignores those needs not expressed, demanded or satisfied and the role of social forces on their expression and satisfaction.

Wants presume norms and to endorse them is to accept the existing pattern of wants as appropriate and desirable. Furthermore, the fact that something is wanted and subjectively valuable does not make it objectively valuable, worth desiring or having. It cannot be assumed that it is good for people to have what they want.

Finally it was argued that political policies based on wants do not avoid coercion since the wants themselves are coercively conditioned and constrained. Nor can it be shown that the capitalist market economy allows people to freely purchase goods and services to meet either their actual needs or their unexpressed needs, since many people do not have the ability, opportunity and resources to do so. In addition, want satisfaction per se cannot guarantee freedom because the desires themselves may frustrate our most significant ends and purposes.

The criticism of liberal theory and the political economy informed by it at a conceptual, empistemological and empirical level did not depend on the division of needs into true or false, real or imaginary, natural or artificial. Criticism has been based on how and why they are conditioned in certain ways, the limitations on their forms of expression and failure to satisfy them, not on their falsity or unreality.

The division of needs into true and false, where these are equated with the natural and social, has been rejected. The distinction between true and false needs cannot rest on the natural/social distinction. All expressions of needs are socially produced. Although some are produced by conscious intention, in the main they are not the result of conditioning but of social conditions. They are indirect results of social relations and the system of production, consumption and distribution. People are not victims of manipulated false needs. Socialised expressions of need represent genuine and real attempts to satisfy them.

The natural and social, though, can be distinguished. They are not either different sets of needs (true and false) or inextricably mixed but are analytically distinct. Abstract general needs are naturally determined while manifestations of them are socially determined and historically specific. The abstract, general natural components of needs are those elements common to all specific needs which are socialised particular developments and expressions of them. This view does not lead to naturalising the social or socialising the natural.

Because all needs that are felt are real, this does not mean that people may not have mistaken perceptions about their felt needs nor that because a need is not felt it is not real. People may be unaware of how and why they come about, their transformability and the consequences of them which may be inadequate satisfaction. People may be unaware of what they need or that they need something.

It has been agreed that fundamental human needs can be defined objectively and empirically. Survival and health were identified as means and ends any human being must have if they are to act successfully and purposively. Survival needs were subsumed under health needs. Health was defined in accordance with the bio-medical model. Health is the absence of disease where disease is considered to be an interference with natural functions (PHN1 and MHN1).

The category of instrumental health is what is necessary to achieve, restore or maintain natural functioning (PHN2 and MHN2). These needs are empirically discoverable by reference to their nature as means to ends and to facts about our constitutions.

The category of instrumental health includes those states or qualities advocated by positive health theorists when these can be shown to be causally connected with and conducive to health. Instrumental health needs also encompass different ways and methods of achieving health other than emphasis on acute or formal health care and point to the socio-economic and environmental causes of and remedies for ill health. Though the presence of certain states, symptoms and behaviours do not prove dysfunction they sometimes indicate malfunction. The criteria for mental and physical health is not provided in terms of normal, socially acceptable behaviour or a set of characteristics valued by some theorist. Health is a function of the internal state of the organism rather than its behaviour. It is possible, moreover, to describe biological and psychological functioning in a non-valuative way as descriptions of causal contributions to goals pursued by the human organism.

Though health is a non-evaluative concept we do make value judgements about health as a goal any human being has good reason to pursue, desire or value as it contributes to all goals neutrally. Objections to this view were challenged and it was concluded that health could be defended as an objectively important means and end.

The empirical content of PHN2 and MHN2 was identified. At an abstract level of generality these needs are naturally determined. Physical health needs were identified as the needs for air, food, water, rest, sleep, recreation and exercise, reproduction, protection against the environment and climate and any physical harm which endangers these. These needs are easily identifiable since we know what is necessary for survival and physical functioning. Mental health needs were identified as the needs for security, love and relatedness, esteem and identity and self-realisation. Evidence for the existence of these needs was provided by arguments from common agreement, causal evidence of the destructive physical and psychopathogenic effects on natural functioning if these needs are frustrated and from behavioural evidence – the use of and striving for certain satisfiers. It was argued that these needs are neither good nor bad, but there are good and bad, appropriate and inappropriate ways of expressing and meeting them. Bad expressions and satisfactions are those which for logical or empirical reasons impede the satisfaction of my own needs or those of others.

At a socially specific level, PHN2 and MHN2 are socially determined. The content of these needs will then include social, material, environmental and cultural factors known to exert a causal influence on health and the expression and satisfaction of health needs. They can be identified by referring to the determinants on their manifestations and satisfactions. Felt needs and demands are inadequate indicators of needs since the socio-economic factors which produce health and illness also determine whether health needs are felt, demanded, acknowledged or satisfied. The social experience of health, illness and of biological and psychological needs is determined by the level and nature of material production, consumption and distribution and the structure of social relations. Indicators of need must be developed which reflect the socio-economic causes of ill health.

Physical health indicators have been developed in medical and social science literature which include living and working conditions, social, economic and environmental factors which influence health, its expression as felt need and its satisfactions. Empirical measures for mental health have been developed through theoretical research into the concept of positive mental health and in social indicator research into the quality of life and the multi-variate structure of well-being. I have argued that it is not necessary to adopt a concept of positive health since the concept of instrumental health includes those factors known to be important in influencing health.

It can be demonstrated that we need certain standards of income, diet, housing, heating, hygiene, transport, communication, rest, exercise, leisure, cultural and social activities and all the goods and services which promote these. We need safe living, working and environmental conditions, meaningful work, education, information, skills, attitudes and beliefs and any other factors known to be conducive to achieving, restoring or maintaining health. Meeting health needs requires access to material and non-material resources and depends on the nature of the production process, patterns of consumption and place in distribution.

Criteria for inclusion in a list of objective indicators are the existence of causal connections between the proposed indicator and the achievement, restoration or maintenance of health. Use of these indicators can measure individuals' health and point to unfelt and unmet needs. They can lead to practical recommendations for health service planning and development, health promotion and education, priorities and target areas as well as the social, economic and political policies and action required to improve health. Some measures are possible now and are feasible within the system but other require a radical re-organisation of the process of capital accumulation, material production, consumption and distribution patterns, the structure of social relations and economic inequalities.

In order to further support and develop the claims made in this book further research is necessary.

I have argued that facts about survival and health needs provide people with prudential and moral reasons for acting to meet their own needs and those of others. Though it may be rational to act in accordance with the needs of others this does not mean that people will do so. A psychological and social theory is needed to supplement this, which would demonstrate the social relations, conditions and circumstances under which the basis of such motivation to action could occur.

It has been argued that theoretical emphasis and social policies based on wants and preferences are not necessarily freedom-preserving. Want satisfaction per se does not guarantee freedom. Capitalist allocation through the market is characterised by mass poverty, unemployment, exploitation and extreme inequalities of material and non-material resources. Consequently market mechanisms fail both to meet the wants and preferences capitalism has engendered as well as failing to meet needs. The theoretical defence of the concept of needs demonstrated that knowledge of our needs and the ability, opportunity and resources to meet them is freedom enhancing. However, allocative priority given to the satisfaction of fundamental needs has in practice led to the experience of bureaucratically centralised economies where priorities have been imposed. In order to demonstrate that this is not the only alternative to market economies, it is necessary to develop a theoretical model of democratically centralised and collective planning where conscious resource allocation renders the satisfaction of fundamental needs for all without imposition.

I have attempted to outline an empirical theory of the abstract, universal general needs for physical and mental health. The needs I have identified are not necessarily exhaustive nor do I claim that the way in which they have been classified is uniquely correct. I do claim though that there is empirical causal evidence to support their status as fundamental human needs. However, further biological and psychological scientific research is necessary to confirm these connections. Similarly, further social scientific research is necessary to refine and develop objective indicators of health status in order to identify health needs and satisfactions the better to meet them.

The point of this book has been to show the following: fundamental human needs are universal and objective matters of fact. Needs are objectively valuable and facts about needs provide prudential and moral reasons for meeting them. They can be empirically identified. They have epistemological, moral and empirical advantages over the concepts of felt needs, wants and preferences. They are the proper criterion for deciding, justifying and evaluating social and economic policies.

These claims have significance in that the concept of need has been defended against traditional liberal criticisms and the epistemological, moral and empirical advantages of the concepts of felt needs, wants and preferences have been challenged.

It has been shown that the concept of needs can be made empirical and actual needs can be empirically identified. Since it is a matter of fact what needs people have, then in principle there can be agreement on these needs since disputes can be settled empirically. It has been established that needs are objectively valuable, for without their satisfaction people are unable to act to achieve any end. They are more important than the satisfaction of any particular want since they are necessary to achieve the whole range of wants people may have. What is needed is not a matter of choice, belief or judgement, for what we need for survival and health is determined by the kind of creatures we are, and is objectively important whether we desire it or not, for we cannot function successfully to achieve our ends when we lack what we need, whether we want it or not, choose it or not. Objective needs provide criteria for criticising any society where needs are not expressed or satisfied. They provide people with reasons for action to achieve their needs. The desirability of these needs is independent of the desires themselves, though unless they become desired people will not act to achieve them.

This is why this book has been written. It began with the presumptions of the centralities of human concerns and purposes and of the task of philosophy to elucidate these in order to actualise theory in practice. This involves clarifying the nature of necessity, knowing what we do need as well as having the ability, opportunity and resources to meet needs. It is rational to suppose, all things being equal, that this knowledge will give reasons for action, that once informed and empowered people will act to satisfy their needs. This is why a theory of objective needs is important as the first stage in the emancipatory process. In a more advanced stage:

> when the enslaving subjugation of individuals to the division of labour, and thereby the antitheses between intellectual and physical labour, have disappeared; when labour is no longer just a means of keeping alive but has itself become a vital need; when the all round development of individuals has also increased their productive powers and all the springs of cooperative wealth flow more abundantly – only then can society wholly cross the narrow horizon of bourgeois right and inscribe on its banner: From each according to his abilities, to each according to his needs (Marx 1974, p. 347).

Bibliography

Adams, E.M. (1984), 'The Subjective Normative Structure of Agency', in Regis, E. Jnr. (ed.), *Gewirth's Ethical Rationalism*, University of Chicago Press, Chicago, pp. 8–23.

Andrews, F.M. and Withey, S.B. (1973), 'Developing measures of perceived life quality', *Social Indicators Research*, 1, pp. 1–26.

Anscombe, G.E.M. (1957), *Intention*, Blackwell, Oxford.

Antonovsky, A. (1970), *Health, Stress and Coping*, Jossey-Bass, San Francisco.

Arber, S., Gilbert, G.N. and Dale, A. (1985), 'Paid Employment and Women's Health: A Benefit or a Source of Role Strain?', *Sociology of Health and Illness*, 7 (3), pp. 375–400.

Aristotle (1962), *Politics*, Sinclair, T.A. (trans.), Penguin, Harmondsworth.

Balint, M. (1968), *The Basic Fault*, Tavistock Publications, London.

Barry, B. (1965), *Political Argument*, Routledge and Kegan Paul, London.

Bay, C. (1968), 'Needs, Wants and Political Legitimacy', *Canadian Journal of Political Science*, Vol. 1, No. 3, pp. 241–60.

Benn, S.I. and Peters, R.S. (1959), *Social Principles and the Democratic State*, Allen and Unwin, London.

Berkman, L.F. (1977), *Social Networks, Host Resistance and Mortality: A Follow-up Study of Almeda Country Residents*, unpublished doctoral dissertation, Department of Epidemiology, School of Public Health, University of California, Berkeley.

Bettleheim, B. (1961), *The Informed Heart*, Thames and Hudson, London.

Birtchnell, J. (1971), 'Social class, parental social class and social mobility in psychiatric patients and general population controls', *Psychological Medicine*, 1, pp. 209–21.

BMA (1987), *Deprivation and Ill Health*, Board of Science and Education, British Medical Association.

Bone, M. (1973), *Family Planning Services in England and Wales*, HMSO.
Boorse, C. (1975), 'On the distinction between disease and illness', *Philosophy and Public Affairs*, 5:1, pp. 49–68.
Boorse, C. (1976a), 'What a theory of mental health should be', *Journal of the Theory of Social Behaviour*, 6:1, pp. 61–84.
Boorse, C. (1976b), 'Wright on Functions', *Philosophical Review*, 85:1, pp. 70–86.
Boorse, C. (1977), 'Health as a Theoretical Concept', *Philosophy of Science*, 44, pp. 542–73.
Bradburn, N.M. and Caplowitz, D. (1965), *Reports on Happiness: A Pilot of Behaviour related to Mental Health*, Aldine Publishing Company, Chicago.
Bradburn, N.M. (1970), *The Structure of Psychological Well Being*, Aldine Publishing Company, Chicago.
Brandt, R.B. (1981), 'The Future of Ethics', *Nous* 15, March, pp. 31–40.
Braren, M. (1973), presentation before Seminar on Socio-Medical Health Indicators, Columbia University, 11 May 1973.
Braybrooke, D. (1987), *Meeting Needs*, Princeton University Press, New Jersey.
Brenner, M.H. (1976), *Estimating the Social Costs of National Economic Policy; implications for mental and physical health and criminal aggression*, Publ. No. 76-6660, U.S. Government Printing Office, Washington, D.C.
Brentano, L., (1908), *Versuch einer Theorie der Bedürfnisse*, Verlag der Königlich Bayerischen Akademie der Wissenschaften, München.
Brown, G.W. and Harris, T. (1978), *Social Origins of Depression: A Study of Psychiatric Disorder in Women*, Tavistock Publications, London.
Brown, G.W. and Harris, T. (1982), 'Social Class and Affective Disorder', in Al-Issa, I. (ed.), *Culture and Psychopathology*, University Park Press, Baltimore.
Bulman, J.S., Richards, N.D., Slack, G.L., and Willcocks, A.J. (1968), *Demand and Need for Dental Care*, Oxford University Press, Oxford.
Campbell, A., Converse, P. E. and Rodgers, W.L. (1976), *The Quality of American Life: Perceptions, Evaluations and Satisfactions*, Russell Sage Foundation, New York.
Caplan, R. (1975), *Job Demands and Workers' Health* NIOSH (National Institute of Safety and Health), Washington, D.C.
Carritt, E.F. (1967), 'Liberty and Equality', in Quinton, A. (ed.), *Political Philosophy*, Oxford University Press, Oxford.
Carr-Hill, R. and Lintott, J. (1986), 'Social Indicators for Popular Planning', in Ekins, P. (ed.), *The Living Economy*, Routledge and Kegan Paul, London, pp. 145–155.
Cartwright, A. and O'Brien, M. (1976), 'Social Class Variations in Health Care', in Stacey, M. (ed.), *The Sociology of the NHS, Sociological Review Monograph 22*.

Cassell, J. (1976), 'The contribution of the social environment to host resistance', *American Journal of Epidemiology*, 104, pp. 107–123.

Catford, J. (1983), 'Positive Health Indicators – towards a new information base for health', *Community Medicine*, 5.

Clarke, Simon. (1982), *Marx, Marginalism and Modern Sociology*, Macmillan, London.

Coates, B. and Rawstron, E. (1971), *Regional Variations in Britain*, Batsford, London.

Coates, K. and Silburn, R. (1967), *St. Anne's: Poverty, Deprivation and Morale*, Nottingham University, Department of Adult Education, Nottingham.

Cobb, S. (1976), 'Social support as a moderator of life stress', *Psychosomatic Medicine*, 38, pp. 300–314.

Cochrane, R. (1983), *The Social Creation of Mental Illness*, Longman, Harlow, Essex.

Cochrane, R. and Stopes-Roe, M. (1980a), 'Factors affecting the distribution of psychological symptoms in urban areas in England', *Acta Psychiatrica Scandinavica*, 61, pp. 445–60.

Cochrane, R. and Stopes-Roe, M. (1980b), 'Women, marriage, employment and mental health', *British Journal of Psychiatry*, 139, pp. 373–81.

Cofer, C.N. and Appleby, M.H. (1964), *Motivation: Theory and Research*, Wiley, New York.

Collier, A. (1973), 'Truth and Practice', *Radical Philosophy*, No.5, pp. 9–17.

Cooper, M.H. (1974), 'Economics of Need: The Experience of the British Health Service', in Perlman, M. (ed.), *The Economy of Health and Medical Care*, Macmillan, London.

Coulter, J. (1973), *Approaches to Insanity: A Philosophical and Sociological Study*, Martin Robertson, London.

Cox, B. et al. (1987), *Health and Lifestyle Survey: Preliminary Report*, Health Promotion Trust.

Dalkey, N.C. (1972), *Studies in the Quality of Life*, Lexington Books, Lexington, Massachussetts.

Daniels, N. (1985), *Just Health Care*, Cambridge University Press, Cambridge.

Davies, J.C. (1977) 'The Development of Individuals and the Development of Politics', in Fitzgerald, R. (ed.), (1977).

Dearden, R. (1972), '"Needs" in Education', in Hirst, P. and Peters R. (eds.), *Development of Reason*, Routledge and Kegan Paul, London, pp. 50–64.

Den Uyl, J. and Machan, T.R. (1984), 'Gewirth and the Supportive State', in Regis, E. Jnr. (ed.), *Gewirth's Ethical Rationalism*, University of Chicago Press, Chicago, pp. 167–180.

Dohrenwend, B.P. and Dohrenwend, B.S. (1969), *Social Status and Psychological Disorder: A Causal Inquiry*, John Wiley, New York.

Douglas, J.W.B. and Rowntree, G. (1949), 'Supplementary Maternal and Child Health Services', *Population Studies*, 2.
Doyal, L. and Gough, I. (1984), 'A Theory of Human Need', *Critical Social Policy* 4 (1), pp. 6–38.
Doyal, L. and Pennell, I. (1979), *The Political Economy of Health*, Pluto, London.
Elinson, J. (1974), 'Towards Socio-Medical Health Indicators', *Social Indicator Research*, 1, pp. 59–71.
Elster, J. (1985), *Making Sense of Marx*, Cambridge University Press, Cambridge.
Erikson, E.H. (1956), 'The Problem of Ego Identity', *Journal of the American Psychoanalytic Association*, 4, pp. 58–121.
Fagin, L. and Little, M. (1984), *The Forsaken Families*, Penguin, Harmondsworth.
Fairburn, W.R.D. (1952), *Psychoanalytic Studies of Personality*, Tavistock, London.
Farrel, E. (1986), 'Marketing Research for Local Health Promotion', *Research Report*, No.7, Health Education Council.
Feinberg, J. (1973), *Social Philosophy*, Prentice Hall, Englewood Cliffs, New Jersey.
Finlay-Jones, R. and Eckhardt, B. (1981), 'Psychiatric disorder among the young unemployed', *Australian and New Zealand Journal of Psychiatry*, 15, pp. 265–70.
Fitzgerald, R. (ed.) (1977), *Human Needs and Politics*, Pergamon, Rushcutters Bay.
Fitzgerald, R. (1977a), 'Abraham Maslow's Hierarchy of Needs – An Exposition and Evaluation', in Fitzgerald, R. (ed.) (1977).
Fitzgerald, R. (1977b), 'The Ambiguity and Rhetoric of "Need"', in Fitzgerald, R. (ed.) (1977), pp. 195–212.
Flew, A. (1973), *Crime or Disease*, Macmillan, London.
Flew, A. (1977), 'Wants or Needs', Choices or Demands, in Fitzgerald, R. (ed.) (1977), pp. 213–218.
Foot, P. (1958), 'Moral Arguments', *MIND*, Vol LXVII, pp. 502–13.
Foot, P. (1969), 'Moral Beliefs', in Hudson, W.D. (ed.) (1969), pp. 196–214.
Forster, D.P. (1976), 'Social Class Differences in Sickness and General Practitioner Consultations', *Health Trends*, 8.
Frankenhaeuser, M., and Gardell, B. (1976), 'Underload and Overload in Working Life: Outline of a Multi-disciplinary approach', *Journal of Human Stress*. 2. pp. 35–46.
Frankfurt, H. (1984), 'Necessity and Desire', *Philosophy and Phenomenological Research*, 45, pp. 1–13.
Friedlander, F. (1967), 'Importance of work versus non-work during socially and occupationally stratified groups', *Journal of Applied Psychology*, 50.
Fromm, E. (1956), *The Sane Society*, Routledge and Kegan Paul, London.

Fromm, E. (1966), *Marx's Concept of Man*, Bottomore, T.B. (trans.), Frederick Ungar, New York.
Fromm, E. (1977), *The Anatomy of Human Destructiveness*, Penguin, Harmondsworth.
Gardell, B. (1972), 'Alienation and Mental Health in the modern industrial environment', in Leads, L. (ed.), *Society, Stress and Disease*, Oxford University Press, Oxford.
Gardell, B (1976a), 'Technology, alienation and mental health: summary of a social psychological research programme on technology and the worker', *Acta Sociologica*, 19, pp. 83–94.
Gardell, B. (1976b) *Arbetsinne hall och Livskualitet* (Job Content and Quality of Life), Prisma, Stockholm.
Gardell, B (1979), *Tjanstemdnnens Arbetsmiljoer: Psyko-social arbetsmiljo och halsa* (Work Environment of White Collar Workers: Psychological Work Environment and Health), Working Paper, Department of Psychology, University of Stockholm.
Gardell, B. (1982), 'Scandinavian Research on Stress in Working Life', *Journal of Health Services*, Vol. 12. No. 1.
Gardell, B., and Gustavsen, B. (1980), 'Work Environment Research and Social Change: current developments in Scandivavia', *Journal of Occupational Behaviour*, 1.
Galtung, J. (1980), 'The Basic Needs Approach', in Lederer, K. (ed.) (1980), pp. 55–130.
Gerrard, D.L. and Houston, L.G. (1953), 'Family setting and the social ecology of schizophrenia', *Psychiatric Quarterly*, 27, pp. 90 – 101.
Gewirth, A. (1978), *Reason and Morality*, University of Chicago Press, Chicago.
Gewirth, A. (1982), *Human Rights: Essays on Justification and Applications*, University of Chicago Press, Chicago.
Gewirth, A. (1984a), 'The Epistemology of Human Rights', *Social Philosophy and Policy*, Vol. 1, No.2, pp. 1–24.
Gewirth, A. (1984b), 'Replies to My Critics', in Regis, E. Jnr. (ed.), *Gewirth's Ethical Rationalism*, University of Chicago Press, Chicago, pp. 192–257.
Gewirth, A. (1987), 'Private Philanthropy and Positive Rights', in Frankel, Paul E., Miller, F.D. Jnr., Paul, J. and Ahrens, J. (eds.), *Beneficence, Philanthropy and the Public Good*, Blackwell, Oxford, pp. 55–79.
Gibbs, B. (1976), *Freedom and Liberation*, Sussex University Press, London.
Goldberg, D.P. (1972), *The Detection of Psychiatric Illness by Questionnaire*, Oxford University Press, London.
Goldman, N. and Ravid, R. (1980), 'Community Surveys: Sex differences in mental Illness', in Guttentag, M., Salasin S., and Belle, D., (eds.), *The Mental Health of Women*, Academic Press, New York, pp. 31–56.
Gordon, I. (1951), 'Social Status and Active Prevention of Disease', *Monthly Bulletin of the Ministry of Health*, 10.

Gove, W.R. (1972), 'The relationship between sex roles, marital status and mental illness', *Social Forces*, 51, pp. 34–44.
Gove, W.R. (1973), 'Sex, marital status and mortality', *American Journal of Sociology*, 79, pp. 45–67.
Gove, W.R. and Herb, T.R. (1974), 'Stress and mental illness among the young', *Social Forces*, 53, pp. 256–65.
Gove, W.R. and Tudor, J.K. (1973), 'Adult Sex Roles and Mental Illness', *American Journal of Sociology*, 78, pp. 812–35.
Goves, P. (1960), 'Indian "Wolf Boy"', *New York Times Magazine*, 30 October.
Gray, P. G. et al. (1970), *Adult Dental Health in England and Wales in 1968*, HMSO.
Greene, G. (1971), *A Sort of Life*, Bodley Head, London.
Guntrip, H. (1961), *Personality Structure and Human Interaction*, Hogarth Press, London.
Gurin, G., Veroff, J. and Held, S. (1960), *Americans View Their Mental Health*, Basic Books, New York.
Guttman, L. (1944), 'A Basic for Scaling Qualitative Data', *American Sociological Review*, 9.
Haavio-Mannila, E. (1986), 'Inequalities in Health and Gender', *Social Science and Medicine*, 22, 2, pp. 141–9.
Halsall, R.W. and Lloyd, W.H. (1961), 'Admission of elderly people to hospital', *British Medical Journal*, 30 December.
Hampshire, S. (1949), 'Fallacies in Moral Philosophy', *MIND* LVIII, pp. 466–82.
Hare, R.M. (1952), *The Language of Morals*, Oxford University Press, Oxford.
Hare, R.M. (1963), *Freedom and Reason*, Oxford University Press, Oxford.
Hare, R.M. (1969), 'Descriptivism', in Hudson, W.D. (ed.) (1969), pp. 240–259.
Hare, R.M. (1981), *Moral Thinking*, Oxford University Press, Oxford.
Hare, R.M. (1984), 'Do Agents Have to be Moralists?', in Regis, E. Jnr. (ed.), *Gewirth's Ethical Rationalism*, University of Chicago Press, Chicago, pp. 52–59.
Hare, R.M. (1988), Comments in Seanor, D. and Fotion, N. (eds.), *Hare and Critics*, Oxford University Press, Oxford, pp. 199–295.
Harlow, H.F. (1958), 'The Nature of Love', *The American Psychologist*, Vol. 1, No. 12, pp. 673–685.
Harlow, H.F. and Zimmerman, R.R. (1958), 'The Development of Affectional Responses in Infant Monkeys', *Proceedings of the American Philosophical Society*, 102, pp. 501–509.
Hart, H.L.A. (1955), 'Are there any natural rights?', *Philosophical Review*, 64, pp. 175–91.

Hegel, G.W.F. (1931), *The Phenomenology of Mind*, Baillie, J.B. (trans.), Harper and Row, London.

Heller, A. (1980), 'Can "True" and "False" Needs be Posited?', in Lederer, K. (ed.) (1980), pp. 213–26.

Hill, J.F. (1984), 'Are Marginal Agents Our Recipients?', in Regis, E. Jnr. (ed.), *Gewirth's Ethical Rationalism*, University of Chicago Press, Chicago, pp. 180 – 92.

Hollingshead, A.B. and Redlich, F.C. (1958), *Social Class and Mental Illness*, John Wiley, New York.

House, J.S. (1981), *Work, Stress and Social Support*, Addison-Wesley, Reading, Massachusetts.

Hudson, W.D. (ed.) (1969), *The Is/Ought Question*, Macmillan, London.

Hudson, W.D. (1970), *Modern Moral Philosophy*, Macmillan, London.

Hudson, W.D. (1984), 'The Is-Ought Problem Resolved', in Regis, E. Jnr. (ed.), *Gewirth's Ethical Rationalism*, University of Chicago Press, Chicago, pp. 108 – 128.

Jackson, P. R and Stafford, E.M. (1980), *Work involvement and employment status as influences on mental health: a test of an interactional model*, paper presented at the British Psychological Society Social Psychology Section Conference, Canterbury.

Jahoda, M. (1958), *Current Conceptions of Positive Mental Health*, Basic Books Inc., New York.

Johnson, J.V. (1980), *Work Fragmentation, Human Degradation and Occupational Stress*, Unpublished Mimeograph.

Johansson. G., Aronsson, G., and Lindstrom, B.O. (1978), 'Social psychological and neuroendrocine stress reactions in highly mechanised work', *Ergonomics*, 21, pp. 583–599.

Johansson, H. (1975), *Industriar loebetarens fritid (The industrial blue collar worker and his leisure)*, Mimeograph, Department of Psychology, University of Gothenburg.

Kalin, J. (1984), 'Public Pursuit and Private Escape: The Persistence of Egoism', in Regis, E. Jnr. (ed.), *Gewirth's Ethical Rationalism*, University of Chicago Press, Chicago, pp. 128 – 147.

Kant, I. (1956), *The Moral Law: Kant's 'Groundwork of the Metaphysic of Morals'*, Paton, H.J. (trans.), Hutchinson, London.

Kaplan, H.B. (1972), 'Towards a general theory of psychosocial deviancy: the case of aggressive behaviour', *Social Science in Medicine* 6, pp. 593–617.

Kaplan, H.B., Cassell. J.C and Gove, S. (1977), 'Social Support and Health', *Medical Care*, 25 (Suppl.), pp. 47–58.

Katz, D., and Kahn, R.L. (1978), *Social Psychology of Organisation*, Wiley, New York.

Kirsh, S. (1983), *Unemployment: Its Impact on Body and Soul*, Canadian Mental Health Association, Toronto.

Knutson, J.N. (1972), *The Human Basis of the Polity*, Aldine-Atherton, Chicago.

Knutson, J.N. (1973), 'The Political Relevance of Self-Actualisation', in Wilcox, A. (ed.) *Public Opinion and Public Attitudes*, Wiley, New York.

Kohn, M.L. (1968), 'Social class and schizophrenia: a critical review', in Rosenthal, D. and Kety, S. (eds.), *The Transmission of Schizophrenia*, Pergamon, Oxford, pp. 155–172.

Kohn, M.L. (1972), 'Class, Family and Schizophrenia: a reformulation', *Social Forces*, 50, 295–304.

Krech, D., Crutchfield, R.S., Livson, N. (1969), *Elements of Psychology*, Knopf, New York.

Kurtzke, J.F. (1981), 'Initial Proposals for a uniform minimal record of disability', *Acta Neurological Scandinavia*, supplement 87, 64, 49.

Lane, R.E. (1969), *Political Thinking and Consciousness*, Markham, Chicago.

Langer, T.S. (1962), 'A 22-Item screening score of psychiatric symptoms indicating impairment', *Journal of Health and Human Behaviour*, III, pp. 269–71.

Langer, T.S. and Michael, S.T. (1962), *Life Stresses and Mental Health: the Midtown Study*, Free Press, Glencoe, Illinois.

Lederer, K. (ed.)(1980), *Human Needs*, Oelgeschlager, Gunn and Hain, Cambridge, Massachusetts.

Lederer, K. (1980), 'Needs Methodology: The Environmental Case', in Lederer, K. (ed.) (1980), pp. 259–278.

Lee, K. (1985), *A New Basis for Moral Philosophy*, Routledge and Kegan Paul, London.

Lee, R.P.L. (1976), 'The causal priority between socio-economic status and psychiatric disorder: a prospective study', *International Journal in Social Psychiatry*, 22, pp. 1–8.

Leiss, W. (1976), *The Limits to Satisfaction: An Essay on the Problems of Needs and Commodities*, University of Toronto Press, Toronto.

Levy, E. (1977), 'Health Indicators and Health Systems Analysis', in Perlman, M. (ed.), *Economics of Health and Health Care*, Martin Robertson, London.

Lowe, C.R. and Garrett, F.N. (1959), 'Sex patterns of admission to mental hospitals in relation to social circumstances', *British Journal of Preventive and Social Medicine*, 13, pp. 88–102.

Lukes, S. (1973), *Individualism*, Blackwell, Oxford.

Lundahl, A. (1971), *Fritid och Rekcreation (Leisure and Recreation)*, Allmanna, Forlaget, Stockholm.

McInnes, N. (1977), 'The Politics of Need or Who Needs Politics', in Fitzgerald, R. (ed.) (1977) pp. 229–34.

MacIntyre, A. (1969), 'Hume on "is" and "ought"', in Hudson, W.D. (ed.) (1969), pp. 35–50.

Macklin, R. (1972), 'Mental health and mental illness: some problems of definition and concept formation', *Philosophy of Science*, 39, pp. 341–65.
Macpherson, C.B. (1973), *Democratic Theory*, Clarendon Press, Oxford.
Mallman, C. A. (1980), 'Society, Needs and Rights: A Systematic Approach', in Lederer, K. (ed.) (1980), pp. 37–54.
Marcuse, H. (1964), *One Dimensional Man: Studies in the Ideology of Advanced Industrial Society*, Beacon Press, Boston, Massachusetts.
Martin, B. (1977), *Abnormal Psychology: Clinical and Scientific Perspectives*, Holt, Rinehart and Winston, New York.
Marx, K. (1967), 'Towards the Critique of Hegel's Philosophy of Laws: Introduction', in Easton, L.D. and Guddat, K.H. (trans.), *Writings of the Young Marx on Philosophy and Society*, Anchor Books, Doubleday, Garden City, New York.
Marx, K. (1973), *Grundrisse*, Penguin, Harmondsworth.
Marx, K. (1974), 'Critique of the Gotha Programme', in Fernbach, D. (ed.), *The First International and After*, Penguin, Harmondsworth.
Marx, K. (1976), *Collected Works*, Vol. 5, Lawrence and Wishart, London.
Maslow, A. (1943), 'A Theory of Human Motivation', *Psychological Review*, Vol. 50.
McColl, S. (1975), 'The Quality of Life', *Social Indicators Research*, 2. pp. 229–248.
Meiksins Wood, E. (1988), 'Prospects of Emancipation', *New Left Review*, 167, pp. 1–22.
Meissner, M. (1971), 'The long arm of the job', *Industrial Relations*, 10, pp. 238–260.
Menniger, K.A. (1930), *The Human Mind*, Knopf, New York.
Miller, D. (1976), *Social Justice*, Oxford University Press, Oxford.
Miller, J.E. (1973), 'Guide-lines for selecting a Health Status Index', in Berg, R. (ed.), *Health Status Indexes*, Hospital Research and Education Trust, Chicago.
Mobasser, N. (1987), 'Marx and Self-Realisation', *New Left Review*, No.1. 61, pp. 119–128.
Morris, P. (1969), *Put Away*, Routledge and Kegan Paul, London.
Myers, J.K. and Bean, L.L. (1968), *A Decade Later: A Follow up of Social Class and Mental Illness*, John Wiley, New York.
Myers, J.K., Lindenthal, J.L. and Pepper, M.P. (1975), 'Life events, social integration and psychiatric symptomatology', *Journal of Health and Social Behaviour*, 16, pp. 421–9.
Myerson, A. (1941), Review of 'Mental Disorders in Urban Areas' by Faris, R.E.L. and Dunham, H.W., *American Journal of Psychiatry*, 96, pp. 995–7.
Narveson, J. '(1984)', 'Negative and Positive Rights in Gewirth's "Reason and Morality"', in Regis, E. Jnr. (ed.), *Gewirth's Ethical Rationalism*, University of Chicago Press, Chicago, pp. 98–108.

Nielsen, K. (1963), 'On Human Needs and Moral Appraisals', *Inquiry*, Vol. 6, pp. 170–183.
Nielsen, K. (1969), 'Morality and Needs', in MacIntosh, J. and Coval, J. (eds.), *The Business of Reason*, Routledge and Kegan Paul, London, pp. 186–206.
Nielsen, K. (1977), 'True Needs, Rationality and Emancipation', in Fitzgerald, R. (ed.) (1977), pp. 142–156.
Nielsen, K. (1984), 'Against Ethical Rationalism', in Regis, E. Jnr. (ed.), *Gewirth's Ethical Rationalism*, University of Chicago Press, Chicago, pp. 59–84.
Nielsen, K. (1985), *Equality and Liberty: A Defence of Radical Egalitarianism*, New Jersey.
Norman, R. (1971), *Reasons for Action*, Blackwell, London.
Norman, R. (1982), 'Does Equality Destroy Liberty?', in Quinton, A. (ed.), *Political Philosophy*, Oxford University Press, Oxford.
Norman, R. (1987), *Free and Equal*, Oxford University Press, Oxford.
OPCS (1981), *General Household Survey for 1979*, HMSO.
Packard, V. (1960), *The Hidden Persuaders*, Penguin, Harmondsworth.
Pearlin, L.I., Lierman, M.A., E.G. and Mullan, J.T. (1981), 'The Stress Process', *Journal of Health and Social Behaviour*, 22, pp. 337–56.
Peters, R.S. (1958), *The Concept of Motivation*, Routledge and Kegan Paul, London.
Phillips, D.Z. and Mounce, H.O. (1969), 'On Morality's Having a Point', in Hudson, W.D. (ed.) (1969) pp. 228–239.
Piaget, J. (1953), *The Origins of Intelligence in the Child*, Routledge and Kegan Paul, London.
Plant, R. (1985), 'Welfare and the value of liberty', *Government and Opposition*, 20, pp. 297–314.
Plant, R., Lesser, H. and Taylor-Gooby, P. (1980), *Political Philosophy and Social Welfare*, Routledge and Kegan Paul, London.
Plog, S.C. and Edgerton, R.B. (eds.) (1969), *Changing Perspectives in Mental Illness*, Holt, Rinehart and Winston, London.
Raphael, D.D. (1984), 'Rights and Conflicts', in Regis, E. Jnr. (ed.), *Gewirth's Ethical Rationalism*, University of Chicago Press, Chicago, pp. 84–96.
Rawls, J. (1971), *A Theory of Justice*, Harvard University Press, Cambridge, Massachusetts.
Redlich, F.C. and Freedman, D.X. (1966), *The Theory and Practice of Psychiatry*, Basic Books, New York.
Regis, E. Jnr. (ed.) (1984), *Gewirth's Ethical Rationalism*, University of Chicago Press, Chicago.
Reich, W. (1975), *The Mass Psychology of Fascism*, Penguin, Harmondsworth.

Renshon, S.A. (1974), *Psychological Needs and Political Behaviour: A Theory of Personality and Political Efficacy*, Free Press, New York.
Renshon, S.A. (1975), 'Psychological Needs, Personal Control and Political Participation', *Canadian Journal of Political Science*, Vol. 22, No.1.
Rickard, J.H. (1976), 'Per capita expenditure of the English Area Health Authorities', *British Medical Journal*, 31 January, pp. 299–350.
Robb, B. (1967), *Sans Everything*, Nelson, London.
Rodgers, W.L. and Converse, P. E. (1975), 'Measures of Perceived Overall Quality of Life', *Social Indicators Research*, pp. 127–153.
Rousseau, J.J. (1964), *Ouvres Completes*, Vol. 3, *Ecrits Politiques*, Vol. 4, Gallimard, Bibliotheque de la Pleiade, Paris.
Runciman, W.G. (1966), *Relative Deprivation and Social Justice*, Routledge and Kegan Paul, London.
Sarbin, T. (1967), 'On the futility of the proposition that some people are labelled "mentally ill"', *Journal of Consulting Psychology*, 31, pp. 447–53.
Sarbin, T. (1969), 'The scientific status of the mental illness metaphor', in Plog, S.C. and Edgerton, R.B. (eds.), *Changing Perspectives in Mental Illness*, Holt, Rinehart and Winston, New York, pp. 9–31.
Sartre, J.P. (1976), *Critique of Dialectical Reason: Theory of Practical Ensembles*, Vol. 1, Lee, J. (ed.), Sheridan-Smith, A. (trans.), New Left Books, London.
Schachtel, E.G. (1962), 'On Alienated Concepts of Identity', in Josephson, E. and Josephson, M. (eds.), *Man Alone*, Dell, New York.
Schwab, J.J., Warheit, R.A. and Schwab, R.B. (1979), *Social Order and Mental Health: the Florida Health Study*, Raven Press, New York.
Seligman, M.E.P. (1975), *Helplessness*, W.H. Freeman, San Francisco.
Sen, A.K. (1985a), *Commodities and Capabilities*, North Holland, Amsterdam.
Sen, A.K. (1985b), 'Well-being, agency and freedom', *Journal of Philosophy*, 1982, pp. 169–21.
Shue, H. (1980), *Basic Rights*, Princeton University Press, p. 99–350.
Singer, M.G. (1984), 'Gewirth's Ethical Monism', in Regis, E. Jnr. (ed.), *Gewirth's Ethical Rationalism*, University of Chicago Press, Chicago, pp. 23–39.
Slater, E. and Roth, M. (1969), *Clinical Psychiatry*, Bailliere, Tindall and Cassell, London.
Smail, D. (1984), *Illusion and Reality: The Meaning of Anxiety*, J.M. Dent and Sons, London.
Smith, R. (1987), *Unemployment and Health*, Oxford University Press, Oxford.

Soloman, E., Boucharchi, N., Denisov, V., Hankiss, E., Mallman, A., Mibrath, L. (1980), 'Unesco's Policy Relevant Quality of Life Research Programme', in Szalai, A. and Andrew, F. (eds.), *The Quality of Life*, Sage Publications, London, Ch.13.

Soper, (1979), 'Marxism, Materialism and Biology', in Mepham, J. and Hillel-Ruben, D. (eds.), *Issues in Marxist Philosophy*, Vol. 2, Harvester, Brighton, pp. 61–99.

Soper, (1981), *On Human Needs*, Harvester, Brighton.

Spitz, R.A. (1949), 'The Role of Ecological Factors in Emotional Development in Infancy', *Child Development*, 20, pp. 145–155.

Springborg, P. (1981), *The Problem of Human Needs and the Critique of Civilisation*, Allen and Unwin, London.

Stafford, E., Jackson, P. and Banks, M. (1980), *Employment, work involvement and mental health in less qualified young people*, Memo 365, MRC Social and Applied Psychology Unit, Department of Psychology, University of Sheffield.

Stokes, G.J. (1981), *The psychological and social consequences of economically precipitated stress*, unpublished Ph.D, University of Birmingham.

Storr, A. (1976), *The Dynamics of Creation*, Penguin, Harmondswick.

Storr, A. (1979), *The Art of Psychotherapy*, Secker, Warburg and Heinemann Medical Books, London.

Strole, L., Langer, T.S., Michael, S.T. and Opler, M.K. (1961), *Mental Health in the Metropolis*, Mc. Graw-Hill, New York.

Szasz, T.S. (1961), *The Myth of Mental Illness*, Hoeber-Harper, New York.

Szasz, T.S. (1963), *Law, Liberty and Psychiatry*, Macmillan, New York.

Szasz, T.S. (1970a), *Ideology and Insanity*, Doubleday, Garden City, New York.

Szasz, T.S. (1970b), *The Manufacture of Madness*, Harper and Row, New York.

Tawney, R.H. (1964), *Equality*, Allen and Unwin, London.

Taylor, C. (1967), 'Neutrality in Political Science', in Laslett, P. and Runciman, W.G. (ed.), *Philosophy, Politics and Society*, Third Series, Blackwell, Oxford.

Taylor, C. (1979), 'What's wrong with Negative Liberty?', in Ryan, A. (ed.), *The Idea of Freedom*, Oxford University Press, Oxford, pp. 175–194.

Taylor, P. (1959), '"Need" Statements', *Analysis*, Vol. 19, No.5, pp. 106–11.

Thomson, G. (1987), *Needs*, Routledge and Kegan Paul, London.

Timpanaro, S. (1975), *On Materialism*, Verso, London.

Townsend, P. and Davidson, N. (eds.) (1982), *Inequalities in Health (The Black Report)*, Penguin, Harmondsworth.

Townsend, P. and Wedderburn, D (1965), *The Aged in the Welfare State*, Bell Occasional Papers on Social Administration.

Verwayen, H. (1980), 'The Specification and Measurement of the Quality of Life in OECD Countries', in Szalai, A. and Andrew, F. (ed.), *The Quality of Life*, Sage Publications, London, Ch.14.

Walzer, M. (1983), *Spheres of Justice*, Oxford University Press, Oxford.

Ware, J.E., Brook, R.H., Davis, A.R. et al (1981), 'Choosing measures of health status for individuals in general populations', *American Journal of Public Health*, 71, 620.

Weale, A. (1978), *Equality and Social Policy*, Routledge and Kegan Paul, London.

Westlander, G. (1976), *Arbetets Villkor och Fritidens Inne hall (Working Conditions and the Content of Leisure)*, Swedish Council for Personnel Administration, Stockholm.

White, A.R. (1971), *Modal Thinking*, Blackwell, Oxford.

Whitehead, M. (1988), 'The Health Divide', in Townsend, P., Davidson, N. and Whitehead, M. (eds.), *Inequalities in Health: The Black Report and the Health Divide*, Penguin, Harmondsworth.

Wiggins, D. (1985), 'Claims of Need', in Honderich, T. (ed.), *Morality and Objectivity*, Routledge and Kegan Paul, London, pp. 149–203.

Williams, A. (1974), '"Need" as a demand concept with special reference to health', in Culyer, A. (ed.), *Economic Policies and Social Goals*, Martin Robertson and Co. Ltd., London, pp. 60 – 78.

Williams, A.W., Ware, J.E. Jnr., and Donald, C.A. (1981), 'A model of mental health, life events and social supports applicable to general populations', *Journal of Health and Social Behaviour* 22, pp. 324–36.

Winnicott, D.W. (1965), *The Maturation Process and the Facilitating Environment*, Hogarth Press, London.

World Health Organisation (1979), 'Measurement of Levels of Health', *WHO European Series*, No.7, Copenhagen, WHO.

Ziller, R.C. (1973), 'Self-Other Orientations and the Quality of Life', *Social Indicator Research*, Vol. 1, D. Reidel Publishing Co, Dordrech, Holland, pp. 301–325.